GW00542579

TABLE OF MEDAL WINNERS*
BY NATIONALITY FROM 1896 TO 1968

SUMMER OLYMPICS
(Excluding Art Competitions)

	GOLD	SILVER	BRONZE	TOTAL
1. United States	545	396½	353½	1,295
2. U.S.S.R. (Russia in 1908, 1912)	161	155	150	466
3. Great Britain	192½	172½	147	461½
4. Germany (from 1968 includes East and West)	122	169	153	444
5. France	116	133	124	373
6. Sweden	115½	110	136	361½
7. Italy	105	92	87	284
8. Hungary	96	77	89	262
9. Finland	80	69	93	242
10. Australia	55	45	59	159
11. Japan	52	52	43	147
12. Switzerland	37	50	48	135
13. Netherlands	38	43	46	127
14. Denmark	28	48	48	124
15. Canada	23	37	46	106
16. Czechoslovakia	36	37	30	103
17. Poland	23	28	51	102
18. Norway	37	28	29	94
19. Greece	21	34	29	84
20. Belgium	20	35	29	84

WINTER OLYMPICS (including 1972)

	GOLD	SILVER	BRONZE	TOTAL
Norway	47	49	42	138
U.S.S.R.	38	26	27	91
United States	27	35	23	85
Finland	22	30	22	74
Austria	20	29	25	74
Sweden	25	23	24	72
Germany (from 1968 includes East and West)	25	20	23	68
Switzerland	14	14	15	43
France	12	9	11	32
Canada	11	6	13	30
Netherlands	8	11	6	25
Italy	9	5	6	20
Great Britain	4	4	10	18
Czechoslovakia	2	4	5	11
Belgium	1	1	3	5
Hungary	0	1	4	5
Japan	1	2	1	4
Poland	1	1	2	4
Rumania	1	0	1	2
Spain	1	0	0	1
North Korea	0	0	1	1

* These tables include medals won in sports and events no longer on the current schedule.

GUINNESS
BOOK OF
OLYMPIC RECORDS

COMPLETE ROLL OF
OLYMPIC MEDAL WINNERS (1896–1968)
FOR THE 22 SPORTS
TO BE COMPETED IN THE 1972 GAMES
AND ALL OTHER ESSENTIAL
INFORMATION

Edited by
NORRIS D. McWHIRTER and
A. ROSS McWHIRTER
(Co-editors of the
Guinness Book of World Records)

Associate Editors
STAN GREENBERG and BOB PHILLIPS

PENGUIN BOOKS

Penguin Books Ltd, Harmondsworth, Middlesex, England
Penguin Books Australia Ltd, Ringwood, Victoria, Australia

—

First published in the U.S.A. by Sterling Publishing Co., Inc. 1964
Published in Penguin Books 1972

—

Copyright © Guinness Superlatives Ltd., 1972

—

Made and printed in France by
Brodard et Taupin, La Flèche
Set in Monotype Times

PICTURE CREDITS

*Aitken, Ltd., 75; Associated Press Ltd., London, 6, 94(r), 144; Central
Press Photos Ltd., London ,173, 181; European Picture Union, 27, 152(r);
Finnish Tourist Association, 16; Global Olympic Picture Association, 141(b);
Keystone Press Agency, Ltd.,51; E. D. Lacey, 38, 47, 93, 97, 109,,111 116(l),
120, 127, 128, 129, 137, 139, 167; London and Wide World Photos, 18,
20, 21(t)(b), 53, 90, 94(l), 110(l)(r), 130, 138, 146, 156, 166; New York
Athletic Club, 113, 133(b); Novosti Press Agency, Moscow, 143; Radio
Times Hulton Picture Library, 12, 83, 115(b), 118, 131, 176; A. G. Spalding
and Bros., 14.; United Press International, 105; United Press International,
Inc., New York, 171; United Press International (U.K.) Ltd., 34, 62, 77,
141(b), 173; Wide World Photos, 23, 122, 134; Wide World Photos Inc.,
126; Wide World Photos, Los Angeles, 17, 48; Wide World Photos, New
York, 29, 112; World Sports, 69, 115(t).*

TABLE OF CONTENTS

The opening ceremony is far and away the most spectacular of all Olympic events. The torch relay, the athlete's march-in, the carrying of the Olympic flag, the oath-taking (shown here)—all are traditional ceremonies.

Authors' Preface

Students of the 75-year-old modern Olympic Games movement seem to be offered in existing books either a bare Roll of Champions since 1896, or else a highly detailed and expensive (in the case of the earlier Games, very rare) report of a single celebration. We have attempted, in an inexpensive form and in as much detail as space permits, to set out *all* the medal winners of all time—that is, the holders of the gold, silver, and bronze awards for every event on the 1972 program.

The Olympics have many fascinations to those who, like us, follow them round the world for television, radio, or the press, but there are two peculiarities perhaps above all others.

First, the competitors themselves make friendships that will last for the rest of their lives. This happens despite the tendencies of some commentators to over-emphasize any disagreement that inevitably occurs in such an exceptionally competitive atmosphere. Occasionally even there are Olympic marriages. Olympic friendships, particularly notable since the custom started in 1932 of lodging the participants in an Olympic village, transcend the mere difficulties of conflicting language, race and creed. The Olympic spirit of common interest in the techniques of sport makes very light of nationalistic differences, which so often leave professional diplomats in deadlock.

Secondly, especially in those sports that enjoy a dependence on absolute measurement of either time, distance, or weight to determine their results—such as track and field athletics, swimming, and weight-lifting—the continuous urge to improve on previous high-water marks is most inspiring. It is practically a law of the Olympics that every record set in previous Games will be in great jeopardy when the next celebration takes place in four years' time.

The 1972 Games see a return of the Olympics to Europe after 12 years and to Germany after 36 years. Nearly every Olympic record for participation and performance will be broken under the world's largest roof.

We would like to acknowledge the enthusiastic and energetic pursuit of detail by Bob Phillips and Stan Greenberg in originally compiling the main section of this book.

We have made reference to all the available Olympic literature of many countries, but are most indebted to the work of the late Dr. Ferenc Mezo, a former representative from the International Olympic Committee to his country of Hungary. Dr. Mezo was a dedicated admirer and student of all things pertaining to the Olympic Games movement, which, after all, is still the greatest show on earth.

Spring 1971   NORRIS and ROSS McWHIRTER

Celebrations of the Modern Olympic Games

I	Athens	April 6–15, 1896
II	Paris	July 2–22, 1900
III	St. Louis	Aug. 29–Sept. 7, 1904
†	Athens	April 22–May 2, 1906
IV	London	July 13–25, 1908
V	Stockholm	July 6–15, 1912
VI	*Berlin	1916
VII	Antwerp	Aug. 14–29, 1920
VIII	Paris	July 5–27, 1924
IX	Amsterdam	July 28–Aug. 12, 1928
X	Los Angeles	July 30–Aug. 14, 1932
XI	Berlin	Aug. 1–16, 1936
XII	*Tokyo, then Helsinki	1940
XIII	*London	1944
XIV	London	July 29–Aug. 14, 1948
XV	Helsinki	July 19–Aug. 3, 1952
XVI	‡Melbourne	Nov. 22–Dec. 8, 1956
XVII	Rome	Aug. 25–Sept. 11, 1960
XVIII	Tokyo	Oct. 10–Oct. 24, 1964
XIX	Mexico City	Oct. 12–27, 1968
XX	Munich	Aug. 26–Sept. 10, 1972
XXI	Montreal	Scheduled July 18–Aug. 1 1976

* Cancelled due to World Wars.
† Intercalated Celebration.
‡ Equestrian events held at Stockholm, Sweden.

The Winter Olympic Games

I	Chamonix	Jan. 25–Feb. 4, 1924
II	St. Moritz	Feb. 11–19, 1928
III	Lake Placid	Feb. 4–13, 1932
IV	Garmisch-Partenkirchen	Feb. 6–16, 1936
V	St. Moritz	Jan. 30–Feb. 8, 1948
VI	Oslo	Feb. 14–25, 1952
VII	Cortina, Italy	Jan. 26–Feb. 5, 1956
VIII	Squaw Valley, Calif.	Feb. 18–28, 1960
IX	Innsbruck	Jan. 29–Feb. 9, 1964
X	Grenoble	Feb. 6–18, 1968
XI	Sapporo, Japan	Feb. 3–13, 1972
XII	Denver, Colorado	Scheduled Feb. 20–29, 1976

Ancient Greek urn
depicting the torch
which symbolizes the
Olympic Games.

History of the Olympic Games

1. THE ANCIENT GAMES

Few human institutions can even remotely approach the antiquity of the Olympic Games. Though precise records of the ancient Games began only in 776 B.C., there is abundant evidence of their occasional celebration up to six centuries earlier. A date conservatively attributed to the Games at Olympia sponsored by Pelops is 1370 B.C. This date is, of course, subject to adjustment in the light of evidence of new archaeological techniques. All the signs are, however, that Olympic history spans some thirty-three centuries.

The Olympic Games faded away about the middle of the 9th century B.C., but were reputedly revived by King Iphitos of Elis. During this period came the idea of a temporary truce among all the warring factions in Greece: the Olympic peace or *ekecheiria* was proclaimed to last for about three months before the Games (which themselves lasted for five days) and long enough after them for the competitors to enjoy a safe passage back to their homes.

The Games of 776 B.C.—the first of which there is an actual record of the name of a champion—seems to have

Early morning rays of the sun strike a concave mirror in the ancient Stadium of Olympia, Greece, and light an impregnated stick held by a kneeling Spartan girl athlete. The flame is immediately transferred to the pottery bowl held by another maiden and carried in procession to a white marble bowl beside the River Alpheus. Then the first of 370 relay runners lights his torch and begins the long carry to Athens. This re-enactment of an ancient custom has been occurring since 1936. The flame has been sent to Berlin, London, Helsinki, Melbourne and Rome—wherever the Games are held.

consisted of merely one event: the stadium race (about 170 metres or 186 yds.), won by Coroibos of Olis. But the Games rapidly expanded in scope—with longer races, plus a pentathlon of running, discus throwing (about 9 lb. in weight), long jump with weights, javelin throwing with a lever, and wrestling; as well as boxing and wrestling. Moreover, the Greeks had to compete soon against the challenge of both Sicilians and Creteans.

Even in those days each celebration had its hero. There were winners of what would now be called the sprint double, there were heats for the shorter events, and eventually women had their own Games.

A famous champion, Chionis, in the middle of the 7th century B.C. is credited by modern researches to have long jumped, almost certainly with the aid of dumb-bell weights, 7 m. 05 cm. or 23 feet 1½ in.

From this time onwards, the names and feats of many champions are recorded and competitions in the fine arts were added.

The original prizes were only olive wreaths, but gradually the champions began to acquire valuable rewards and the Games became corrupted. The long Roll of Champions ends in A.D. 369, and in 393 the Emperor Theodosius decreed from Milan the end of the Olympic Games. So the Olympic torch went out for 1,503 summers.

2. THE MODERN (OR REVIVED) GAMES

The germ of the idea of reviving the Ancient Olympic Games was born in Germany. J. C. F. Guts-Muths (1759–1839), the founder of the notable German gymnastics movement, put forward the idea. Ernst Curtius (1814–96) gave a lecture on the Ancient Games in Berlin on 10 January 1852. His researches aroused interest in Greece where the wealthy Major Euangelis Zappas organized the first "Pan-Hellenic Games," in 1859 watched by 20,000 spectators. These games—a purely national affair—were repeated in

Olympic torch on the way to Rome in 1960. After being carried in the traditional manner by relays, the flame was carried from Athens to Syracuse, Sicily, on board the Italian naval training ship, Amerigo Vespucci. From there it was carried, again by relay of runners to Naples and eventually Rome. The torch was lit on August 12 and the Games began on August 25.

Athens was the scene of the first modern Olympic Games in 1896—and again in an intercalated celebration in 1906. Crowds in Athens at the marble stadium with the tight end turns were tremendous, but the times achieved by the runners were relatively slow. In ancient Greece all hostilities ceased during the Olympic Games while athletes contested for crowns of wild olive.

1870, 1875, 1888 and 1889. They at least kindled a spark of interest in other countries.

It is Baron Pierre de Coubertin (1863–1937) of France who is, however, rightly styled the "Founder of the Modern Olympic Games." This wealthy young nobleman was commissioned by the French Government in 1889 to study physical culture throughout the civilized world. His enquiries produced a disquieting picture of feuding and dissension between sport and sport, nation and nation, and the already apparent commercial spirit in sport.

On 25 November 1892, de Coubertin in a lecture at the Sorbonne in Paris for the first time publicly advanced his conviction that there should be a modern revival of the Ancient Games. His lecture was received with an ovation. In 1893, de Coubertin convened an international conference at the Hall of Sciences at the Sorbonne from 16 to 23 June 1894. Thirteen countries sent representatives and 21 others sent messages of support. On the last day a resolution was passed that "sport competitions should be held every fourth year on the lines of the Greek Olympic Games and every nation should be invited to participate."

De Coubertin envisaged the first Games being in Paris at the beginning of the century, but a Greek motion was passed giving the Greeks the privilege of holding the First Celebration at Athens in 1896. Accordingly, the International Olympic Committee (IOC) then 12 strong—was formed.

1896—The First Games at Athens

On 5 April after a gap of 1,503 years, 80,000 Athenians witnessed the revival of the Olympics.

Despite the support of 34 nations at the Paris Conference only 12 sent representatives to Athens. The white marble stadium was a splendid sight, but too long and narrow for track events. The small American team won 9 out of the 12 track and field events, while the Germans dominated the gymnastics, and the French the cycling. The Greeks became depressed as all the titles, even what they regarded as their own national specialty, the discus throw, were won by foreigners. Happily the last event—the Marathon—(24 miles 1500 yds.) was dramatically won by Spyros Louis, a post office messenger from Marusi near Athens, one of 21 Greek starters.

1900—The IInd Games at Paris

It was feared that the Second Games would rival the World Exhibition in Paris in the same year, so de Coubertin was subdued and the Games were allowed to be nothing more than a side-show. Another factor that reduced interest was that the Games in the Bois de Boulogne, Paris, were spread over more than five months. Despite these drawbacks, the standards shot up and quite a few world best performances were set. The hero of the Games was Alvin Kraenzlein (U.S.) who won the 60 metres, 110 metres hurdles, 200 metres hurdles, and long jump.

U.S. athletes who competed in Olympics at Paris in 1900. Hero of the meet was Alvin C. Kraenzlein (fifth from left in back row), who was the first to win 4 gold medals in a single celebration—in a sprint, two hurdle races, and the long jump. Also in this group is Ray C. Ewry (fourth from left in middle row), who won 8 gold medals (an Olympic record for individual performance that still stands) between 1900 and 1908, in the now uncontested standing high jump, standing broad jump and standing triple jump

1904—The IIIrd Games at St. Louis

Again the Olympics were organized as a mere side show to a World Fair. Because of the distance and expense of travel, only four European and four other countries were represented. Interest in the 85 Olympic events was minimal: the record crowd was 2,000.

Despite the rather crude facilities, mostly at Washington University, the competitive spirit and advancing skill of the contestants—the golden thread of the whole Olympic tapestry—was undiminished. There was a major scandal in the Marathon when an American (Lorz) got a clandestine 10 miles' lift in a car in the middle section of the Marathon and naturally arrived in the Stadium first. When the truth dawned, wild applause soon thinned to vituperative abuse and immediate expulsion.

Harry L. Hillman (U.S.) was a triple winner in St. Louis in 1904. Here he is shown winning the 400-metre race.

1908—The IVth Games at London

The Greeks held an unofficial, but nonetheless valuable, celebration of the Games at Athens in 1906. Their intention, however, of always holding an Olympic Games mid-way between the official Games ended after this first interpolated celebration.

Italy was originally awarded the IVth Games but resigned them and London took on the job. With the White City Stadium that could hold 100,000, full royal patronage, a vast schedule, good publicity, and 1,500 competitors from 19 nations, the Olympics at last broke through as a World event.

The two most memorable incidents were in the track and field athletics, and both sadly involved disqualification. There was an unfortunate rumpus over the 400 metres final in which the U.S. runner Carpenter was disqualified for obstruction. His compatriots Robbin and Taylor then scratched in protest, so the only remaining competitor, Lt. William Halswell (G.B.), had a 50.0 sec. walk-over for the gold medal.

Johny Hayes, a department store assistant from New York, won the marathon in 1908. The 26-mile 385-yard course was from Windsor Castle to Shepherd's Bush, West London, and in this photo he is shown passing through Ruislip with his handler following on a bicycle. A crowd estimated at 250,000 watched the race.

The marathon from Windsor to the Stadium was watched by the then world's largest recorded sports crowd—an estimated 250,000 people. The leader, a frail looking little Italian, Dorando Pietri, tottered into the Stadium in the last stages of exhaustion. Harassed officials aided him when he fell for a second time, so he had to be disqualified for receiving aid, and the race went to the U.S. runner Johnny Hayes, who took the gold medal while Pietri got a gold cup from a sympathetic Queen Alexandra.

Wearing a laurel wreath just presented to him by King Gustavus V of Sweden is Duke Kahanamoku from Hawaii (U.S.), who won the 100-metre free-style swimming gold metal in 1912 at Stockholm.

Statue of Paavo Nurmi (Finland), star distance runner of the 1920, 1924 and 1928 Olympics, stands outside the stadium in Helsinki which was the scene of the 1952 Olympics. Counting individual and team gold medals, Nurmi has 9, one more than Ewry (see page 13). Today a businessman in Finalnd, Nurmi set 24 world records during his career.

1912—The Vth Games at Stockholm, Sweden

Following the success of the London Games, this celebration at Stockholm confirmed and cemented world-wide interest in the Olympics. The number of participants doubled to 3,100, drawn from 18 countries. The hero of the Games was the American Indian, Jim Thorpe, who won both the pentathlon and the decathlon. Thorpe was later discovered by the A.A.U. to have rather thoughtlessly transgressed their amateur rules by earlier acceptance of payment for some minor baseball appearances. Inevitably he was struck off the Roll of Champions and his two gold medals were re-awarded to his runners-up.

1916—The VIth Games, awarded to Berlin

Owing to the World War which developed following Germany's invasion of Belgium and part of France, in August, 1914, the Games inevitably had to be cancelled.

1920—The VIIth Games at Antwerp, Belgium

The Olympics were resumed at Antwerp but were without any representation from the defeated central European countries or the Russians, who remained absent until 1952. The Games were highly successful, with the Finns challenging even the Americans in the track events.

1924—The VIIIth Games at Paris

The Olympic Games again leapt forward in growth—44 countries entered 5,533 competitors. The Finn, Paavo Nurmi, won 5 gold medals—for the 1,500 metres, 5,000 metres, 10,000 metres cross-country race (both team and individual), and the 3,000 metres team event. The American, Johnny Weismuller, later to be the most famous of Hollywood's dynasty of Tarzans, won 3 gold medals for sprint swimming.

1928—The IXth Games at Amsterdam, Holland

At Amsterdam the Germans reappeared. Olympic medals tended to be more widely distributed among the nations. The Finns were again dominant in distance running, but this time Nurmi won only the 10,000 metres. Weismuller won two more swimming gold medals. Women's events were successfully introduced in track and field with world records being set in all five events.

...art of the 1500-metre race in the great oval Los Angeles Olympic stadium ...1932. This was the race in which the leading contender, Glenn Cunning-...m (U.S.) came in fourth, behind the surprise winner, Luigi Beccali of Italy.

1932—The Xth Games at Los Angeles

Under the famous sunny California climatic conditions a profusion of Olympic and world records were set. Every single track and field Olympic record, except the long jump, was improved. America's black sprinters and jumpers excelled while the Japanese collected five gold medals in the men's swimming events. It was wrongly predicted that records made under these "freak California conditions" would remain unbroken for years.

Olympic flame being lit in Berlin in 1936—the first time the torch relay became a part of the opening ceremony. Faces of Nazi youths are peering interestedly from the uniformed mass.

1936—The XIth Games at Berlin

At Berlin the Nazi government of Germany disgracefully attempted to turn the Olympic movement into a propaganda vehicle for the glorification of their creed. The strong internationalism of the Games prevented complete subversion. The levels of performance in most events left many of the 1932 "super-records" well behind, against all prediction. The hero of the Games was the modest American Negro, J. C. Owens*, who won the 100 metres, 200 metres, 4×100 metres relay, and the long jump. The Japanese marathon runners (gold and bronze medals) and the Dutch women's swimmers made a strong impression.

---

*Commonly called Jesse Owens because of his initials, J. C.

1940-44—The XIIth Games, awarded to Tokyo and then Helsinki; the XIIIth Games awarded to London

Neither of these two celebrations could be held because of the World War. The 1940 Games were originally awarded to Tokyo but when the Japanese became involved in war with China, they were re-awarded to Helsinki. The 1944 Games were hopefully given to London but the war still had a year to run.

1948—The XIVth Games at London

London and the Wembley Stadium attracted 4,106 competitors from 59 countries. For the first time a woman became the Victrix Ludorum and Mvr. Fanny Blankers-Koen, the mother of two children, won the 100 metres, 200 metres, 80 metre hurdles, and the 4×100 metres relay for the Netherlands. Other athletes who attracted great interest were Harrison Dillard (U.S.) in the 100 metres and 4×100 metres relay; Emil Zatopek (Czechoslovakia) in the 10,000 metres; Bob Mathias (U.S.) in the decathlon; and Willi Grut (Sweden) in the modern pentathlon.

(See photograph, next page)

1952—The XVth Games at Helsinki, Finland

Sixty-nine nations and 4,925 competitors came to the Finnish capital city, Helsinki (population 350,000) in 1952 The Games were notable for the reappearance of the Russians after an absence of 40 years. The undoubted heroes of the Games were the Zatopeks of Czechoslovakia. Emil won the unprecedented triple—the 5,000 metres, 10,000 metres, and the marathon—all in Olympic record time. On the day he won the 5,000 metres, his wife, Dana, won the women's javelin throwing title, also with an Olympic record.

1956—The XVIth Games at Melbourne, Australia

The Games were celebrated in the Southern Hemisphere for the first and so far only time. Inevitably, the difficulties of season, distances, and expense reduced the entries, but only slightly. The equestrian events had to be held separately in Stockholm because of rigid horse quarantine laws in Australia. Outstanding on the track was Vladimir Kuts (U.S.S.R.) with a great 5,000 metres and 10,000 metres double victory; and the sprinters Bobby-Joe Morrow (U.S.) and Miss Betty Cuthbert of Australia, each of whom won three gold medals in the 100 metres, 200 metres and 4×100 metres relay. The Australians dominated the swimming, winning 8 out of 13 events.

(See photograph, page 21)

...the march past at Wembley in 1948. The electric scoreboard reads "The important thing in the Olympic Games is not... ...it is not conquering but fighting well."

Hundreds of pigeons being released at the opening of the 1956 Olympics in Melbourne—the first in the Southern Hemisphere.

1960—The XVIIth Games at Rome

Rome, which missed its opportunity of staging the Games in 1908, made a magnificent setting for the XVIIth Games.

Australian athletes carry the official Olympic flag into the stadium in Rome to open the 1960 Olympics.

Eighty-four nations contributed nearly 6,000 competitors to a fortnight of the most intense competition, for the most part in exceptionally hot conditions. Awards were widely spread with 23 countries gaining at least one gold medal. Outstanding achievements were the 1,500 metres world record by the Australian, Herbert Elliott, and the unexpected marathon success of the Ethiopian, Bikila Abebe. In the women's events, Miss Wilma Rudolph, a black American runner, dominated the sprints and won three gold medals. The Australians in equestrianism and the Russian girl gymnasts left a great impression.

1964—The XVIIIth Games at Tokyo

The first celebration in Asia was the organizational high-water mark of the Games, thanks to meticulous attention to detail by the Japanese. A conservative estimate is that the cost of all the public works and other expenses with a direct bearing on the Games was $560,000,000.

The growth of the Games is well illustrated by this table:

	1896	1964
Number of countries	12	94
Number of sports	10	20
Number of competitors	under 300	5,711

Vast crowds, undeterred by frequent rain, added atmosphere to a celebration in which Olympic records again fel wholesale, though, perhaps significantly, the number o world records set was fewer than in past Games. The high lights included the unique Marathon double by Abeb Bikila (Ethiopia); a blazing finish in the 10,000 metres b Billy Mills (U.S.) with less than 1½ seconds between the thre medalists; the four swimming gold medals won by Do Schollander (U.S.); and the third successive win in the 10 metres freestyle by Dawn Fraser (Australia).

1968—XIXth Games at Mexico City

A record seven and a half thousand competitors from 11 nations did battle at nearly seven and a half thousand fe above sea level—these are the two salient figures to rememb for the first Games in Latin America—the size and th height.

The technical organization in Mexico was excelle while the brilliantly colourful fiesta atmosphere excus the few flaws in the ancillary arrangements for progran information to the public, and transport.

Because nobody dropped dead it did not mean that t altitude problem was insignificant. Just as predicted t performances in the "explosive" events—memorably B Beamon's almost incredible long jump of 29 feet 2½ inches were records, while those involving more than three minut continuous effort were in some cases back to standa achieved as long ago as 1948.

And the future . . .

Up 90 steps to the Olympic flame cauldron in 1968 in Mexico City ran the first woman to take the final pass of the torch and to light the Olympic flame.

1972—XXth Games at Munich

This will be the third occasion in which Germany has received the nomination as host country by the International Olympic Committee. The first occasion was the cancelled Games of 1916 scheduled for Berlin and the second the Games of 1936, which were duly staged in the capital of the then unified Germany.

The XXth Games will be more exhaustively covered by the press, radio and television than any previous celebration. For sheer scale of planning, expenditure and striving after perfection of planning, it will exceed anything in the three-quarter century long history of the modern Games.

Among the many superlatives will be the giant computorized instant score board and the transparent roof over the stadium which will cover 21 acres (8.5 hectares).

Handball will be contested for the first time since 1936 and after 52 years archery will also be restored to the competitions making 22 sports in all.

A record number among the 146 sovereign nations of the world will be represented with Mainland China being probably the only highly populous absentee.

1976—The XXIst Games at Montreal

The Olympic Games for 1976 were awarded to Montreal 1970. They are the first to be held in Canada, and the first held in North America since the 1932 Games at Los Angeles.

Canada's long amateur sporting record and support for the Games from the beginnings of the movement, coupled with their successful staging of the Commonwealth Games in 1930 and 1954 and their experience from Expo '68 augur well for a triumphant celebration.

ROLL OF OLYMPIC MEDAL WINNERS SINCE 1896 IN THE 20 CURRENT SPORTS

* Indicates Olympic record.
d.n.a.—Data not available.

1a. Archery (Men)

(Archery is re-introduced to the 1972 Olympic Games, having been previously included in the Games of 1900, 1904, 1908 and 1920. But none of the events in those celebrations compare with the championship events of 1972. Gold, silver and bronze medals up to and including 1920 were won by the following countries: MEN—Belgium 10–5–2; France 4–5–6; U.S. 3–3–5; G.B. 1–1–0; Australia 1–0–0; Netherlands 1–0–0; Spain 0–1–0. WOMEN—U.S. 3–3–2; G.B. 2–2–2. The greatest number of individual gold medals won is four by Hubert Van Innis (BELGIUM) with two in 1900 and two more in 1920.)

1972   Men's International Round (36 arrows each at 90, 70, 50 and 30 metres.

1b. Archery (Women)

1972   Women's International Round (36 arrows each at 70, 60, 50 and 30 metres.)

(For previous medal winners, see headnote above).

2. Basketball

1896–1932 Event not held[1]

	GOLD	SILVER	BRONZE
1936	U.S.[2]	CANADA	MEXICO
	Francis Johnson	J. Stewart	C. Borja Morco
	Carl Knowles	J. Allison	V. Borja Morco
	Joe Fortenberry	Charles Chapman	Leija de la Vega
	William Wheatley	A. Wiseman	Pamplona Lecunda
	Jack Ragland	G. Atchison	Choperanna Irizarri
	Ralph Bishop	D. Peden	J. Olmos Moreno
	Carl Shy	A. Chapman	Robert Fernandez
	Duane Swanson	Meretsky	Skousen Spilsbury
	Samuel Balter	Dawson	F. Martinez Cordero
	John Gibbons		Hernandez del Valle
	Frank Lubin		Gomez Domingues
	Arthur Mollner		
	Donald Piper		
	Willard Schmidt		
1948	U.S.[3]	FRANCE	BRAZIL
	Clifford Barker	André Barrais	Zenny de Azevedo
	Donald Barksdale	Michel Bonnevie	Joao Braz
	Ralph Beard	André Buffière	Marcus Dias
	Louis Beck	René Chocat	Alfonso Evora
	Vincent Boryla	René Derency	Ruy de Freitas
	Gordon Carpenter	Maurice Desaymonnet	Alexandre Gemigniani
	Alexander Groza	André Even	Alberto Marson
	Wallace Jones	Fernand Guillou	Alfredo da Mota
	Robert Kurland	Maurice Girardot	Nilton de Oliveira
	Raymond Lumpp	Raymond Offner	Massinet Sorcinelli
	R. C. Pitts	Jacques Perrier	Guilherme Rodrigues
	Jesse Renick	Yvan Quenin	
	R. Jackie Robinson	Lucien Rebuffic	
	Kenneth Rollins	Pierre Thiolon	
1952	U.S.[4]	U.S.S.R.	URUGUAY
	Charles Hoag	Viktor Vlasov	Martins Acosta y Lara
	William Houghland	Styapas Butautas	Enrique Balino
	John Keller	Ivan Lysov	Victorio Gieslinkas
	Dean Kelley	Kazis Petkyavichus	Hector Costa
	Robert Kenney	Nodar Dzhordzhikiya	Nelson Demarco
	William Lienhard	Anatoliy Konev	Hector Garcia Otero
	Clyde Lovelette	Otar Korkiya	Tabare Larre Borges
	Marcus Frieberger	Ilmar Kullam	Adesio Lombardo
	Wayne Glasgow	Yuriy Ozerov	Roberto Lovera
	Frank McCabe	Aleksandr Moiseyev	Sergio Matto
	Daniel Pippin	Kheino Kruus	W. Pelaez
	Howard Williams	Yustinas Lagunavichus	Carlos Rossello
	Ronald Bontemps		
	Robert Kurland		

---

[1] There were basketball competitions in the 1904, 1924 and 1928 Games, but they were only demonstration events.

[2] Semi-finals: U.S. bt MEXICO 25–10; CANADA bt POLAND 42–15. Final: U.S. bt CANADA 19–8. Third-place: MEXICO bt POLAND 26–12.

[3] Semi-finals: U.S. bt MEXICO 71–40; FRANCE bt BRAZIL 43–33. Final: U.S. bt FRANCE 65–21. Third-place: BRAZIL bt MEXICO 52–47.

[4] Semi-finals: U.S.S.R. bt URUGUAY 61–57; U.S. bt ARGENTINA 85–76. Final: U.S. bt U.S.S.R. 36–25. Third-place: URUGUAY bt ARGENTINA 68–59.

[5] Final: U.S. bt U.S.S.R. 89–55. Third-place: URUGUAY bt FRANCE 71–62.

[6] Also well known as a high jumper, with best mark of 6 ft. 9¼ in. set in 1956.

Russian player (dark shirt) shoots a basket while surrounded by three Mexican opponents in a match in 1960 at Rome, won by the U.S.S.R., 66-49. The Russians lost the finals to the U.S. team which included such stars as Oscar Robertson and Jerry Lucas. The U.S. has won the basketball tournament on 5 occasions out of 5.

	GOLD	SILVER	BRONZE
1956	U.S.[5]	U.S.S.R.	URUGUAY
	Carl Cain	Valdis Muizhnieks	Carlos Blixen
	William Houghland	Maigonis Valdmanis	Ramiro Cortes
	K. C. Jones	Vladimir Torban	Hector Costa
	William Russell[6]	Stassis Stonkius	Nelson Chelle
	James Walsh	Kazis Petkyavichus	Nelson Demarco
	William Evans	Arkhadiy Bochkaryev	Hector Garcia Otero
	Burdette Haldorson	Janis Krumins	Carlos Gonzalez
	Ronald Tomsic	Mikhail Semyonov	Sergio Matto
	Richard Boushka	Alguirdas Lauritanas	Oscar Moglia
	Gilbert Ford	Yuriy Ozerov	Raul Mera
	Robert Jeangerard	Viktor Zoubkov	Ariel Olascoaga
	Charles Darling	Mikhail Studenetskiy	Milton Scarón

	GOLD	SILVER	BRONZE
1960	U.S.[7]	U.S.S.R.	BRAZIL
	Jerry West	Valdis Muizhnieks	Zenny de Azevedo
	Walter Bellamy	Maigonis Valdmanis	Amaury Pasos
	Robert Boozer	Tsezars Ozers	Wlamir Marques
	Terry Dischinger	Guram Minashvili	Moyses Blas
	Burdette Haldorson	Viktor Zoubkov	Carlo Domingos
	Darrall Imhoff	Vladimir Ugrekhilidze	Fernando Pereira
	Allen Kelley	Janis Krumins	Carmo de Souza
	Lester Lane	Mikhail Semyonov	Jatyr Schall
	Jerry Lucas	Yuriy Korneyev	Edson Bispo dos Santos
	Adrian Smith	Aleksandr Petrov	Antonio Salvador
	Jay Arnette		Waldyr Geraldo
	Oscar Robertson[8]		Waldemar Blatkauskas
1964	U.S.[9]	U.S.S.R.	BRAZIL
	Jim Barnes	Valdis Muizhnieks	Amaury Pasos
	William Bradley	Nikolay Bagley	Wlamir Marques
	Lawrence Brown	Armenak Alachachian	Maciel Pereira
	Joe Caldwell	Aleksandr Travin	Carlo Domingos
	Mel Counts	Vyacheslav Khrynin	Friedrich Wilhelm Bran-
	Richard Davies	Janis Krumins	Carmo de Souza
	Walter Hazzard	Levan Mosheshvili	Jathyr Schall
	Lucious Jackson	Yuriy Korneyev	Edson Bispo dos Santos
	John McCaffrey	Aleksandr Petrov	Antonio Salvador
	Jeffrey Mullins	Gennadiy Volnov	Victor Mirshawka
	Jerry Shipp	Yaak Lipso	Sagio de Toledo
	George Wilson	Yuris Kalniush	Machado
			José Edvar
1968	U.S.	YUGOSLAVIA	U.S.S.R.
	Michael Barrett	Dragutin Cermac	Vladimir Andreyev
	John Clawson	Kresimir Cosic	Sergei Belyov
	Donald Dee	Vladimir Cvetkovic	Vadim Kapranov
	Calvin Fowler	Ivo Daneu	Sergei Kovalenko
	Spencer Haywood	Radivou Korac	Anatoly Krikun
	William Hosket	Zoran Maroevic	Yaak Lipso
	James King	Nikola Plecas	Anatoly Polivoda
	Glynn Saulters	Trajko Rajkovic	Modest Paulauskas
	Charles Scott	Dragoslav Raznotovic	Zurab Sakandelidze
	Michael Silliman	Petar Skansi	Yuri Selikhov
	Kenneth Spain	Damir Solman	Priit Tomson
	Joseph White	Aljosa Zorga	Gennady Volnov

1972

---

[7] U.S. bt U.S.S.R. 81–57 in semi-final pool, and bt ITALY 112–81 and BRAZIL 90–63 in final pool; U.S.S.R. bt BRAZIL 64–62 and ITALY 78–70 in final pool.

[8] Lists of team-members include, where known, names of all who played in preliminaries as well as finals.

[9] U.S. bt U.S.S.R. 73–59 in match for first place, and BRAZIL bt PUERTO RICO 76–60 in the match for third place.

Cassius M. Clay (U.S.) became the 1960 Olympic light-heavyweight gold medal winner. Then an 18-year-old schoolboy, the future world heavyweight champion is shown here bouncing a right off the head of Tony Madigan of Australia, bronze medal winner.

3. Boxing

LIGHT FLYWEIGHT

GOLD	SILVER	BRONZE
1968[1] Francisco Rodriguez (VENEZUELA)	Yong-Ju Jee (S. KOREA)	Harlan Marbley (U.S.) H. Skrzypczak (POLAND)
1972		

[1] weight up to 48 kilograms (105.8 lbs).

FLYWEIGHT

1896–1900   Event not held

GOLD	SILVER	BRONZE
1904[1] George Finnegan (U.S.)	Miles Burke (U.S.)	d.n.a.
1908–1912 Event not held		
1920[2] Frank De Genaro (U.S.)	Anders Petersen (DENMARK)	W. Cuthbertson (G.B.)
1924[2] Fidel La Barba (U.S.)	James McKenzie (G.B.)	Raymond Fee (U.S.)
1928[2] Antal Kocsis (HUNGARY)	Armand Apell (FRANCE)	Carlo Cavagnoli (ITALY)
1932[2] Istvan Enekes (HUNGARY)	Francisco Cabanas (MEXICO)	Louis Salica (U.S.)
1936[2] Willi Kaiser (GERMANY)	Gavino Matta (ITALY)	Louis Laurie (U.S.)

	GOLD	SILVER	BRONZE
1948[3]	Paschal Perez (ARGENTINA)	Spartaco Bandinelli (ITALY)	Soo Ann Han (KOREA)
1952[3]	Nathan Brooks (U.S.)	Edgar Basel (GERMANY)	Anatoliy Bulakov[4] (U.S.S.R.) William Towell (S. AFRICA)
1956[3]	Terence Spinks (G.B.)	Mircea Dobrescu (RUMANIA)	John Caldwell (EIRE) René Libeer (FRANCE)
1960[3]	Gyula Torok (HUNGARY)	Sergey Sivko (U.S.S.R.)	Kiyoshi Tanabe (JAPAN) Abdelmoneim Elgvindi (U.A.R.)
1964[3]	Fernando Atzori (ITALY)	Artur Olech (POLAND)	Robert Carmody (U.S.) Stanislav Sorokin (U.S.S.R.)
1968	Ricardo Delgado (MEXICO)	Artur Olech (POLAND)	Servilio Oliveira (BRAZIL) Leo Rwabwogo (UGANDA)
1972			

---

[1] Weight up to 47.6 kilograms (105 lbs).
[2] Weight up to 50.8 kilograms (112 lbs).
[3] Weight up to 51 kilograms (112½ lbs).
[4] From 1952, both losing semi-finalists are awarded bronze medals.

BANTAMWEIGHT

	GOLD	SILVER	BRONZE
1896–1900	Event not held		
1904[1]	O. L. Kirk (U.S.)	George Finnegan (U.S.)	d.n.a.
1908[2]	H. Thomas (G.B.)	J. Condon (G.B.)	W. Webb (G.B.)
1912	Event not held		
1920[3]	Clarence Walker (S. AFRICA)	C. G. Graham (CANADA)	James McKenzie (G.B.)
1924[3]	William Smith (S. AFRICA)	Salvatore Tripoli (U.S.)	Jean Ces (FRANCE)
1928[3]	Vittorio Tamagnini (ITALY)	John Daley (U.S.)	Harry Isaacs (S. AFRICA)
1932[4]	Horace Gwynne (CANADA)	Hans Ziglarski (GERMANY)	José Villanueva (PHILIPPINES)
1936[4]	Ulderico Sergo (ITALY)	Jack Wilson (U.S.)	Fidel Ortiz (MEXICO)
1948[5]	Tibor Csik (HUNGARY)	Giovanni Zuddas (ITALY)	Juan Venegas (PUERTO RICO)
1952[5]	Pentti Hämäläinen (FINLAND)	John McNally (EIRE)	Gennadiy Garbuzov[6] (U.S.S.R.) Joon Kang (S. KOREA)
1956[5]	Wolfgang Behrendt (GERMANY)	Soon Chun Song (KOREA)	Frederick Gilroy (EIRE) Claudio Barrientos (CHILE)
1960[5]	Olyeg Grigoryev (U.S.S.R.)	Primo Zamparini (ITALY)	Brunoh Bendig (POLAND) Oliver Taylor (AUSTRALIA)
1964[5]	Takao Sakurai (JAPAN)	Shin Cho Chung (S. KOREA)	Juan Fabila (MEXICO) Washington Rodriguez (URUGUAY)

GOLD	SILVER	BRONZE
1968	Valeriy Sokolov (U.S.S.R.)	Eridadi Mukwanga (UGANDA)	Eiji Morioka (JAPAN) Kyou Chull Chang (S. KOREA)
1972			

---

[1] Weight up to 52.1 kilograms (115 lbs).
[2] Weight up to 52.6 kilograms (116 lbs).
[3] Weight up to 53.6 kilograms (118¼ lbs).
[4] Weight up to 53.5 kilograms (118 lbs).
[5] Weight up to 54 kilograms (119 lbs).
[6] From 1952 both losing semi-finalists are awarded bronze medals.

FEATHERWEIGHT

1896–1900 Event not held

	GOLD	SILVER	BRONZE
1904[1]	O. L. Kirk (U.S.)	Frank Haller (U.S.)	d.n.a.
1908[2]	Richard Gunn (G.B.)	C. W. Morris (G.B.)	Hugh Roddin (G.B.)
1912	Event not held		
1920[2]	Paul Fritsch (FRANCE)	Gauchet (FRANCE)	Edoardo Garzena (ITALY)
1924[2]	John Fields (U.S.)	Joseph Salas (U.S.)	Pedro Quartucci (ARGENTINA)
1928[2]	Bep van Klaveren (NETHERLANDS)	Victor Peralta (ARGENTINA)	Harold Devine (U.S.)
1932[2]	Carmelo Robledo (ARGENTINA)	Josef Schleinkofer (GERMANY)	Carl Carlsson (SWEDEN)
1936[2]	Oscar Casanovas (ARGENTINA)	Charles Catterall (S. AFRICA)	Joseph Miner (GERMANY)
1948[3]	Ernesto Formenti (ITALY)	Denis Shepherd (S. AFRICA)	Aleksey Antkiewicz (POLAND)
1952[4]	Jan Zachara (CZECHO.)	Sergio Caprari (ITALY)	Joseph Ventaja[5] (FRANCE) Leonard Leisching (S. AFRICA)
1956[4]	Vladimir Safronov (U.S.S.R.)	Thomas Nicholls (G.B.)	Henryk Niedzwiedzki (POLAND) (Pentti Hämäläinen (FINLAND)
1960[4]	Francesco Musso (ITALY)	Jerzy Adamski (POLAND)	William Meyers (S. AFRICA) Jorma Limmonen (FINLAND)
1964[4]	Stanislav Stepashkin (U.S.S.R.)	Antony Villanueva (PHILIPPINES)	Charles Brown (U.S.) Heinz Schultz (GERMANY)
1968	Antonio Roldan (MEXICO)	Albert Robinson (U.S.)	Philip Warurngi (KENYA) Ivan Michailov (BULGARIA)
1972			

Weight up to 56.7 kilograms (125 lbs).
Weight up to 57.15 kilograms (126 lbs).
Weight up to 58 kilograms (127¾ lbs).
Weight up to 57 kilograms (125¾ lbs).
From 1952 both losing semi-finalists are awarded bronze medals.

	GOLD	SILVER	BRONZE

LIGHTWEIGHT

Year	GOLD	SILVER	BRONZE
1896–1900	Event not held		
1904[1]	H. J. Spanger (U.S.)	James Eagan (U.S.)	R. Van Horn (U.S.)
1908[2]	Frederick Grace (G.B.)	F. Spiller (G.B.)	H. H. Johnson (G.B.)
1912	Event not held		
1920[1]	Samuel Mosberg (U.S.)	Gotfred Johanssen (DENMARK)	Newton (CANADA)
1924[1]	Hans Nielsen (DENMARK)	Alfredo Copello (ARGENTINA)	Frederick Boylstein (U.S.)
1928[1]	Carlo Orlandi (ITALY)	Stephen Halaiko (U.S.)	Gunnar Berggren (SWEDEN)
1932[1]	Lawrence Stevens (S. AFRICA)	Thure Ahlquist (SWEDEN)	Nathan Bor (U.S.)
1936[1]	Imre Harangi (HUNGARY)	Nikolai Stepulov (ESTONIA)	Erik Agren (SWEDEN)
1948[3]	Gerald Dreyer (S. AFRICA)	Joseph Vissers (BELGIUM)	Svend Wad (DENMARK)
1952[4]	Aureliano Bolognesi (ITALY)	Aleksey Antkiewicz (POLAND)	Gheorghe Fiat[5] (RUMANIA) Erkki Pakkanen (FINLAND)
1956[4]	Richard McTaggart (G.B.)	Harry Kurschat (GERMANY)	Anthony Byrne (EIRE) Anatoliy Laguetko (U.S.S.R.)
1960[4]	Kazimierz Pazdzior (POLAND)	Sandro Lopapoli (ITALY)	Richard McTaggart (G.B.) Abel Laudonio (ARGENTINA)
1964[4]	Jozef Grudzien (POLAND)	Vellikton Barannikov (U.S.S.R.)	Ronald Harris (U.S.) James McCourt (IRELAND)
1968	Ronnie Harris (U.S.)	Josef Grudzien (POLAND)	Calistrat Cutov (RUMANIA) Vujin Zvonimir (YUGOSLAVIA)
1972			

---

[1] Weight up to 61.2 kilograms (135 lbs).
[2] Weight up to 63.5 kilograms (140 lbs).
[3] Weight up to 62 kilograms (136¾ lbs).
[4] Weight up to 60 kilograms (132 lbs).
[5] From 1952 both losing semi-finalists are awarded bronze medals.

LIGHT-WELTERWEIGHT

Year	GOLD	SILVER	BRONZE
1896–1948	Event not held		
1952[1]	Charles Adkins (U.S.)	Viktor Mednov (U.S.S.R.)	Erkki Mallenius (FINLAND) Bruno Visintin (ITALY)
1956[1]	Vladimir Jengibarian (U.S.S.R.)	Franco Nenci (ITALY)	Henry Loubscher (S. AFRICA) Constantin Dumitrescu (RUMANIA)
1960[1]	Bohumil Nemecek (CZECHO.)	Clement Quartey (GHANA)	Quincy Daniels (U.S.) Marian Kasprzyk (POLAND)
1964[1]	Jergy Kulej (POLAND)	Evgeniy Frolov (U.S.S.R.)	Eddie Blay (GHANA) Habib Galhia (TUNISIA)

GOLD	SILVER	BRONZE
1968 Jerzy Kulej (POLAND)	Enrique Regueiferos (CUBA)	Arto Nilsson (FINLAND) James Wallington (U.S.)
1972		

---

[1] Weight up to 63.5 kilograms (140 lbs).
[2] Both losing semi-finalists are awarded bronze medals.

WELTERWEIGHT

1896–1900 Event not held		
1904[1] Albert Young (U.S.)	H. J. Spanger (U.S.)	Joseph Lydon (U.S.)
1908–1912 Event not held		
1920[2] T. Schneider (CANADA)	A. Ireland (G.B.)	Frederick Colberg (U.S.)
1924[2] Jean Delarge (BELGIUM)	Hector Mendez (ARGENTINA)	Douglas Lewis (CANADA)
1928[2] Edward Morgan (NEW ZEALAND)	Paul Landini (ARGENTINA)	Raymond Smillie (CANADA)
1932[2] Edward Flynn (U.S.)	Erich Campe (GERMANY)	Bruno Ahlberg (FINLAND)
1936[2] Sten Suvio (FINLAND)	Michael Murach (GERMANY)	Gerhard Petersen (DENMARK)
1948[3] Julius Torma (CZECHO.)	Horace Herring (U.S.)	Alessandro Ottavio (ITALY)
1952[3] Zyugmunt Chychla (POLAND)	Sergey Shcherbakov (U.S.S.R.)	Victor Jörgensen[4] (DENMARK) Günther Heidemann (GERMANY)
1956[3] Nicolae Linca (RUMANIA)	Frederick Tiedt (EIRE)	Kevin Hogarth (AUSTRALIA) Nicholas Gargano (G.B.)
1960[3] Giovanni Benvenuti (ITALY)	Yuriy Radnoyak (U.S.S.R.)	Leszek Drogosz (POLAND) James Lloyd (G.B.)
1964[3] Marian Kasprzyk (POLAND)	Richardas Tamulis (U.S.S.R.)	Pertti Purhonen (FINLAND) Silvano Bertini (ITALY)
1968 Manfred Wolke (E. GERMANY)	Joseph Bessala (CAMEROON)	Vladimir Musalinov (U.S.S.R.) Mario Guilloti Gonzalez (ARGENTINA)
1972		

---

[1] Weight up to 65.2 kilograms (143 lbs).
[2] Weight up to 66.6 kilograms (147 lbs).
[3] Weight up to 67 kilograms (147¾ lbs).
[4] From 1952 both losing semi-finalists are awarded bronze medals.

LIGHT-MIDDLEWEIGHT

1896–1948 Event not held		
1952[1] Laszlo Papp (HUNGARY)	Theunis van Schalkwyk (S. AFRICA)	Boris Tishin[2] (U.S.S.R.) Eladio Herrera (ARGENTINA)

Laszlo Papp (Hungary), a southpaw, is the only boxer to win 3 gold medals —in the light-middleweight class in 1952 and 1956, and as a middleweight in 1948.

	GOLD	SILVER	BRONZE
1956[1]	Laszlo Papp (HUNGARY)	José Torres (U.S.)	John McCormack (G.B.) Zbigniew Pietrzykowski (POLAND)
1960[1]	Wilbert McClure (U.S.)	Carmelo Bossi (ITALY)	Boris Lagutin (U.S.S.R.)
1964[1]	Boris Lagutin (U.S.S.R.)	Josef Gonzales (FRANCE)	William Fisher (G.B.) Nojim Maiyegun (NIGERIA) Jozef Grzesiak (POLAND)
1968	Boris Lagutin (U.S.S.R.)	Rolando Garbey (CUBA)	John Baldwin (U.S.) Gunther Meier (W. GERMANY)
1972			

---
[1] Weight up to 71 kilograms (156¼ lbs).
[2] Both losing semi-finalists are awarded bronze medals.

MIDDLEWEIGHT

	GOLD	SILVER	BRONZE
1896–1900	Event not held		
1904[1]	Charles Mayer (U.S.)	Benjamin Spradley (U.S.)	d.n.a.
1908[1]	John Douglas (G.B.)	Reginald Baker (AUSTRALASIA)	W. Philo (G.B.)
1912	Event not held		
1920[2]	Harry Mallin (G.B.)	Prudhomme (CANADA)	Herzowitch (CANADA)

	GOLD	SILVER	BRONZE
1924[2]	Harry Mallin (G.B.)	John Elliott (G.B.)	Joseph Beecken (BELGIUM)
1928[2]	Piero Toscani (ITALY)	Jan Hermanek (CZECHO.)	Leonard Steyaert (BELGIUM)
1932[2]	Carmen Barth (U.S.)	Amado Azar (ARGENTINA)	Ernest Pierce (S. AFRICA)
1936[2]	Jean Despeaux (FRANCE)	Henry Tiller (NORWAY)	Raul Villareal (ARGENTINA)
1948[3]	Laszlo Papp (HUNGARY)	John Wright (G.B.)	Ivano Fontana (ITALY)
1952[4]	Floyd Patterson (U.S.)	Vasile Tita (RUMANIA)	Boris Nikolov[5] (BULGARIA) Karl Sjölin (SWEDEN)
1956[4]	Genadiy Schatkov (U.S.S.R.)	Ramón Tapia (CHILE)	Gilbert Chapron (FRANCE) Victor Zalazar (ARGENTINA)
1960[4]	Edward Crook (U.S.)	Tadeusz Walasek (POLAND)	Ion Monea (RUMANIA) Evgeniy Feofanov (U.S.S.R.)
1964[4]	Valeriy Popenchenko (U.S.S.R.)	Emil Schultz (GERMANY)	Franco Valla (ITALY) Tadensz Walasek (POLAND)
1968	Christopher Finnegan (G.B.)	Aleksey Kiselyov (U.S.S.R.)	Agustin Zaragoza (MEXICO) Alfred Jones (U.S.)
1972			

[1] Weight up to 71.65 kilograms (158 lbs).
[2] Weight up to 72.5 kilograms (160 lbs).
[3] Weight up to 73 kilograms (161 lbs).
[4] Weight up to 75 kilograms (165¼ lbs).
[5] From 1952 both losing semi-finalists are awarded bronze medals.

LIGHT-HEAVYWEIGHT

	GOLD	SILVER	BRONZE
1896–1912	Event not held		
1920[1]	Edward Eagan (U.S.)	Sverre Sörsdal (NORWAY)	H. Franks (G.B.)
1924[1]	Harry Mitchell (G.B.)	Thyge Petersen (DENMARK)	Sverre Sörsdal (NORWAY)
1928[1]	Victorio Avendano (ARGENTINA)	Ernst Pistulla (GERMANY)	Karel Miljon (NETHERLANDS)
1932[1]	David Carstens (S. AFRICA)	Gino Rossi (ITALY)	Peter Jörgensen (DENMARK)
1936[1]	Roger Michelot (FRANCE)	Richard Voigt (GERMANY)	Francisco Risiglione (ARGENTINA)
1948[2]	George Hunter (S. AFRICA)	Donald Scott (G.B.)	M. Cia (ARGENTINA)
1952[3]	Norvel Lee (U.S.)	Antonio Pacenza (ARGENTINA)	Anatoliy Perov[4] (U.S.S.R.) Harry Siljander (FINLAND)
1956[3]	James Boyd (U.S.)	Gheorghe Negrea (RUMANIA)	Carlos Lucas (CHILE) Romualdas Morauskas (U.S.S.R.)
1960[3]	Cassius Clay (U.S.)	Zbigniew Pietrzykowski (POLAND)	Anthony Madigan (AUSTRALIA) Giulio Saraudi (ITALY)
1964[3]	Cosimo Pinto (ITALY)	Aleksey Kiselyov (U.S.S.R.)	Alexander Nicolov (BULGARIA) Zbigniew Pietrzykowski (POLAND)

	GOLD	SILVER	BRONZE
1968	Dan Pozdiak (U.S.S.R.)	Ion Monea (RUMANIA)	Gueorgui Stankov (BULGARIA) Stanislaw Dragan (POLAND)
1972			

---

[1] Weight up to 79.3 kilograms (175 lbs).
[2] Weight up to 80 kilograms (176¼ lbs).
[3] Weight up to 81 kilograms (178¼ lbs).
[4] From 1952 both losing semi-finalists are awarded bronze medals.

HEAVYWEIGHT

	GOLD	SILVER	BRONZE
1896–1900	Event not held		
1904[1]	Samuel Berger (U.S.)	Charles Mayer (U.S.)	d.n.a.
1908[1]	A. L. Oldman (G.B.)	S.C.H. Evans (G.B.)	F. Parks (G.B.)
1912	Event not held		
1920[2]	Ronald Rawson (G.B.)	Sören Petersen (DENMARK)	Elvère (FRANCE)
1924[2]	Otto von Porath (NORWAY)	Sören Petersen (DENMARK)	Alfredo Porzio (ARGENTINA)
1928[2]	Arturo Rodriguez Jurado (ARGENTINA)	Nils Ramm (SWEDEN)	Michael Michaelsen (DENMARK)
1932[2]	Alberto Lovell (ARGENTINA)	Luigi Rovati (ITALY)	Frederick Feary (U.S.)
1936[2]	Herbert Runge (GERMANY)	Guillermo Lovell (ARGENTINA)	Erling Nilsen (NORWAY)
1948[3]	Rafael Iglesias (ARGENTINA)	Gunnar Nilsson (SWEDEN)	John Arthur (S. AFRICA)
1952[4]	Edward Sanders (U.S.)	[5] —	Andries Nieman[6] (S. AFRICA) Ilkka Koski (FINLAND)
1956[4]	T. Peter Rademacher (U.S.)	Lev Mukhin (U.S.S.R.)	Daniel Bekker (S. AFRICA) Giacomo Bozzano (ITALY)
1960[4]	Franco de Piccoli (ITALY)	Daniel Bekker (S. AFRICA)	Josef Nemec (CZECHO.) Günter Siegmund (GERMANY)
1964[4]	Joe Frazier (U.S.)	Hans Huber (GERMANY)	Giuseppe Ros (ITALY) Vadim Yemelyanov (U.S.S.R.)
1968	George Foreman (U.S.)	Iones Chepulis (U.S.S.R.)	Giorgio Bambini (ITALY) Joaquin Roacha (MEXICO)
1972			

---

[1] Weight over 71.65 kilograms (158 lbs).
[2] Weight over 79.3 kilograms (175 lbs).
[3] Weight over 80 kilograms (176¼ lbs).
[4] Weight over 81 kilograms (178¼ lbs).
[5] No silver medal awarded due to disqualification of J. Ingemar Johansson (SWEDEN) in final bout.
[6] From 1952 both losing semi-finalists are awarded bronze medals.

4a. Canoeing (Men)

KAYAK SINGLES[1]

1896–1932   Event not held

	GOLD	SILVER	BRONZE
1936	Gregor Hradetzky (AUSTRIA) 4m 22.9s	Helmut Cämmerer (GERMANY) 4m 25.6s	Jacob Kraaier (NETHS.) 4m 35.1s
1948	Gert Frederiksson (SWEDEN) 4m 33.2s	J. Andersen (DENMARK) 4m 39.9s	Henri Eberhardt (FRANCE) 4m 41.4s
1952	Gert Frederiksson (SWEDEN) 4m 07.9s	Thorvald Strömberg (FINLAND) 4m 09.7s	Louis Gantois (FRANCE) 4m 20.1s
1956	Gert Frederiksson (SWEDEN) 4m 12.8s	Igor Pisaryev (U.S.S.R.) 4m 15.3s	Lajos Kiss (HUNGARY) 4m 16.2s
1960	Erik Hansen (DENMARK) 3m 53.0s	Imre Szöllosi (HUNGARY) 3m 54.0s	Gert Fredriksson (SWEDEN) 3m 55.8s
1964	Rolf Peterson (SWEDEN) 3m 57.13s	Mihaly Hesz (HUNGARY) 3m 57.28s	Aurel Vernescu (RUMANIA) 4m 00.7s
1968	Mihaly Hesz (HUNGARY) 4m 02.63s	Alexander Shaporenko (U.S.S.R.) 4m 03.58s	Erik Hansen (DENMARK) 4m 04.39s
1972			

---

[1] Course of 1,000 metres (1,094 yards).

KAYAK PAIRS[1]

1896–1932   Event not held

1936	AUSTRIA 4m 03.8s Adolf Kainz Alfons Dorfner	GERMANY 4m 08.9s Ewald Tilker Fritz Bondroit	NETHS. 4m 12.2s Nicolaas Tates Willem van der Kroft
1948	SWEDEN 4m 07.3s Hans Berglund Lennart Klingström	DENMARK 4m 07.5s Eivind Hansen Bernard Jensen	FINLAND 4m 08.7s Ture Axelsson Nils Björklöf
1952	FINLAND 3m 51.1s Kurt Wires Yrjö Hietanen	SWEDEN 3m 51.1s Lars Glasser Harald Hedberg	AUSTRIA 3m 51.4s Max Raub Herbert Wiedermann
1956	GERMANY 3m 49.6s Michel Scheuer Meinrad Miltenberger	U.S.S.R. 3m 51.4s Mikhail Kaaleste Anatoliy Demitkov	AUSTRIA 3m 55.8s Max Raub Herbert Wiedermann
1960	SWEDEN 3m 34.7s Gert Fredriksson Sven Olof Sjodelius	HUNGARY 3m 34.9s Andras Szente Gyorgy Meszaros	POLAND 3m 37.3s Stefan Kaplaniak Wladyslaw Zieliski
1964	SWEDEN 3m 38.54s Sven Olof Sjodelius Gunnar Utterberg	NETHS. 3m 39.30s Antonius Geurts Paul Hoekstra	GERMANY 3m 40.69s Heinz Bueker Holger Zander
1968	U.S.S.R. 3m 37.54s Alexander Shaporenko Vladimir Morozov	HUNGARY 3m 38.44s Csaba Giczi Istvan Timar	AUSTRIA 3m 40.71s Gerhard Seibold Gunther Pfaff
1972			

---

[1] Course of 1,000 metres (1,094 yards).

KAYAK FOURS
(not previously held)

1964	U.S.S.R. 3m 14.67s N. Chuzhikov A. Grishin V. Ionov V. Morozov	GERMANY 3m 15.39s G. Perleberg B. Schulze F. Wentzke H. Zander	RUMANIA 3m 15.51s S. Cuciuc A. Sciotnic M. Turcas A. Vernescu
1968	NORWAY 3m 14.38s Steinar Amundsen Egil Soby Tore Berger Jan Johansen	RUMANIA 3m 14.81s Anton Calenic Dimitrie Ivanov Haralambie Ivanov Mimai Turcas	HUNGARY 3m 15.10s Csaba Giczi Istvan Timar Imre Szollosi Istvan Csizmadia
1972			

The Rumanian pair, Patzaichin and Covaliov, winning the 1968 Canadian Pairs event on the artificial lake Canal de Quemanco, which was also used for rowing.

CANADIAN SINGLES[1]

	GOLD	SILVER	BRONZE
1896–1932	Event not held		
1936	Francis Amyot (CANADA) 5m 32.1s	Bohuslav Karlik (CZECHO.) 5m 36.9s	Erich Koschik (GERMANY) 5m 39.0s
1948	Josef Holecek (CZECHO.) 5m 42.0s	D. Bennett (CANADA) 5m 53.3s	Robert Boutigny (FRANCE) 5m 55.9s
1952	Josef Holecek (CZECHO.) 4m 56.3s	János Parti (HUNGARY) 5m 03.6s	Olavi Ojanperä (FINLAND) 5m 08.5s
1956	Leon Rottman (RUMANIA) 5m 05.3s	István Hernek (HUNGARY) 5m 06.2s	Gennadiy Bukharin (U.S.S.R.) 5m 12.7s
1960	János Parti (HUNGARY) 4m 33.9s	Aleksandr Silayev (U.S.S.R.) 4m 34.4s	Leon Rottman (RUMANIA) 4m 35.8s
1964	J. Eschert (GERMANY) 4m 35.14s	A. Igorov (RUMANIA) 4m 37.89s	E. Penyayev (U.S.S.R.) 4m 38.31s
1968	Tibor Tatai (HUNGARY) 4m 36.14s	Detlef Lewe (GERMANY) 4m 25.50s	Vitaly Galkov (U.S.S.R.) 4m 40.42s
1972			

---

[1] Course of 1,000 metres (1,094 yards).

CANADIAN PAIRS[1]

	GOLD	SILVER	BRONZE
1896–1932	Event not held		
1936	CZECHO. 4m 50.1s Vladimir Syróvátka Jan Brzák	AUSTRIA 4m 53.8s Rupert Weinstabl Karl Proisl	CANADA 4m 56.7s Frank Saker Harvey Charters
1948	CZECHO. 5m 07.1s Jan Brzak Bohumil Kudrna	U.S. 5m 08.2s Stephen Lysak Stephen Macknowski	FRANCE 5m 15.2s Georges Dransart Georges Gandil
1952	DENMARK 4m 38.3s Bent Peder Rasch Finn Haunstoft	CZECHO. 4m 42.9s Jan Brzak Bohumil Kudrna	GERMANY 4m 48.3s Egon Drews Wilfried Soltau
1956	RUMANIA 4m 47.4s Alexe Dumitru Simion Ismailciuc	U.S.S.R. 4m 48.6s Pavel Kharin Gratsian Botyev	HUNGARY 4m 54.3s Károly Wieland Ferenc Mohácsi

	GOLD	SILVER	BRONZE
1960	U.S.S.R. 4m 17.9s	ITALY 4m 20.7s	HUNGARY 4m 20.8s
	Leonid Geyshter	Aldo Dezi	Imre Farkas
	Sergey Makharenko	Francesco Lamacchia	Andras Toro
1964	U.S.S.R. 4m 04.65s	FRANCE 4m 06.52s	DENMARK 4m 07.48s
	Andrey Khimich	Jean Boudehen	Peer Nielsen
	Stepan Oschepkov	Michel Chapuis	John Sorenson
1968	RUMANIA 4m 07.18s	HUNGARY 4m 08.77s	U.S.S.R. 4m 11.30s
	Ivan Patzaichin	Tamas Wichmann	Naum Prokupets
	Serghei Covaliov	Gyula Petrikovics	Mikhail Zamotin
1972			

---

[1] Course of 1,000 metres (1,094 yards).

4×500 METRES (547 yards)

	GOLD	SILVER	BRONZE
1896–1956	Event not held		
1960	GERMANY 7m 39.4s	HUNGARY 7m 44.0s	DENMARK 7m 46.0s
	Paul Lange	Imbre Szoellosi	Helmut Sörensen
	Günther Perleberg	Imre Kemecsi	Arne Hoyer
	Friedhelm Wentzke	Andras Szente	Erling Jessen
	Dieter Krause	György Meszaros	Erik Hansen
1964–1968	(Event not held)		

4b. Canoeing (Women)

KAYAK SINGLES[1]

	GOLD	SILVER	BRONZE
1896–1936	Event not held		
1948	Karen Hoff (DENMARK) 2m 31.9s	Alide Van de Anker-Doedans (NETHS.) 2m 32.8s	Fritzi Schwingl (AUSTRIA) 2m 32.9s
1952	Sylvi Saimo (FINLAND) 2m 18.4s	Gertrude Liebhart (AUSTRIA) 2m 18.8s	Nina Savina (U.S.S.R.) 2m 21.6s
1956	Elisaveta Dementyeva (U.S.S.R.) 2m 18.9s	Therese Zenz (GERMANY) 2m 19.6s	Tove Soby (DENMARK) 2m 22.3s
1960	Antonina Seredina (U.S.S.R.) 2m 08.0s	Therese Zenz (GERMANY) 2m 08.2s	Daniela Walkowiak (POLAND) 2m 10.4s
1964	Ludmila Khvedosink (U.S.S.R.) 2m 12.87s	Hilde Lauer (RUMANIA) 2m 15.35s	Marcia Jones (U.S.) 2m 15.68s
1968	Ludmila Pinayeva (U.S.S.R.) 2m 07.10s	Renate Breuer (GERMANY) 2m 12.71s	Viorica Dumitru (RUMANIA) 2m 13.22s
1972			

KAYAK PAIRS[1]

	GOLD	SILVER	BRONZE
1896–1956	Event not held		
1960	U.S.S.R. 1m 54.7s	GERMANY 1m 56.6s	HUNGARY 1m 58.2s
	Maria Zhubina	Therese Zenz	Virman Egresi
	Antonina Seredina	Ingrid Hartmann	Klara Fried
1964	GERMANY 1m 56.95s	U.S. 1m 59.16s	RUMANIA 2m 00.25s
	Roswitha Esser	Francine Fox	Hilde Lauer
	Anne Marie Zimmermann	Glorianne Perrier	Cornelia Sideri
1968	GERMANY 1m 56.44s	HUNGARY 1m 58.60s	U.S.S.R. 1m 58.61s
	Anne Marie Zimmermann	Anna Pfeffer	Ludmila Pinayeva
	Roswitha Esser	Katalin Roszynoi	Antonina Seredina
1972			

---

[1] Course of 500 metres (547 yards).

5. Cycling

1,000 METRES SPRINT[1]

1896   Event not held

	GOLD	SILVER	BRONZE
1900	G. Taillandier (FRANCE) 2m 16.0s	Ferdinand Vasserot (FRANCE)	Lanz (FRANCE)
1904–08–12	Event not held		
1920	Mauritius Peeters (NETHS.) 1m 38.3s	H. T. Johnson (G.B.)	Harry Ryan (G.B.)
1924[2]	Lucien Michard (FRANCE)	Jacob Meyer (NETHS.)	Jean Cugnot (FRANCE)
1928	R. Beaufrand (FRANCE)	Antoine Mazairac (NETHS.)	Willy Falck-Hansen (DENMARK)
1932	Jacobus van Egmond (NETHS.)	Louis Chaillot (FRANCE)	Bruno Pellizzari (ITALY)
1936	Toni Merkens (GERMANY)	Arie van Vliet (NETHS.)	Louis Chaillot (FRANCE)
1948	Mario Ghella (ITALY)	Reginald Harris (G.B.)	Axel Schandorff (DENMARK)
1952	Enzo Sacchi (ITALY)	Lionel Cox (AUSTRALIA)	Werner Potzernheim (GERMANY)
1956	Michel Rousseau (FRANCE)	Guglielmo Pesenti (ITALY)	Richard Ploog (AUSTRALIA)
1960	Sante Gaiardoni (ITALY)	Leo Sterckx (BELGIUM)	Valentino Gasparella (ITALY)
1964	Giovanni Pettenella (ITALY)	Sergio Bianchetto (ITALY)	Daniel Morelon (FRANCE)
1968	Daniel Morelon (FRANCE)	Giordano Turrini (ITALY)	Pierre Trentin (FRANCE)
1972			

---

[1] There was a 1,000 metres sprint event in the 1908 Games, but it was declared void because "the riders exceeded the time limit, in spite of repeated warnings."
[2] Since 1924 only times over the last 200 metres of the event have been recorded.

1,000 METRES TIME-TRIAL

1896–1924   Event not held

1928	Willy Falck-Hansen (DENMARK) 1m 14.4s*	Gerard Bosch van Drakesstein (NETHS.) 1m 15.2s	Edgar Gray (AUSTRALIA)1m15.6s
1932	Edgar Gray (AUSTRALIA) 1m 13.0s*	Jacobus van Egmond (NETHS.) 1m 13.3s	Charles Rampelberg (FRANCE) 1m 13.4s
1936	Arie van Vliet (NETHS.) 1m 12.0s*	Pierre Georget (FRANCE) 1m 12.8s	Rudolf Karsch (GERMANY) 1m 13.2s
1948	Jacques Dupont (FRANCE) 1m 13.5s	Pierre Nihant (BELGIUM) 1m 14.5s	Thomas Godwin (G.B.) 1m 15.0s
1952	Russell Mockridge (AUSTRALIA) 1m 11.1s*	Marino Morettini (ITALY) 1m 12.7s	Raymond Robinson (S. AFRICA) 1m 13.0s
1956	Leandro Faggin (ITALY) 1m 09.8s*	Ladislav Foucek (CZECHO.) 1m 11.4s	J. Alfred Swift (S. AFRICA) 1m 11.6s
1960	Sante Gaiardoni (ITALY) 1m 07.27s*[1]	Dieter Gieseler (GERMANY) 1m 08.75s	Rostislav Vargashkin (U.S.S.R.) 1m 08.86s
1964	Patrick Sercu (BELGIUM) 1m 09.59s	Giovanni Pettenella (ITALY) 1m 10.09s	Pierre Trentin (FRANCE) 1m 10.42s
1968	Pierre Trentin (FRANCE) 1m 03.91s	Niels Fredborg (DENMARK) 1m 04.61s	Janusz Kierzkowski (POLAND) 1m 04.61s
1972			

---

[1] Electrical timing.

2,000 METRES TANDEM

	GOLD	SILVER	BRONZE
1896–1904	Event not held		
1908	FRANCE 3m 07.6s*	G.B.	G.B.
	Maurice Schilles	F. G. Hamlin	C. Brooks
	André Auffray	H. T. Johnson	W. H. T. Isaacs
1912	Event not held		
1920	G.B. 2m 49.4s*	S. AFRICA	NETHS.
	Harry Ryan	J. R. Walker	Devreugit
	Thomas Lance	W. R. Smith	Piet Ikelaar
1924	FRANCE 2m 40.0s*	DENMARK	NETHS.
	Jean Cugnot	Edmund Hansen	Mauritius Peeters
	Lucien Choury	Willy Falck-Hansen	Gerard Bosch van Drakestein
1928[1]	NETHS.	G.B.	GERMANY
	Bernhard Leene	Jack Sibbit	Bernhardt
	Daan van Dijk	Ernest Chambers	Köther
1932	FRANCE	G.B.	DENMARK
	Maurice Perrin	Ernest Chambers	Harald Christensen
	Louis Chaillot	Stanley Chambers	Willy Gervin
1936	GERMANY	NETHS.	FRANCE
	Ernst Ihbe	Bernhard Leene	Pierre Georget
	Carl Lorenz	Hendrik Ooms	Georges Maton
1948	ITALY	G.B.	FRANCE
	Renato Perona	Reginald Harris	Georges Dron
	Ferdinando Teruzzi	Alan Bannister	René Faye
1952	AUSTRALIA	S. AFRICA	ITALY
	Russell Mockridge	Raymond Robinson	Antonio Maspes
	Lionel Cox	Thomas Shardelow	Cesare Pinarello
1956	AUSTRALIA[2]	CZECHO.	ITALY
	Ian Browne	Václav Machek	Giuseppe Ogna
	Anthony Marchant	Ladislav Foucek	Cesare Pinarello
1960	ITALY	GERMANY	U.S.S.R.
	Sergio Bianchetto	Jürgen Simon	Boris Vasiliyev
	Giuseppe Beghetto	Lothar Stäber	Vladimir Leonov
1964	ITALY	U.S.S.R.	GERMANY
	Sergio Bianchetto	Imant Bodniex	Willi Fuggerer
	Angelo Damiano	Victor Logunov	Klaus Kobusch
1968	FRANCE	NETHS.	BELGIUM
	Pierre Trentin	Johannes Jansen	Daniel Goens
	Daniel Morelon	Leijn Loevesijn	Robert Van Lancker
1972			

[1] Since 1928 only times over the last 200 metres of the event have been recorded.
[2] The AUSTRALIAN pair were last of three teams in their first-round heat, and were beaten by CZECHOSLOVAKIA in the repechage (consolation heat for losers); but they won their second repechage heat, quarter-final and semi-final.

4,000 METRES INDIVIDUAL PURSUIT
(not previously held)

1964	Jiri Daler	Giorgio Ursi	Preben Isaksson
	(CZECH.) 5m 04.75s	(ITALY) 5m 05.96s	(DENMARK) 5m 01.90s
1968	Daniel Rebillard	Frey Jensen	Xaver Kurmann
	(FRANCE) 4m 41.71s	(DENMARK) 4m 42.43s	(SWITZ.) 4m 39.42s
1972			

4,000 METRES TEAM PURSUIT

1896–1912	Event not held		
1920	ITALY 5m 20.0s*	G.B.	S. AFRICA
	Franco Giorgetti	Albert White	J. R. Walker
	Ruggero Ferrario	H. T. Johnson	W. R. Smith
	Arnaldo Carli	William Stewart	Henry Kaltenbrun
	Primo Magnani	C. Albert Alden	H. W. Goosen

	GOLD	SILVER	BRONZE
1924	ITALY 5m 12.0s*	POLAND	BELGIUM
	Alfredo Dinale	Josef Lange	Léon Dahelinczky
	Francesco Zucchetti	Franciszek Szymczyk	Henry Hoevenaers
	Angelo de Martino	Jan Lazarski	Ferdinand Saive
	Alerado Menegazzi	Tomas Sztankiewicz	Jean van den Bosch
1928	ITALY 5m 01.8s*	NETHS. 5m 06.2s	G.B.
	Luigi Tasselli	Adrianus Braspenninx	Frank Wyld
	Giacomo Gaioni	Jan Maas	Harry Wyld
	Cesare Facciani	Johannes Pijnenburg	Percy Wyld[1]
	Mario Lusiani	Piet van der Horst	Frank Southall
1932	ITALY 4m 52.9s*	FRANCE 4m 55.7s	G.B. 4m 56.0s
	Marco Cimatti	Amadé Fournier	Ernest Johnson
	Paolo Pedretti	René Legrèves	William Harvell
	Alberto Ghilardi	Henri Mouillefarine	Frank Southall
	Nino Borsari	Paul Chocque	Charles Holland
1936	FRANCE 4m 45.0s*	ITALY 4m 51.0s	G.B. 4m 52.6s
	Robert Charpentier	Bianco Bianchi	Harry Hill
	Jean Goujon	Mario Gentili	Ernest Johnson
	Guy Lapébie	Armando Latini	Charles King
	Roger Le Nizerhy	Severino Rigoni	Ernest Mills
1948	FRANCE 4m 57.8s	ITALY 5m 36.7s	G.B. 4m 55.8s[3]
	Pierre Adam	Arnaldo Benfenati	Alan Geldard
	Serge Blusson	Guido Bernardi	Thomas Godwin
	Charles Coste	Anselmo Citterio	David Ricketts
	Ferdinand Decanali	Rino Pucci	Wilfred Waters
1952	ITALY 4m 46.1s	S. AFRICA 4m 53.6s	G.B. 4m 51.5s[4]
	Marino Morettini	Thomas Shardelow	Ronald Stretton
	Guido Messina	Alfred Swift	Alan Newton
	Mino de Rossi	Robert Fowler	George Newberry
	Loris Campana	George Estman	Donald Burgess
1956	ITALY 4m 37.4s*	FRANCE 4m 39.4s[5]	G.B. 4m 42.2s
	Leandro Faggin	René Bianchi	Thomas Simpson
	Valentino Gasparella[6]	Jean Graczyk	Donald Burgess
	Franco Gandini	Jean-Claude Lecante	John Geddes
	Tonino Domenicali	Michel Vermeulin	Michael Gambrill
1960	ITALY 4m 30.90s[7]	GERMANY 4m 35.78s	U.S.S.R. 4m 34.05s[8]
	Luigi Arienti	Peter Gröning	Stanislav Moskvin
	Franco Testa	Manfred Klieme	Viktor Romanov
	Mario Vallotto	Siegfried Köhler	Leonid Kolumbert
	Marino Vigna	Bernd Barleben	Arnold Belygaert
1964	GERMANY 4m 35.67s	ITALY 4m 35.74s	NETHS. 4m 38.99s[9]
	Lothar Claesges	Luigi Roncaglia	Gerard Koel
	Karl-Heinz Henrichs	Vincenzo Mantovani	Hendrik Cornelisse
	Karl Link	Carlo Rancati	Jacob Oudkerk
	Ernest Streng	Franco Testa	Cornelis Schuuring
1968	DENMARK 4m 22.44s	GERMANY 4m 18.94s	ITALY 4m 18.35s
	Gunnar Asmussen	Udo Hempel	Lorenzo Bosisio
	Per Lyngemark	Karl Link	Cipirano Chemello
	Reno Olsen	Karl-Heinz Henrichs	Luigi Roncaglia
	Frey Jensen	Jurgen Kissner	Giorgio Morbiato
1972			

---

[1] The Wylds were brothers; set record of 5:01.6 in preliminaries.
[2] Set record of 4:41.8 in preliminaries.
[3] Time recorded in third-place race against Uruguay. Times for French and Italian teams are those recorded in final.
[4] Time recorded in third-place race against FRANCE. Times for ITALIAN and SOUTH AFRICAN teams are those recorded in final. In preliminaries ITALY recorded 4:45.7, SOUTH AFRICA 4:50.6 and G.B. 4:49.4.
[5] FRANCE recorded 4:39.0 and G.B. 4:40.6 in preliminaries.
[6] Virginio Pizzali rode in first-round heat, but fell and was injured. Gasparella replaced him for remainder of event.
[7] Electrical timing.
[8] Time recorded in third-place race against FRANCE. Times for ITALIAN and GERMAN teams are those recorded in final. In preliminaries ITALY re-recorded 4:28.88 (O.R.). GERMANY 4:29.32 and U.S.S.R. 4:29.97.
[9] Time recorded in third-place race against AUSTRALIA.

ROAD-RACE
(first held 1896)

GOLD	SILVER	BRONZE
1896[1] A. Konstantinidis	A. Goedrich	F. Battel
(GREECE) 3h 22m 31.0s	(GERMANY)	(G.B.)
	3h 42m 18.0s	
1900–08 Event not held[2]		
1912[3] Rudolph Lewis	Frederick Grubb	Carl Schutte
(S. AFRICA)	(G.B.) 10h 51m 24.2s	(U.S.) 10h 52m 38.8s
10h 42m 39.0s		
Teams—		
SWEDEN 44h 35m 33.6s	G.B. 44h 44m 39.2s	U.S. 44h 47m 55.5s
Eric Friborg	Frederick Grubb	Carl Schutte
Ragnar Malm	Leonard Meredith	Alvin Loftes
Axel Persson	Charles Moss	Albert Krushel
Algot Lönn	V. R. Hammond	W. C. Martin
1920[4] Harry Stenquist	Henry Kaltenbrun	F. Canteloube
(SWEDEN)	(S. AFRICA)	(FRANCE)
4h 40m 01.8s	4h 41m 26.6s	4h 42m 54.4s
*Teams—*FRANCE	SWEDEN	BELGIUM
19h 16m 43.2s	19h 23m 10.0s	19h 28m 44.4s
F. Canteloube	Harry Stenquist	Janssens
Georges Detreille	Ragnar Malm	Debunne
Achille Souchard	Axel Persson	Vercruysse
Marcel Gobillot	Sigfrid Lundberg	Wyckmann
1925[5] Armand Blanchonnet	Henry Hoevenaers	René Hamel
(FRANCE)	(BELGIUM)	(FRANCE)
6h 20m 48.0s	6h 30m 27.0s	6h 30m 51.6s
*Teams—*FRANCE	BELGIUM	SWEDEN
19h 30m 14.0s	19h 46m 55.4s	19h 59m 41.6s
Armand Blanchonnet	Henry Hoevenaers	Gunnar Sköld
René Hamel	A. Parfondry	Erik Bohlin
Georges Wambst	Jean van den Bosch	Ragnar Malm
1928[6] Henry Hansen	Frank Southall	Gösta Carlsson
(DENMARK)	(G.B.) 4h 54m 44.0s	(SWEDEN)
4h 47m 18.0s		4h 59m 55.0s
*Teams—*DENMARK	G.B. 15h 14m 29.0s	SWEDEN
15h 09m 14.0s		15h 27m 22.0s
Henry Hansen	Frank Southall	Gösta Carlsson
Leo Nielsen	Jack Lauterwasser	Georg Johnsson
Orla Jörgensen	Jack Middleton	Erik Jansson
1932[7] Attilio Pavesi	Guglielmo Segato	Bernhard Britz
(ITALY) 2h 28m 05.6s	(ITALY) 2h 29m 21.4s	(SWEDEN)
		2h 29m 45.2s
*Teams—*ITALY	DENMARK	SWEDEN
7h 27m 15.2s	7h 38m 50.2s	7h 39m 12.6s
Attilio Pavesi	Frede Sörensen	Bernhard Britz
Guglielmo Segato	Leo Nielsen	Arne Berg
Giuseppe Olmo	Henry Hansen	S. Hoglund
1936[7] Robert Charpentier	Guy Lapébie	Ernst Nievergelt
(FRANCE)	(FRANCE)	(SWITZ.)
2h 33m 05.0s	2h 33m 05.2s	2h 33m 05.8s
*Teams—*FRANCE	SWITZ.	BELGIUM
7h 39m 16.2s	7h 39m 20.4s	7h 39m 21.0s
Robert Charpentier	Ernst Nievergelt	Auguste Garrebeeck
Guy Lapébie	Edgar Buchwalder	Armand Putzeys
Robert Dorgebray	Kurt Otto	Francois vander Motten
1948[8] José Beyaert	Geerit Voorting	Louis Wouters
(FRANCE)	(NETHS.)	(BELGIUM)
5h 18m 12.6s	5h 18m 16.2s	5h 18m 16.2s
*Teams—*BELGIUM	G.B. 16h 03m 31.6s	FRANCE
15h 58m 17.4s		16h 08m 19.4s
Louis Wouters	Robert Maitland	José Beyaert
Léon Delathouwer	Gordon Thomas	Alain Moineau
Eugène van Roosbroeck	C. S. Ian Scott	Jacques Dupont
1952[9] André Noyelle	Robert Grondelaers	Edi Ziegler
(BELGIUM)	(BELGIUM)	(GERMANY)
5h 06m 03.4s	5h 06m 51.2s	5h 07m 47.5s

GOLD	SILVER	BRONZE
Teams—BELGIUM 15h 20m 46.6s	ITALY 15h 33m 27.3s	FRANCE 15h 38m 58.1s
André Noyelle	Dino Bruni	Jacques Anquetil
Robert Grondelaers	Vincenzo Zucconelli	Alfred Tonello
Lucien Victor	Gianni Ghidini	Claude Rouer
1956[10] Ercole Baldini (ITALY) 5h 21m 17.0s	Arnaud Geyre (FRANCE) 5h 23m 16.0s	Alan Jackson (G.B.) 5h 23m 17.0s
Teams—FRANCE 22 pts.[11]	G.B. 23 pts.	GERMANY 27 pts.
Arnaud Geyre	Alan Jackson	Horst Tüller
Maurice Moucheraud	A. Stanley Brittain	Gustav Schur
Michel Vermeulin	William Holmes	Reinhold Pommer
1960[12] Viktor Kapitonov (U.S.S.R.) 4h 20m 37.0s	Livio Trapé (ITALY) 4h 20m 37.0s	Willy van den Berghen (BELGIUM) 4h 20m 57.0s
	Team event not held	
1964 Mario Zanin (ITALY) 4h 39m 51.63s	Kjell Rodian (DENMARK) 4h 39m 51.65s	Walter Godefroot (BELGIUM) 4h 39m 51.74s
1968 Pierfranco Vianelli (ITALY) 4h 41m 25.24s	Leif Mortensen (DENMARK) 4h 42m 49.71s	Gosta Pettersson (SWEDEN) 4h 43m 15.24s
1972		

[1] Held over 87 kilometres (54 miles).
[2] In 1904 there were events over two miles (3,218 metres), five miles (8,045 metres) and 25 miles (40,225 metres), but all were on the track.
[3] Held over 320 kilometres (199 miles).
[4] Held over 175 kilometres (109 miles).
[5] Held over 188 kilometres (117 miles).
[6] Held over 169 kilometres (105 miles).
[7] Held over 100 kilometres (62 miles).
[8] Held over 199.6 kilometres (124 miles).
[9] Held over 190.4 kilometres (118 miles).
[10] Held over 187.7 kilometres (117 miles).
[11] Time aggregates: FRANCE 16:10.36; G.B. 16:10.46 and GERMANY 16:11.10.
[12] Held over 175.4 kilometres (109 miles).

ROAD TEAM TIME-TRIAL
(first held 1960)

	GOLD	SILVER	BRONZE
1960[1]	ITALY[2] 2h 14m 33.53s	GERMANY 2h 16m 56.31s	U.S.S.R. 2h 18m 41.67s
	Antonio Bailetti	Gustav Schur	Viktor Kapitonov
	Ottavio Cogliati	Egon Adler	Eugen Klevzov
	Giacomo Fornoni	Erich Hagen	Yuriy Melikhov
	Livio Trapé	Günter Lörke	Aleksey Petrov
1964	NETHS. 2h 16m 31.19s	ITALY 2h 26m 55.39s	SWEDEN 2h 27m 11.52s
	Gerben Karstens	Severino Andreoli	Sven Hamrin
	Evert Dolman	Luciano della Bona	Erik Pettersson
	Johannes Pieterse	Pietro Guerra	Gosta Pettersson
	Hubertus Zort	Ferniccio Manza	Sven Pettersson
1968	NETHS. 2h 07m 49.06s	SWEDEN 2h 09m 26.60s	ITALY 2h 10m 18.74s
	Marinus Pijnen	Gosta Pettersson	Vittorio Marcelli
	Fedor den Hertog	Sture Pettersson	Mauro Simonetti
	Jan Krekels	Erik Pettersson	Pierfranco Vianelli
	Gerardes Zoetemelk	Tomas Pettersson	Giovanni Bramucci
1972			

[1] Held over 100 kilometres.
[2] Electrical timing.

6. Equestrian Sports

GRAND PRIX (JUMPING)

GOLD	SILVER	BRONZE
1896–1908 Event not held		
1912 Jean Cariou	von Kröcher	Emanuel Blommaert de Soye
(FRANCE) 186 pts.	(GERMANY) 186	(BELGIUM) 185
Teams—SWEDEN 545 pts.	FRANCE 538	GERMANY 530
Casimir Lewenhaupt	Jean Cariou	Sigismund Freyer
Hans von Rosen	d'Astafort	Graf von Hohenau
Gustaf Kilman	F. Meyer	Ernst Deloch
1920 Tommaso Lequio	Alessandro Valerio	Gustaf Lewenhaupt
(ITALY) no faults	(ITALY) 3	(SWEDEN) 4
Teams—SWEDEN 14 faults	BELGIUM 16.25	ITALY 18.75
Hans von Rosen	Count de Oultremont	Ettore Caffaratti
Claes König	Commans	Giuseppe Cacciandra
Daniel Norling	Baron de Gaiffier	Alessandro Alvisi
1924 Alphons Gemuseus	Tommaso Lequio	Adam Królikiewicz
(SWITZ.) 6 pts.	(ITALY) 8.75	(POLAND) 10
Teams—SWEDEN 42.5 pts.	SWITZ. 50	PORTUGAL —
Ake Thelning	Alphons Gemuseus	Borges d'Almeida
Axel Stähle	Werner Stüber	Martins de Souza
Age Lundström	Hans Bühler	Mouzinho d'Albuquerque
1928 Frantisek Ventura	Pierre Bertran de Balanda	Chasimir Kuhn
(CZECHO.) no faults	(FRANCE) 2	(SWITZ.) 4
Teams—SPAIN 4 faults	POLAND 8	SWEDEN 10
Marquis de los Trujillos	Kazimierz Gzowski	Karl Hansen
J. Morenes Navarro	Kazimierz Szosland	Carl Björnstjerna
J. Garcia Fernandez	Michael Antoniewicz	Ernst Hallberg
1932[1] Takeichi Nishi	Harry Chamberlin	Clarence von Rosen
(JAPAN) 8 pts.	(U.S.) 12	(SWEDEN) 16
1936 Kurt Hasse	Henri Rang	József Platthy
(GERMANY) 4 pts.	(RUMANIA) 4	(HUNGARY) 8
Teams—GERMANY 44 pts.	NETHS. 51.5	PORTUGAL 56
Kurt Hasse	Jan de Bruine	Luis Mena e Silva
Marten von Barnekow	Johan Greter	Marquez de Funchal
Heinz Brandt	Henri van Schaik	José Beltrao
1948 Humberto Mariles	Ruben Uriza	Jean d'Orgeix
(MEXICO) 6.25 pts.	(MEXICO) 8	(FRANCE) 8
Teams—MEXICO 34.25 pts.	SPAIN 56	G.B. 67
Humberto Mariles	J. Garcia Cruz	H. M. V. Nicoll
Ruben Uriza	M. Ponce de Leon	Arthur Carr
R. Valdes	J. Morenes Navarro	Henry Llewellyn
1952 Pierre Jonquères d'Oriola	Oscar Cristi	Fritz Thiedemann
(FRANCE) no faults	(CHILE) 4	(GERMANY) 8
Teams—G.B. 40.75 faults	CHILE 45.75	U.S. 52.25
Douglas Stewart	Oscar Cristi	Arthur McCashin
Wilfred White	Ricardo Echeverria	John Russel
Henry Llewellyn	Cesar Mendoza	William Steinkraus
1956 Hans Günter Winkler	Raimondo d'Inzeo	Piero d'Inzeo
(GERMANY) 4 faults	(ITALY) 8	(ITALY) 11
Teams—GERMANY 40	ITALY 66	G.B. 69
Hans Günter Winkler	Raimondo d'Inzeo	Wilfred White
Fritz Thiedemann	Piero d'Inzeo	Patricia Smythe
August Lütge-Westhues	Salvatore Oppes	Peter Robeson
1960 Raimondo d'Inzeo	Piero d'Inzeo	David Broome
(ITALY) 12 faults	(ITALY) 16	(G.B.) 23
Teams—GERMANY 46.50	U.S. 66	ITALY 80.50
Alwin Schockemöhle	George Morris	Raimondo d'Inzeo
Fritz Thiedemann	Frank Chapot	Piero d'Inzeo
Hans Günter Winkler	William Steinkraus	Antonio Oppes

---

[1] There was also a teams competition, but there was no nation of which all three riders completed the course.

GOLD	SILVER	BRONZE
1964 Pierre Jonquières d'Oriola (FRANCE) 9 faults	Herman Schridde (GERMANY) 13.75 faults	Peter Robeson (G.B.) 16 faults
Teams—GERMANY 68.50 Herman Schridde Kurt Jarasinki Hans Günter Winkler	FRANCE 77.75 Pierre Jonquières d'Oriola Janon Lefebvre Guy Lefrant	ITALY 88.50 Piero d'Inzeo Raimondo d'Inzeo Graziano Mancinelli
1968 William Steinkraus (U.S.) 4 faults	Marian Coates (G.B.) 8 faults	David Broome (G.B.) 12 faults
Teams—CANADA 102.75 Thomas Gayford James Day James Elder	FRANCE 110.50 Jean Rozier Janon Lefebvre Pierre Jonquières d'Oriola	GERMANY 117.25 Hermann Schridde Alwin Schockemohle Hans Günther Winkler
1972		

GRAND PRIX (DRESSAGE)

1896 Event not held		
1900 C. Haegeman (BELGIUM)	van der Poele (BELGIUM)	de Champsavin (FRANCE)
1904–08 Event not held		
1912 Carl Bonde (SWEDEN) 15 pts.	Gustaf-Adolf Boltenstern (SWEDEN) 21	Hans von Blixen-Finecke (SWEDEN) 32
1920 Janne Lundblad (SWEDEN) 27,937 pts.	Bertil Sandström (SWEDEN) 26,312	Hans von Rosen (SWEDEN) 25,125
1924 Ernst von Linder (SWEDEN) 276.4 pts.	Bertil Sandström (SWEDEN) 275.8	Francois Lesage (FRANCE) 268.5
1928 Carl von Langen (GERMANY) 237.42pts.	Charles Marion (FRANCE) 231.00	Ragnar Olsson (SWEDEN) 229.78
Teams—GERMANY 669.72 pts. Carl von Langen Hermann Linkenbach Eugen von Lotzbeck	SWEDEN 650.86 Ragnar Olsson Carl Bonde Janne Lundblad	NETHS. 642.96 Jan van Reede Pierre Versteegh Gérard le Heux
1932 Xavier Lesage (FRANCE) 1,031.25 pts.	Charles Marion (FRANCE) 916.25	Hiram Tuttle (U.S.) 901.50
Teams—FRANCE 2,818.75 pts. Xavier Lesage Charles Marion André Jousseaume	SWEDEN 2,678.00 Thomas Byström Gustaf-Adolf Boltenstern Bertil Sandström	U.S. 2,576.75 Hiram Tuttle Isaac Kitts Alvin Moore
1936 Heinrich Pollay (GERMANY) 1,760.0 pts.	Friedrich Gerhard (GERMANY) 1,745.5	Alois Podhajsky (AUSTRIA) 1,721.5
Teams—GERMANY 5,074 pts. Heinrich Pollay Friedrich Gerhard Hermann von Oppeln Bronikowski	FRANCE 4,846 André Jousseaume Daniel Gillois Gérard de Ballorre	SWEDEN 4,660.5 Gregor von Adlercreutz Folke Sandström Sven Colliander
1948 Hans Moser (SWITZ.) 492.5 pts.	André Jousseaume (FRANCE) 480.0	Gustaf-Adolf Boltenstern (SWEDEN) 477.5
Teams—FRANCE 1,269 pts.[1] André Jousseaume Jean Paillard Maurice Buret	U.S. 1,256 Robert Borg Earl Thomson Frank Henry	PORTUGAL 1,182 Fernando da Silva Paes Francisco Valadas Luis Mena e Silva

Canada won its only gold medal with the last event of the 1968 Games when Jim Elder (seen above), Thomas Gayford and James Day were victorious in the Grand Prix Jumping Team Championship.

	GOLD	SILVER	BRONZE
1952	Henri St. Cyr (SWEDEN) 556.5 pts.	Lis Hartel (DENMARK) 541.5	André Jousseaume (FRANCE) 541.0
	Teams—SWEDEN 1,597.5pts.	SWITZ. 1,579.0	GERMANY 1,501.0
	Gustaf-Adolf Boltenstern	Gustav Fischer	Ida von Nagel
		Gottfried Trachsel	Fritz Thiedemann
	Henri St. Cyr	Henri Chammartin	Heinrich Pollay
	Gehnäll Persson		
1956	Henri St. Cyr (SWEDEN) 860 pts.	Lis Hartel (DENMARK) 850	Liselott Linsenhoff (GERMANY) 832
	Teams—SWEDEN 2,475 pts.	GERMANY 2,346	SWITZ. 2,346
	Henri St. Cyr	Liselotte Linsenhoff	Gustav Fischer
	Gehnäll Persson	Hannelore Weygand	Gottfried Trachsel
	Gustaf-Adolf Boltenstern	Anneliese Küppers	Henri Chammartin
1960	Sergey Filatov (U.S.S.R.) 2,144 pts.	Gustav Fischer (SWITZ.) 2,087	Josef Neckermann (GERMANY) 2,082
		Team event not held	
1964	Henri Chammartin (SWITZ.) 1,504 pts.	Harry Boldt (GERMANY) 1,503 pts.	Sergey Filatov (U.S.S.R.) 1,486 pts.
	Teams—GERMANY 2,558 pts.	SWITZ. 2,526 pts.	U.S.S.R. 2,311 pts.
	Harry Boldt	Henri Chammartin	Sergey Filatov
	Josef Neckermann	Gustav Fischer	Ivan Kizimov
	Reiner Klimke	Marianne Gossweiler	Ivan Kalita
1968	Ivan Kizimov (U.S.S.R.) 1,572 pts.	Josef Neckermann (GERMANY) 1,546	Rainer Klimke (GERMANY) 1,537
	Teams—GERMANY 2,699 pts.	U.S.S.R. 2,657 pts.	SWITZ. 2,547 pts.
	Josef Neckermann	Elena Petuchkova	Henri Chammartin
	Liselott Linsenhoff	Ivan Kizimov	Marianne Gossweiler
	Rainer Klimke	Ivan Kalita	Gustav Fischer
1972			

---

[1] SWEDEN were originally declared winners with 1,366 pts., but were subsequently disqualified—five years later.

Grand Prix jumping is a test of the stamina and ability of both horse and man. Captain Ernst Hallberg of the Swedish team in 1932 and his highly-strung horse, Marokann, stumbled on the difficult water jump in the steeplechase that makes up the second day of the three-day event, but stayed in the contest the third day in spite of injuries sustained.

THREE-DAY EVENT

	GOLD	SILVER	BRONZE
1896–1908	Event not held		
1912	Axel Nordlander (SWEDEN) 46.59 pts.	von Rochow (GERMANY) 46.42	J. Cariou (FRANCE) 46.32
Teams—	SWEDEN 139.06pts. Nils Adlercreutz Axel Nordlander E. G. Casparsson	GERMANY 138.48 von Ruchow von Lütcken Rudolf Thannheim	U.S. 137.33 Benjamin Lear John Montgomery Guy Henry
1920	Helmer Mörner (SWEDEN) 1,775 pts.	Age Lundström (SWEDEN) 1,738	Ettore Caffaratti (ITALY) 1,733.75
Teams—	SWEDEN 5,057.5pts. Helmer Mörner Age Lundström Georg von Braun	ITALY 4,735 Ettore Caffaratti Garibaldi Sprighi Giuseppe Cacciandra	BELGIUM 4,660 Mooremans d'Emars Lints J. Bonvalet
1924	Adolph van Zijp (NETHS.) 1,976 pts.	Fröde Kirkjeberg (DENMARK) 1,873.5	Sloan Doak (U.S.) 1,845.5
Teams—	NETHS. 5,294.5pts. Adolph van Zijp Ferdinand de Mortanges Gerard de Kruyff	SWEDEN 4,743.5 Claes König Torsten Sylvan Gustaf Hagelin	ITALY 4,512 Alberto Lombardi Alessandro Alvisi Emanuele di Pralormo
1928	Ferdinand de Mortanges (NETHS.) 1,969.82 pts.	Gerard de Kruyff (NETHS.) 1,967.26	Bruno Neumann (GERMANY) 1,934.42
Teams—	NETHS. 5,865.68 pts. Ferdinand de Mortanges Gerard de Kruyff Adolph van Zijp	NORWAY 5,395.68 Arthur Quist Bjart Ording Eugen Johansen	POLAND 5,067.92 Josef Trenkwald Michael Antoniewicz Karol Rómmel
1932	Ferdinand de Mortanges (NETHS.) 1,813.83 pts.	Earl Thompson (U.S.) 1,811	Clarence von Rosen (SWEDEN) 1,809.42

	GOLD	SILVER	BRONZE
	Teams—U.S. 5,038.08 pts.	NETHS. 4,689.08	—
	Earl Thomson	Ferdinand de Mortanges	
	Harry Chamberlin	Karel Schummelketel	
	Edwin Argo	Aernout van Lennep	
1936	Ludwig Stubbendorff	Earl Thomson	Hans Lunding
	(GERMANY) 37.7 faults	(U.S.) 99.9	(DENMARK) 102.2
	Teams—		
	GERMANY 676.75 pts.	POLAND 991.70	G.B. 1,195.50
	Ludwig Stubbendorff	Severyn Kulesza	Edward Howard-Vyse
	Rudolf Lippert	Henryk Rojcewicz	Alec Scott
	Konrad von Wangenheim	Zdislaw Kawecki	Richard Fanshawe
1948	Bernard Chevallier	Frank Henry	J. Robert Selfelt
	(FRANCE) plus 4 pts.	(U.S.) minus 21	(SWEDEN) minus 25
	Teams—U.S. 161.50 faults	SWEDEN 165.00	MEXICO 305.25
	Frank Henry	J. Robert Selfelt	Humberto Mariles
	Charles Anderson	Olof Stahre	Raul Campero
	Earl Thomson	Sigurd Svensson	Joaquin Solano
1952	Hans von Blixen-Finecke	Guy Lefrant	Wilhelm Büssing
	(SWEDEN) 28.33 faults	(FRANCE) 54.50	(GERMANY) 55.50
	Teams—SWEDEN 221.94	GERMANY 235.49	U.S. 587.16
	Hans von Blixen-Finecke	Wilhelm Büssing	Charles Hough
	Nils Stahre	Klaus Wagner	Walter Staley
	Karl Frölen	Otto Rothe	John Wofford
1956	Petrus Kastenman	August Lütge-Westhues	Francis Weldon
	(SWEDEN) 66.53 faults	(GERMANY) 84.87	(G.B.) 85.48
	Teams—G.B. 355.48	GERMANY 475.61	CANADA 572.72
	Albert Hill	August Lütge-Westhues	James Elder
	Francis Weldon	Klaus Wagner	Brian Herbinson
	A. Lawrence Rook	Otto Rothe	John Rumble
1960	Laurence Morgan	Neale Lavis	Anton Bühler
	(AUSTRALIA)	(AUSTRALIA)	(SWITZ.)
	plus 7.15 pts.	minus 16.50	minus 51.21
	Teams—		
	AUSTRALIA 128.18 pts.	SWITZ. 386.02	FRANCE 515.71
	Laurence Morgan	Anton Bühler	Jack Le Goff
	Neale Lavis	Hans Schwarzenbach	Jean Le Roy
	William Roycroft	Rudolf Gunthardt	Guy Lefrant
1964	Mauro Checcoli	Carlos Moratorio	Fritz Ligges
	(ITALY) 64.40 pts.	(ARGENTINA) 56.40 pts.	(GERMANY) 49.20 pts.
	Teams—ITALY 85.80 pts.	U.S. 56.86 pts.	GERMANY 56.73 pts.
	Mauro Checcoli	Michael Page	Fritz Ligges
	Paolo Angioni	Kevin Freeman	Horst Karsten
	Giuseppe Ravano	Michael Plumb	Gerhard Schultz
1968	Jean-Jacques Guyon	Derek Allhusen	Michael Page
	(FRANCE) 38.86 pts.	(G.B.) 41.61 pts.	(U. S.) 52.31 pts.
	Teams—G.B. 175.93 pts.	U.S. 245.93 pts.	AUSTRALIA 331.26
	Derek Allhusen	Michael Page	Wayne Roycroft
	Richard Meade	James Wofford	Brien Cobcroft
	Sgt. Jones	Michael Plumb	William Roycroft
	Jane Bullen (non-scorer)		

972

7a. Fencing (Men)

FOIL (INDIVIDUAL)

	GOLD	SILVER	BRONZE
1896	E. Gravelotte (FRANCE) 4 wins	Henri Callott (FRANCE) 3	Perikles Pierrakos (GREECE) 2
1900	C. Coste (FRANCE) 6 wins	Henry Masson (FRANCE) 5	Jacques Boulanger (FRANCE) 4
1904	Ramon Fonst (CUBA)	Albertson Post (CUBA)	Charles Tatham (CUBA)
1908	Event not held		
1912	Nedo Nadi (ITALY) 7 wins	Pietro Speciale (ITALY) 5	Richard Verderber (AUSTRIA) 4
1920	Nedo Nadi (ITALY) 10 wins	Philippe Cattiau (FRANCE) 9	Roger Ducret (FRANCE) 9
1924	Roger Ducret (FRANCE) 6 wins	Philippe Cattiau (FRANCE) 5	Maurice van Damme (BELGIUM) 4
1928	Lucien Gaudin (FRANCE) 9 wins	Erwin Casmir (GERMANY) 9	Giulio Gaudini (ITALY) 9
1932	Gustavo Marzi (ITALY) 9 wins	Joseph Levis (U.S.) 6	Giulio Gaudini (ITALY) 5
1936	Giulio Gaudini (ITALY) 7 wins	Edouard Gardère (FRANCE) 6	Giorgio Bocchino (ITALY) 4
1948	Jean Buhan (FRANCE) 7 wins	Christian d'Oriola (FRANCE) 5	Lajos Maszlay (HUNGARY) 4
1952	Christian d'Oriola (FRANCE) 8 wins	Edoardo Mangiarotti (ITALY) 6	Manlio di Rosa (ITALY) 5
1956	Christian d'Oriola (FRANCE) 6 wins	Giancarlo Bergamini (ITALY) 5	Antonio Spallino (ITALY) 5
1960	Viktor Zhdanovich (U.S.S.R.) 7 wins	Yuriy Sisikin (U.S.S.R.) 5	Albert Axelrod (U.S.) 3
1964	Egon Franke (POLAND)	Jean Magnan (FRANCE)	Daniel Revenu (FRANCE)
1968	Ileana Drimba (RUMANIA) 4 wins	Jeno Kamuti (15) (HUNGARY) 3	Daniel Revenu (17) (FRANCE) 3

FOIL (TEAM)

	GOLD	SILVER	BRONZE
1896–1912	Event not held[1]		
1920	ITALY[2]	FRANCE	U.S.
	Nedo Nadi	André Labattut	F. W. Honeycutt
	Aldo Nadi	Georges Trombert	Henry Breckinridge
	Abelardo Olivier	Perrot	Brooks Parker
	Pietro Speciale	Lucien Gaudin	Leon Schoonmaker
	Rodolfo Terlizzi	Philippe Cattiau	Arthur Lyon
	Tomasso Costantino	Roger Ducret	R. V. Sears
	Baldo Baldi		Harold Raynor
	Oreste Puliti		
1924	FRANCE[3]	BELGIUM	HUNGARY
	Lucien Gaudin	Désiré Beaurain	László Berti
	Roger Ducret	Charles Grahay	István Lichteneckert
	Philippe Cattiau	Fernand de Montigny	Sándor Posta
	Henri Jobier	Maurice van Damme	Zoltán Schenker
	Jacques Coutrot	Marcel Berré	Odön Tersztyánszky
	Guy de Luget	Albert de Roocker	
	André Labattut	Xaver Beckelaere	
	Joseph Peroteaux		
1928	ITALY[4]	FRANCE	ARGENTINA
	Ugo Pignotti	Lucien Gaudin	Roberto Larraz
	Oreste Puliti	Philippe Cattiau	Raul Anganuzzi
	Giulio Gaudini	Roger Ducret	Luis Lucchetti
	Giorgio Pessina	André Labattut	Hector Lucchetti
	Giorgio Chiavacci	Raymond Flacher	Carmelo Camet
	Gioacchino Guaragna	André Gaboriaud	Oscar Vinas
1932	FRANCE[5]	ITALY	U.S.
	Edouard Gardère	Gustavo Marzi	George Calnan
	René Lemoine	Ugo Pignotti	Frank Righeimer
	René Bougnol	Gioacchino Guaragna	Richard Steere
	Philippe Cattiau	Giulio Gaudini	Hugh Alessandroni
	René Bondoux	Giorgio Pessina	Dernell Every
	Jean Piot	Rodolfo Terlizzi	Joseph Levis

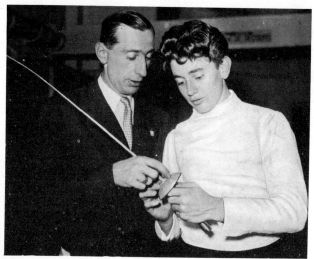

Winner of the Olympic gold medal twice (1952 and 1956) and the silver medal once (in 1948), Christian d'Oriola of France has won the most world and Olympic titles with the foil. He is shown here with his coach.

	GOLD	SILVER	BRONZE
1936	ITALY[6]	FRANCE	GERMANY
	Gustavo Marzi	André Gardère	Erwin Casmir
	Gioacchino Guaragna	René Bougnol	Julius Eisenecker
	Manlio di Rosa	René Lemoine	August Heim
	Ciro Verratti	Jacques Coutrot	Siegfrid Lerdon
	Giulio Gaudini	Edouard Gardère	Otto Adam
	Giorgio Bocchino	René Bondoux	Stefan Rosenbauer
1948	FRANCE[7]	ITALY	BELGIUM
	André Bonin	Renzo Nostini	Georges de Bourguignon
	Christian d'Oriola	Manlio di Rosa	Henry Paternoster
	Jean Buhan	Edoardo Mangiarotti	Edoardo Yves
	René Bougnol	Giuliano Nostini	Raymond Bru
	Jacques Latasse	Giorgio Pellini	André de Vorsselaere
	Adrien Rommel	Saverio Ragno	Paul Valcke
1952	FRANCE[8]	ITALY	HUNGARY
	Jean Buhan	Giancarlo Bergamini	Endre Tilli
	Christian d'Oriola	Antonio Spallino	Aladár Gerevich
	Adrien Rommel	Manlio di Rosa	Endre Palócz
	Claude Netter	Edoardo Mangiarotti	Lajos Maszlay
	Jacques Noel	Renzo Nostini	Tibor Berczelly
	Jacques Latasse	Giorgio Pellini	József Sákovits
1956	ITALY[9]	FRANCE	HUNGARY
	Edoardo Mangiarotti	Christian d'Oriola	Lajos Somodi
	Giancarlo Bergamini	Jacques Latasse	József Gyuricza
	Antonio Spallino	René Coicaud	Endre Tilli
	Vittorio Lucarelli	Claude Netter	József Marosi
	Manlio di Rosa	Roger Closset	Mihaly Fulop
	Luigi Carpaneda	Bernard Baudoux	József Sákovits
60	U.S.S.R.[10]	ITALY	GERMANY
	Viktor Zhdanovich	Alberto Pellegrino	Jürgen Theuerkauff
	Mark Midler	Luigi Carpaneda	Tim Gerresheim
	Yuriy Sisikin	Mario Curletto	Eberhard Mehl
	Gherman Sveshnikov	Aldo Aureggi	Jürgen Brecht
	Yuriy Rudov	Edoardo Mangiarotti	

	GOLD	SILVER	BRONZE
1964	U.S.S.R.[11]	POLAND	FRANCE
	Gherman Sveshnikov	Zbigniew Skrudlik	Daniel Revenu
	Yuriy Sisikin	Witold Woyda	Jacky Courtillat
	Viktor Zhdanovich	Ryszard Parulski	Pierre Rhadocanachi
	Mark Midler	Egon Franke	Christian Noel
1968	FRANCE[12]	U.S.S.R.	POLAND
	Daniel Revenu	German Sveshnikov	Witold Woyda
	Gilles Berolatti	Yury Sharov	Zbigniew Skrudlik
	Christian Noel	Vasily Stankovich	Ryszard Parulski
	Jean Magnan	Victor Putiatin	Egon Franke
1972			

---

[1] There was, however, a foil (team) competition in the 1904 Games when CUBA (Fonst, van zo Post, Manuel Diaz) bt an international team composed of Charles Tatham (CUBA), Townsend (U.S.) and John Fox (U.S.).
[2] ITALY bt FRANCE 9–7, and U.S. 13–3; FRANCE bt U.S. 14–2.
[3] FRANCE bt HUNGARY 15–1; BELGIUM bt HUNGARY 9–7.
[4] ITALY bt FRANCE 10–6, bt ARGENTINA 11–5; FRANCE bt ARGENTINA 9–7.
[5] FRANCE bt ITALY 8–8 (hits received, 58–62), and bt U.S. 11–5; ITALY bt U.S. 9–1.
[6] ITALY bt FRANCE 9–4, and bt GERMANY 16–0; FRANCE bt GERMANY 12–4.
[7] FRANCE bt ITALY 8–8 (60–62), and bt BELGIUM 9–5; ITALY bt BELGIUM 11–5.
[8] FRANCE bt ITALY 8–6, and bt HUNGARY 12–4; ITALY bt HUNGARY 13–3.
[9] ITALY bt FRANCE 9–7, and bt HUNGARY 8–8 (59–63); FRANCE bt HUNGARY 11–5.
[10] U.S.S.R. bt ITALY 9–4, and bt GERMANY 9–3.
[11] U.S.S.R. bt POLAND 9–7, and bt FRANCE 9–6.
[12] FRANCE bt U.S.S.R. 9-6; bt POLAND 9-7.

EPEE (INDIVIDUAL)

1896	Event not held		
1900	Ramon Fonst (CUBA)	Louis Perée (FRANCE)	Léon Sée (FRANCE)
1904	Ramon Fonst (CUBA)	Charles Tatham (CUBA)	Albertson Post (CUBA)
1908	Gaston Alibert (FRANCE) 5 wins	Alexandre Lippmann (FRANCE) 4	Eugène Olivier (FRANCE) 4
1912	Paul Anspach (BELGIUM) 6 wins	Ivan Osiier (DENMARK) 5	Philippe Le Hardy de Beaulieu (BELGIUM) 4
1920	Armand Massard (FRANCE)	Alexandre Lippmann (FRANCE)	Ernest Gevers (BELGIUM)
1924	Charles Delporte (BELGIUM)	Roger Ducret (FRANCE)	Nils Hellsten (SWEDEN)
1928	Lucien Gaudin (FRANCE) 8 wins	Georges Buchard (FRANCE) 7	George Calnan (U.S.) 6
1932	Giancarlo Medici (ITALY) 9 wins	Georges Buchard (FRANCE) 7	Carlo Agostoni (ITALY) 7
1936	Franco Riccardi (ITALY) 13 pts.	Saverio Ragno (ITALY) 12	Giancarlo Medici (ITALY) 12
1948	Luigi Cantone (ITALY) 7 wins	Oswald Zappelli (SWITZ.) 5	Edoardo Mangiarotti (ITALY) 5
1952	Edoardo Mangiarotti (ITALY) 7 wins	Dario Mangiarotti (ITALY) 6	Oswald Zappelli (SWITZ.) 6
1956	Carlo Pavesi (ITALY) 5 wins	Giuseppe Delfino (ITALY) 5	Edoardo Mangiarotti (ITALY) 5
1960	Giuseppe Delfino (ITALY) 5 wins	Allan Jay (G.B.) 5	Bruno Khabarov (U.S.S.R.) 5
1964	Grigory Kriss (U.S.S.R.)	William Hoskyns (G.B.)	Guram Kostava (U.S.S.R.)

Action during the sabre event in Rome, 1960, with Fimamizu of Japan (right) duelling with Van Celden of Israel.

	GOLD	SILVER	BRONZE
1968	Gyozo Kulcsar (HUNGARY)	Grigory Kriss (U.S.S.R.)	Gianluigi Saccaro (ITALY)
1972			

EPEE (TEAM)

1896–1904 Event not held

	GOLD	SILVER	BRONZE
1908	FRANCE[1]	G.B.	BELGIUM
	Gaston Alibert	C. Leaf Daniell	Paul Anspach
	Bernard Gravier	Cecil Haig	Désiré Beaurain
	Alexandre Lippmann	Martin Holt	Ferdinand Feyerick
	Eugène Olivier	Robert Montgomerie	Francois Rom
	Jean Stern	Edward Amphlett	Fernand de Montigny
	Henry Berger	Edgar Seligman	Victor Willems
	Charles Collignon	Sydney Martineau	Ferdinand Bosman
1912	BELGIUM	G.B.	NETHS.
	Paul Anspach	Edgar Seligman	A. E. W. de Jong
	Henry Anspach	Edward Amphlett	Hubert van Bijlenburgh
	Fernand de Montigny	Robert Montgomerie	J. Doorman
	Jacques Ochs	John Blake	George van Rossem
	Gaston Salmon	Percival Davson	Leo Nardus
	Francois Rom	Arthur Everitt	Perk
	Victor Willems	Sydney Martineau	Bos
	Robert Hennet	Martin Holt	Beaufort
1920	ITALY[2]	BELGIUM	FRANCE
	Nedo Nadi	Paul Anspach	Armand Massard
	Aldo Nadi	Léon Tom	Alexandre Lippmann
	Abelardo Olivier	Ernest Gevers	Gustave Buchard
	Giovanni Canova	Félix d'Alviella	Roger Ducret
	Dino Urbani	Fernand de Montigny	Casanova
	Giovanni Bozza	Victor Boin	Frédéric Dubordieu
	Andrea Marrazzi	Joseph de Craecker	
	Antonio Allocchio		
	Paolo Thaón di Revel		

[1] FRANCE bt G.B. 12–5, and bt BELGIUM 9–7; G.B. bt BELGIUM 9–5.
[2] ITALY bt BELGIUM 10–6, and bt FRANCE 9–7; BELGIUM bt FRANCE 8–6.

Fencing (Men) ■ 53

	GOLD	SILVER	BRONZE
1924	FRANCE[2]	BELGIUM	ITALY
	Lucien Gaudin	Fernand de Montigny	Vincenzo Cuccia
	Roger Ducret	Joseph de Craecker	Giovanni Canova
	Alexandre Lippmann	Paul Anspach	Giulio Basletta
	Gustave Buchard	Ernest Gevers	Marcello Bertinetti
	André Labattut	Léon Tom	Virgilio Mantegazza
	Georges Teinturier	Charles Delporte	Oreste Moricca
	Lionel Liottel		
1928	ITALY[3]	FRANCE	PORTUGAL
	Carlo Agostoni	Armánd Massard	Paolo Eca Leal
	Marcello Bertinetti	Georges Buchard	Mario Noronha
	Giancarlo Medici	Gaston Amson	Jorge Paiva
	Renzo Minoli	Emile Cornic	Frederico Paredes
	Giulio Basletta	Bernard Schmetz	Joao Sasetti
	Franco Riccardi	René Barbier	Enrique Silveira
1932	FRANCE[4]	ITALY	U.S.
	Bernard Schmetz	Carlo Agostoni	George Calnan
	Philippe Cattiau	Franco Riccardi	Gustave Heiss
	Georges Buchard	Saverio Ragno	Tracy Jackel
	Jean Piot	Giancarlo Medici	Frank Righeimer
	Fernand Jourdant	Renzo Minoli	Curtis Shears
	Georges Teinturier		Miguel de Capriles
1936	ITALY[5]	SWEDEN	FRANCE
	Giancarlo Medici	Sven Thofelt	Georges Buchard
	Edoardo Mangiarotti	Gustaf Dyrssen	Paul Wormser
	Saverio Ragno	Gösta Almgren	Philippe Cattiau
	Alfredo Pezzano	Hans Granfelt	Michel Dulieux
	Giancarlo Brusati	Birger Cederin	Bernard Schmetz
	Franco Riccardi	Hans van Drakenberg	Michel Pécheux
1948	FRANCE[6]	ITALY	SWEDEN
	Henri Guérin	Edoardo Mangiarotti	Carl Forssell
	Henri Lepage	Carlo Agostini	Arne Tollbom
	Marcel Desprets	Fiorenzo Marini	Bengt Ljungquist
	Michel Pécheux	Antonio Mandruzzato	Sven Thofelt
	Maurice Huet	Luigi Cantone	Frank Cervell
	Edouard Artigas	Dario Mangiarotti	Per Carleson
1952	ITALY[7]	SWEDEN	SWITZ.
	Edoardo Mangiarotti	Lennart Magnusson	Willy Fitting
	Dario Mangiarotti	Carl Forssell	Otto Rufenacht
	Carlo Pavesi	Berndt-Otto Rehbinder	Oswald Zappelli
	Giuseppe Delfino	Per Carleson	Paul Barth
	Franco Bertinetti	Sven Fahlman	Mario Valota
	Roberto Battaglia	Bengt Ljungquist	Paul Meister
1956	ITALY[8]	HUNGARY	FRANCE
	Giuseppe Delfino	Béla Rerrich	Yves Dreyfus
	Franco Bertinetti	Ambrus Nagy	René Queyroux
	Alberto Pellegrino	Barnabás Berszenyi	Daniel Dagallier
	Giorgio Anglesio	József Marosi	Claude Nigon
	Carlo Pavesi	József Sákovits	Armand Mouyal
	Edoardo Mangiarotti	Lajos Balthazár	
1960	ITALY[9]	G.B.	U.S.S.R.
	Alberto Pellegrino	Allan Jay	Valentin Chernikov
	Carlo Pavesi	Michael Howard	Arnold Chernusevich
	Giuseppe Delfino	John Pelling	Guram Kostava
	Edoardo Mangiarotti	H. William Hoskyns	Bruno Khabarov
	Gian Luigi Saccaro	Michael Alexander	
	Fiorenzo Marini	Raymond Harrison	

---

[2] FRANCE bt BELGIUM 10–6 and bt ITALY 8–8 (20–21); BELGIUM ▮
ITALY 11–5.
[3] ITALY bt FRANCE 9–7, and bt PORTUGAL 9–6; FRANCE bt PORTUGA▮
9–7.
[4] FRANCE bt ITALY 9–7, and bt U.S. 10–5; ITALY bt U.S. 9–6.
[5] ITALY bt SWEDEN 10–5, and bt FRANCE 9–5; SWEDEN bt FRANC▮
8–8 (31–32).
[6] FRANCE bt ITALY 11–5, and bt SWEDEN 11–4; ITALY bt SWEDEN 8–▮
[7] ITALY bt SWEDEN 8–5, and bt SWITZ. 12–4; SWEDEN bt SWITZ. 8–▮
[8] ITALY bt HUNGARY 9–3, and bt FRANCE 15–1; HUNGARY bt FRANC▮
9–7.
[9] ITALY bt G.B. 9–5, and bt U.S.S.R. 9–6.

GOLD	SILVER	BRONZE
1964 **HUNGARY**[10]	**ITALY**	**FRANCE**
Gyozo Kulscar	Gian Luigi Saccaro	Jacques Brodin
Zoltan Nemere	Gian Battista Breda	Yves Dreyfus
Tamas Gabor	Gianfranco Paolucci	Claude Bourquard
Istvan Kausz	Giuseppe Delfino	Jack Quittet
1968 **HUNGARY**[11]	**U.S.S.R.**	**POLAND**
Csaba Fenyvesi	Grigory Kriss	Bohdan Andrzejewski
Zoltan Nemere	Iosif Vitebsky	Michal Butkiewicz
Pal Schmitt	Aleksey Nikanchikov	Bogdan Gonsior
Gyozo Kulcsar	Yury Smolyakov	Henryk Nielaba
1972		

---

[10] HUNGARY bt ITALY 8–3 and FRANCE 9–3.
[11] HUNGARY bt U.S.S.R. 7–4; bt POLAND 9–5. POLAND bt W. GERMANY 9–6.

SABRE (INDIVIDUAL)

1896	Jean Georgiadis (GREECE) 4 wins	Telemachos Karakalos (GREECE) 3	Holger Nielsen (DENMARK) 2
1900	G. de la Falaise (FRANCE)	Léon Thiébaut (FRANCE)	Siegfried Flesch (AUSTRIA)
1904	Manuel Diaz (CUBA)	William Grebe (U.S.)	Albertson Post (CUBA)
1908	Jenö Fuchs (HUNGARY) 6 wins	Béla Zulavsky (HUNGARY) 6	Vilem Goppold (BOHEMIA[1]) 4
1912	Jenö Fuchs (HUNGARY) 6 wins	Béla Békessy (HUNGARY) 5	Ervin Mészáros (HUNGARY) 5
1920	Nedo Nadi (ITALY)	Aldo Nadi (ITALY)	A. E. W. de Jong (NETHS.)
1924	Sándor Posta (HUNGARY) 5 wins	Roger Ducret (FRANCE) 5	János Garai (HUNGARY) 5
1928	Odön Tersztyánszky (HUNGARY) 9 wins	Attila Petschauer (HUNGARY) 9	Bino Bini (ITALY) 8
1932	György Piller (HUNGARY) 8 wins	Giulio Gaudini (ITALY) 7	Endre Kabos (HUNGARY) 5
1936	Endre Kabos (HUNGARY) 7 wins	Gustavo Marzi (ITALY) 6	Aladár Gerevich (HUNGARY) 6
1948	Aladár Gerevich (HUNGARY) 7 wins	Vincenzo Pinton (ITALY) 5	Pál Kovács (HUNGARY) 5
1952	Pál Kovács (HUNGARY) 8 wins	Aladár Gerevich (HUNGARY) 7	Tibor Berczelly (HUNGARY) 5
1956	Rudolf Kárpáti (HUNGARY) 6 wins	Jerzy Pawlowski (POLAND) 5	Lev Kuznyetsov (U.S.S.R.) 4
1960	Rudolf Kárpáti (HUNGARY) 5 wins	Zoltán Horvath (HUNGARY) 4	Wladimiro Calarese (ITALY) 4
1964	Tibor Pezsa (HUNGARY)	Claude Arabo (FRANCE)	Umar Mavlikhanov (U.S.S.R.)
1968	Jerzy Pawlowski (POLAND) 4 wins (16 hits)	Mark Rakita (U.S.S.R.) 4 wins (18 hits)	Tibor Pezsa (HUNGARY) 3 wins
1972			

Now part of CZECHOSLOVAKIA.

SABRE (TEAM)

1896–1904 Event not held		
1908 **HUNGARY**[1]	**ITALY**	**BOHEMIA**[14]
Jenö Fuchs	Riccardo Nowak	Vilem Goppold
Oszkár Gerde	Alessandro Biroli	Jaroslav Tucek
Péter Tóth	Abelardo Olivier	Vaclav Lada
Lajos Werkner	Marcello Bertinetti	P. Lada
Dezsö Földes	Sante Ceccherini	Schéjbal

	GOLD	SILVER	BRONZE
1912	HUNGARY[2] László Berti Jenö Fuchs Ervin Mészáros Zoltán Schenker Dezsö Földes Oszkár Gerde Péter Tóth Lajos Werkner	AUSTRIA Richard Verderber Otto Herschmann R. Cvetko F. Golling	NETHS. Hubert van Bijlenburgh A. E. W. de Jong D. Scalongne J. Doorman George van Rossem H. de Jongh
1920	ITALY[3] Nedo Nadi Aldo Nadi Oreste Puliti Federico Cesarano Baldo Baldi Francesco Gargano Giorgio Santelli	FRANCE Lucien Gaudin Gustave Buchard Armand Massard Philippe Cattiau Perrodon	NETHS. J. van der Wiele A. E. W. de Jong J. Doorman Hubert van Bijlenburgh L. Delaunoy S. Feldenrust
1924	ITALY[4] Oreste Puliti Giulio Sarrocchi Marcello Bertinetti Oreste Moricca Renato Anselmi Guido Balzarini Bino Bini Vincenzo Cuccia	HUNGARY László Berti János Garai Sándor Posta József Rády Zoltán Schenker Jenö Uhlyárik Lászlo Széchy Odön Tersztyánszky	NETHS. A. E. W. de Jong J. Doorman H. Scherpenhuysen J. van der Wiele M. van Dulm H. J. M. Daniels
1928	HUNGARY[5] János Garai Gyula Glykais Sándor Gombos József Rády Odön Tersztyánszky Attila Petschauer	ITALY Renato Anselmi Bino Bini Gustavo Marzi Oreste Puliti Emilio Salafia Giulio Sarrocchi	POLAND Kazimierz Laskowski Aleksander Malecki Adam Papée Ladislaw Segda Friedrich Thadée Georg Zabielski
1932	HUNGARY[6] Endre Kabos Aladár Gerevich György Piller Gyula Glykais Attila Petschauer Ernö Nagy	ITALY Renato Anselmi Gustavo Marzi Arturo de Vecchi Giulio Gaudini Ugo Pignotti Emilio Salafia	POLAND Tadeusz Lubicz-Nycz Marian Suski Wladyslaw Dobrowolski Adam Papée Friedrich Thadée Ladislaw Segda
1936	HUNGARY[7] Tibor Berczelly Aladár Gerevich Endre Kabos László Rajcsányi Imre Rajczy Pál Kovács	ITALY Giulio Gaudini Gustavo Marzi Aldo Masciotta Aldo Montano Vincenzo Pinton Athos Tanzini	GERMANY Richard Wahl Erwin Casmir Julius Eisenecker August Heim Hans Jörger Hans Esser
1948	HUNGARY[8] Aladár Gerevich Rudolf Kárpáti Pál Kovács Tibor Berczelly László Rajcsányi Bertalan Papp	ITALY Gastone Daré Carlo Turcato Vincenzo Pinton Mauro Racca Renzo Nostini Aldo Montano	U.S. Norman Armitage George Worth Tibor Nyilas Dean Cetrulo Miguel de Capriles James Flynn
1952	HUNGARY[9] Rudolf Kárpáti Pál Kovács Tibor Berczelly Aladár Gerevich László Rajcsányi Bertalan Papp	ITALY Gastone Daré Roberto Ferrari Renzo Nostini Giorgio Pellini Vincenzo Pinton Mauro Racca	FRANCE Jean Laroyenne Bernard Lefèvre Jean Levavasseur Bernard Morel Maurice Piot Maurice Tournon
1956	HUNGARY[10] Atilla Kereszetes Aladár Gerevich Rudolf Kárpáti Jenö Hámori Pál Kovács Dániel Magai	POLAND Zygmunt Pawlas Jerzy Pawlowski Wojciech Zablocki Andrzej Piatkowski Marian Kuszewski Ryszard Zub	U.S.S.R. Iakov Rylskiy David Tychler Lev Kuznyetsov Evgeniy Cherepovskiy Leonid Bogdanov

GOLD	SILVER	BRONZE
1960 HUNGARY[11]	POLAND	ITALY
Zoltán Horvath	Jerzy Pawlowski	Pierluighi Chicca
Rudolf Kárpáti	Wojciech Zablocki	Wladimiro Calarese
Tamas Mendelenyi	Ryszard Zub	Mario Ravagnan
Pál Kovács	Emil Ochyra	Roberto Ferrari
Gabor Delneki	Andrzej Piatkowski	Giampaolo Calanchini
Aladár Gerevich	Marian Kuszewski	
1964 U.S.S.R.[12]	ITALY	POLAND
Nagzar Asatiani	Wladimiro Calarese	Emil Ochyra
Yakov Rylsky	Cesare Salvadori	Jerzy Pawlowski
Mark Rakita	Gianpaolo Calanchini	Ryszard Zub
Umar Mavlikhanov	Pierluigi Chicca	Andrzej Piatowski
1968 U.S.S.R.[13]	ITALY	HUNGARY
Vladimir Nazlimov	Wladimiro Calarese	Tamas Kovacs
Viktor Sidiak	Michele Maffei	Janos Kalmar
Eduard Vinokurov	Cesare Salvadori	Peter Bakonyi
Mark Rakita	Pierluigi Chicca	Miklos Maszena
Umar Mavlikhanov	Rolando Rigoli	Tibor Pezsa
1972		

---

[1] HUNGARY bt ITALY 11–5, and BOHEMIA 9–7; ITALY bt BOHEMIA by default.
[2] HUNGARY bt AUSTRIA 11–5, and bt NETHERLANDS 13–3.
[3] ITALY bt FRANCE 13–3, and bt NETHS. 12–4; FRANCE bt NETHS. 9–7.
[4] HUNGARY bt HUNGARY 8–8 (46–50), and bt NETHS. 14–2.
[5] HUNGARY bt ITALY 9–7, and bt POLAND 14–2.
[6] HUNGARY bt ITALY 14–2; ITALY bt POLAND 15–1.
[7] HUNGARY bt ITALY 9–6, and bt GERMANY 13–3; ITALY bt GERMANY 13–3.
[8] HUNGARY bt ITALY 10–6, and bt U.S. 10–6; ITALY bt U.S. 8–8 (59–61).
[9] HUNGARY bt ITALY 8–7, and bt FRANCE 13–3; ITALY bt FRANCE 13–3.
[10] HUNGARY bt ITALY 9–4, and bt U.S.S.R. 9–7; POLAND bt U.S.S.R. 9–7.
[11] HUNGARY bt POLAND 9–7, and ITALY 9–6.
[12] U.S.S.R. bt ITALY 9–6, and bt POLAND 9–7.
[13] U.S.S.R. bt ITALY 9–7. ITALY bt HUNGARY 9–6. HUNGARY bt FRANCE 9–5.
[14] Now part of CZECHOSLOVAKIA.

7b. Fencing (Women)

FOIL (INDIVIDUAL)

	GOLD	SILVER	BRONZE
1896–1920	Event not held		
1924	Ellen Osiier (DENMARK) 5 wins	Gladys Davis (G.B.) 4	Grete Heckscher (DENMARK)
1928	Helene Mayer (GERMANY) 7 wins	Muriel Freeman (G.B.) 6	Olga Oelkers (GERMANY) 4
1932	Ellen Preis (AUSTRIA) 9 wins	Heather Guinness (G.B.) 8	Ena Bogen (HUNGARY) 7
1936	Ilona Elek[1] (HUNGARY) 7 wins	Helene Mayer (GERMANY) 5	Ellen Preis (AUSTRIA) 5
1948	Ilona Elek (HUNGARY) 6 wins	Karen Lachmann (DENMARK) 5	Ellen Preis (AUSTRIA) 5
1952	Irene Camber (ITALY) 5 wins	Ilona Elek (HUNGARY) 5	Karen Lachmann (DENMARK) 4
1956	Gillian Sheen (G.B.) 6 wins	Olga Orban (RUMANIA) 6	Renée Garilhe (FRANCE) 5
1960	Heidi Schmid (GERMANY) 6 wins	Valentina Rastvorova (U.S.S.R.) 5	Maria Vicol (RUMANIA) 4

[1] full surname was Schacherer-Elek, later shortened to Elek.

	GOLD	SILVER	BRONZE
1964	Ildiko Rejto (HUNGARY)	Helga Mees (GERMANY)	Antonella Ragno (ITALY)
1968	Elena Novikova (U.S.S.R.) 4 wins	Pilar Roldan (MEXICO) 3 wins (14 hits)	Ildiko Rejto (HUNGARY) 3 wins (16 hits)
1972			

FOIL (TEAM)

	GOLD	SILVER	BRONZE
1896–1956	Event not held		
1960	U.S.S.R.[1] Valentina Rastvorova Tatyana Petrenko Valentina Prudskova Lyudmila Shishova Galina Ghorokova Aleksandra Zabelina	HUNGARY Etelka Juhasz Lidia Sakovits Ildiko Rejto Magda Kovács Tiborne Szekely	ITALY Irene Camber Velleda Cesari Antonella Ragno Bruna Colombetti Claudia Paisni
1964	HUNGARY[2] Ildiko Rejto Katalin Juhasz Lidia Domolky Judit Agoston	U.S.S.R. Galina Gorokhova Valentina Prudskova Tatyana Samusenko Lyudmila Shishova	GERMANY H. Schmid Helga Mees Rosemarie Scherberger Gudrun Theuerkauff
1968	U.S.S.R.[3] Alexandra Zabelina Tatjana Samusenko Elena Novikova Galina Gorokhova Svetlana Chirkova	HUNGARY Lidia Sakovics Ildiko Farkasinszky Ildiko Rejto Maria Gulacsy Paula Marosi	RUMANIA Clara Stahl-Iencic Ileana Drimba Maria Vicol Olga Szabo Ana Ene-Dersidan
1972			

---

[1] U.S.S.R. bt HUNGARY 9–3; HUNGARY bt ITALY 9–3.
[2] HUNGARY bt U.S.S.R. 9–7, and bt GERMANY 9–6.
[3] U.S.S.R. bt HUNGARY 9–3; HUNGARY bt RUMANIA 8 (49 hits)–8 (5 hits); RUMANIA bt FRANCE 8 (45 hits)–8 (47 hits).

8. Field Hockey

FIELD HOCKEY

GOLD	SILVER	BRONZE
1896–1904 Event not held		
1908 ENGLAND[1]	IRELAND	SCOTLAND
H. J. Wood	E. P. C. Holmes	WALES[2]
L. C. Baillon	Henry Brown	
H. Scott-Freeman	Walter Peterson	
A. H. Noble	Henry Murphy	
Edgar Page	W. I. H. Campbell	
J. Y. Robinson	W. E. Graham	
Eric Green	R. L. Kennedy	
R. G. Pridmore	F. L. Robinson	
Stanley Shoveller	E. P. Allman-Smith	
Gerald Logan	R. C. G. Gregg	
P. M. Rees	C. F. Power	
1912 Event not held		
1920 G.B.[3]	DENMARK	BELGIUM
Harry Haslam	Andreas Rasmussen	—
John Bennett	Hans-Christian Herlak	
Charles Atkin	Frans Faber	
H. D. R. Cooke	Erik Husted	
Eric Crockford	Henning Holst	
Cyril Wilkinson	Hans-Jörgen Hansen	
William Smith	Hans-Adolf Bierrum	
George McGrath	Thorvald Eigenbrod	
John McBryan	Sven Blach	
Stanley Shoveller	Steen Due	
R. W. Crummack	Eivind Blach	
Arthur Leighton	H. Hjaer	
C. H. Campbell	P. Koefoed	
Charles Marcon	C. Pantmann-Hansen	
1924 Event not held		
1928 INDIA[4]	NETHS.	GERMANY
Richard Allan	T. Hubrechts	Georg Brunner
M. E. Rocque	A. J. L. Katte	Werner Proft
L. C. Hammond	A. W. Tresling	Heinz Wöltje
R. A. Norris	Reindert de Waal	Werner Freyberg
B. E. Penniger	J. W. Brand	Theo Haag
S. M. Yusuf	E. P. J. Duson	Erwin Zander
W. John Goodsir-Cullen	J. G. Ankerman	Helmut Horn
M. A. Gateley	H. P. Visser t'Hooft	Herbert Müller
G. E. Marthins	R. van der Veen	Benno Boche
Dhyan Chand	P. van de Rovaert	Herbert Hobein
F. S. Seaman	G. J. A. Jannink	Herbert Kemmer
Shaukat Singh	A. J. Kop	
1932 INDIA[5]	JAPAN	U.S.
Mohammed Jaffar	Junzo Inohara	David McMullin
Bais Roopsingh	Toshio Usami	William Boddington
Dhyan Chand	Kanicho Konishi	James Gentle
Gurmit Singh	Hiroshi Nagata	Charles Sheaffer
R. J. Carr	Haruhiko Kon	Laurence Knapp
Lal Shah Bokhari	Eiichi Nakamura	Horace Disston
B. E. Penniger	Joshio Sakai	Samuel Ewing
M. A. K. Minhas	Katsumi Shibata	Henry Greer
L. C. Hammond	Sadayoshi Kobayashi	Leonard O'Brien
Carlyle Tapsell	Akio Sohda	Frederick Wolters
A. C. Hind	Shundkichi Hamada	Harold Brewster
Richard Allan		
Masud Minhas		

ENGLAND bt IRELAND 8–1.
Tie for third place.
G.B. bt DENMARK 5–1, and BELGIUM 12–1; DENMARK bt BELGIUM 5–2.
INDIA bt NETHS. 3–0; GERMANY bt BELGIUM 3–0.
INDIA bt JAPAN 11–1, and U.S. 24–1; JAPAN bt U.S. 9–2.

	GOLD	SILVER	BRONZE
1936	INDIA[6]	GERMANY	NETHS.
	Richard Allan	Karl Dröse	Jan de Looper
	Carlyle Tapsell	Erich Zander	Reindert de Waal
	Mohammed Hussain	Herbert Kemmer	Max Westerkamp
	Baboo Nimal	Heinz Schmalix	Hendrik de Looper
	W. John Goodsir-Cullen	Erwin Keller	Rudolf van der Haar
	Joseph Galibardy	Alfred Gerdes	Anton van Lierop
	Shabban Singh	Fritz Messner	Pieter Gunning
	Jatidar Dara	Hans Scherbart	Henri Schnitger
	Dhyan Chand	Kurt Weiss	Ernst van den Berg
	Bais Roopsingh	Werner Hamel	Agathon de Roos
	Mohammed Jaffar	Harald Huffmann	René Sparenberg
	L. Fernandes	Werner Kubitzki	
	Emmet Dara		
	Ahmed Sher		
1948	INDIA[7]	G.B.	NETHS.
	L. H. K. Pinto	D. L. S. Brodie	A. M. Richter
	T. Singh	G. B. Sime	Henri Derckx
	Randhir Gentle	W. L. C. Lindsay	Johan Drijver
	Keshav Datt	Michael Walford	J. Langhout
	Amir Kumar	Frank Reynolds	Hermanus Loggere
	Maxie Vaz	F. R. Lindsay	Edvard Tiel
	Kishan Lal	J. M. Peak	Willem van Heel
	Kunwar Singh	W. N. White	Andries Boerstra
	Glacken Singh	R. E. Adlard	P. M. J. Bromberg
	P. A. Jansen	Norman Borrett	Jan Kruize
	L. Fernandes	W. S. Griffiths	Rius Esser
	Balbir Singh	R. Davies	
		G. Hudson	
		R. T. Lake	
		Peter Whitbread	
1952	INDIA[8]	NETHS.	G.B.
	Runganadhan Francis	Laurens Mulder	Graham Dadds
	Dharan Singh	Henri Derckx	Roger Midgley
	Randhir Gentle	Johan Drijver	Denys Carnill
	Leslie Claudius	Julius Ancion	John Cockett
	Keshav Datt	Hermanus Loggere	Dennis Eagan
	Govind Perumal	Edvard Tiel	Anthony Robinson
	Raghbir Lal	Willem van Heel	Anthony Nunn
	Kunwar Singh	Rius Esser	Robin Fletcher
	Balbir Singh	Jan Kruize	Richard Norris
	Udham Singh	Andries Boerstra	John Conroy
	Muniswamy Rajagopal	Leonard Wery	John Taylor
	Richard Daluz		D. M. Day
	Nandu Singh		S. T. Theobald
1956	INDIA[9]	PAKISTAN	GERMANY
	Shankar Laxman	Hussain Zakir	Alfred Lücker
	Bakshish Singh	Rahman Latif	Helmut Nonn
	Randhir Gentle	Ghulam Rasul	Günther Ullerich
	Leslie Claudius	Anwar Ahmad	Günther Brennecke
	Amir Kumar	Hussain Mussarat	Werner Delmes
	Govind Perumal	Noor Alam	Eberhard Ferstl
	S. Charles	Abdul Hamid	Hugo Dollheiser
	Gurdev Singh	Rahman Habib	Heinz Radzikowski
	Balbir Singh	Moti Ullah	Wolfgang Nonn
	Udham Singh	Hussain Akhtar	Hugo Budinger
	Raghbir Bhola	Naseer Ahmed	Werner Rosenbaum
	Runganadhan Francis	Manzur Atif	
	Balkishan Singh	Ali Habib	
	Amit Singh	Ahmad Munir	
	Hari Pal Kaushik		
	Hardyal Singh		
	Rachbir Lal		

---

[6] Semi-finals: GERMANY bt NETHS. 3–0; INDIA bt FRANCE 10–0. Final:
INDIA bt GERMANY 8–1. Third-place: NETHS. bt FRANCE 4–3.
[7] Semi-finals: INDIA bt NETHS. 2–1; G.B. bt PAKISTAN 2–0. Final: INDIA
bt G.B. 4–0. Third-place: NETHS. bt PAKISTAN 4–1, after 1–1 draw.
[8] Semi-finals: INDIA bt G.B. 3–1; NETHS. bt PAKISTAN 1–0. Final: INDIA
bt NETHS. 6–1. Third-place: G.B. bt PAKISTAN 2–1.

	GOLD	SILVER	BRONZE
1960	PAKISTAN[10]	INDIA	SPAIN
	Abdul Rashid	Shankar Laxman	Carlos Iglesias
	Bashir Ahmed	Prithipal Singh	José Colomer
	Manzur Atif	Jamanlal Sharma	Rafael Egusquiza
	Ghulam Rasul	Leslie Claudius	Juan Angel Calzado
	Anwar Ahmed	Joseph Antic	José Antonio Dinares
	Ali Habib	Mohinder Lal	Edouardo Dualde
	Noor Alam	Joginder Singh	Joachim Dualde
	Abdul Hamid	John Peter	Pedro Amat
	Abdul Waheed	Jaswant Singh	Francisco Caballer
	Naseer Ahmed	Udham Singh	Ignacio Macaya
	Moti Ullah	Raghbhir Bhola	Pedro Murua
	Khurshid Aslam	Charanjit Singh	Pedro Roig
	Mushtag Ahmed[11]	Govind Sawant	Luis Maria Usoz
	Ahmad Munir	Khullar Singh	Narciso Ventallo
1964	INDIA[12]	PAKISTAN	AUSTRALIA
	Shankar Laxman	Abdul Hamid	Paul Dearing
	Prithipal Singh	Munir Ahmed	Donald McWatters
	Dhara Singh	Manzoor Atif	Brian Glencross
	Lal Mohinder	Saeed Anwar	John McBride
	Charanjit Singh	Anwar Ahmed	Julian Pearce
	Gurbux Singh	Muhammad Rashid	Graham Wood
	Joginder Singh	Khalid Mahmood	Robin Hodder
	John Peter	Zaka Din	Raymond Evans
	Harbinder Singh	Muhammad Afzal	Eric Pearce
	Haripal Kashik	Muhammad Asad	Patrick Nilan
	Darshan Singh	Moti Ullah	Donald Smart
	Jagjit Singh[11]	Tariq Aziz[11]	Antony Waters[11]
	Bandu Patil[11]	Zafar Hayat[11]	Mervyn Crossman[11]
	Udhum Singh[11]	Tariq Naizi[11]	Desmond Piper[11]
	Ali Sayeed[11]	Khurshid Azam[11]	
1968	PAKISTAN	AUSTRALIA	INDIA
	Zakir Hussain	Paul Dearing	Rajendra Christy
	Tanvir Dar	James Mason	Gurbux Singh
	Tariq Aziz	Brian Glencross	Prithipal Singh
	Saeed Anwar	Gordon Pearce	Balbir Singh
	Riaz Ahmed	Julian Pearce	Ajitpal Singh
	Gulrez Akhtar	Robert Haigh	Perumal Krishnamurthy
	Khalid Mahmood	Donald Martin	Balbir Singh
	Mohammad Ashfaq	Eric Pearce	Balbir Singh
	Abdat Rashid	Raymond Evans	Harbinder Singh
	Mohammad Asad	Frederick Quine	Inamur-Rehman
	Jehangir Butt	Ronald Riley	Inder Singh
	Riaz Ud Din	Patrick Nilan	Munir Sait
	Tariq Niazi	Donald Smart	Harmik Singh
		Desmond Piper	Jhon Peter
			Tarsem Singh
1972			

Semi-finals: INDIA bt GERMANY 1–0; PAKISTAN bt G.B. 3–2. Final:
INDIA bt PAKISTAN 1–0. Third-place: GERMANY bt G.B. 3–1.
Semi-finals: INDIA bt G.B. 1–0; PAKISTAN bt SPAIN 1–0. Final: PAKIS-
TAN bt INDIA 1–0. Third-place: SPAIN bt G.B. 2–1.
Lists of team-members include, where known, names of those who played in
preliminaries as well as finals.
Semi-finals: PAKISTAN bt SPAIN 3–0; INDIA bt AUSTRALIA 3–1. Final:
INDIA bt PAKISTAN 1–0.

Victor Chukarin of the Soviet team performing on the pommelled horse, an Olympic event in which he gained the gold medal in 1952. He also won gold medals in the combined exercises in 1952 and 1956. The Russian team with Chukarin won the combined team exercises in the same years, so he is one of very few individuals holding 5 gold medals.

9a. Gymnastics (Men)

COMBINED EXERCISES (INDIVIDUAL)

	GOLD	SILVER	BRONZE
1896	Event not held		
1900	Gustave Sandras (FRANCE)	J. Bass (FRANCE)	G. Demanet (FRANCE)
1904	Adolf Spinnler (GERMANY) 43.49 pts.	Wilhelm Weber (GERMANY) 41.60	Hugo Peitsch (GERMANY) 41.56
1908	Alberto Braglia (ITALY) 317 pts.	S. W. Tysal (G.B.) 312	Louis Segura (FRANCE) 297
1912	Alberto Braglia (ITALY) 135 pts.	Louis Segura (FRANCE) 132.5	Adolfo Tunesi (ITALY) 113.5
1920	Giorgio Zampori (ITALY) 88.35 pts.	Marcel Torres (FRANCE) 87.62	Jean Gounot (FRANCE) 87.45
1924	Leon Skutelj (YUGO.) 110.34 pts.	Robert Prazak (CZECHO.) 110.323	Bedrich Supcik (CZECHO.) 106.903
1928	Georges Miez (SWITZ.) 247.625 pts.	Hermann Hänggi (SWITZ.) 246.625	Leon Stukelj (YUGO.) 244.875
1932	Romeo Neri (ITALY) 140.625 pts.	István Pelle (HUNGARY) 134.925	Heikki Savolainen (FINLAND) 134.575
1936	Karl Schwarzmann (GERMANY) 113.100 pts.	Eugen Mack (SWITZ.) 112.334	Konrad Frey (GERMANY) 111.532
1948	Veikkö Huhtanen (FINLAND) 229.7 pts.	Walter Lehmann (SWITZ.) 229.0	Paavo Aaltonen (FINLAND) 228.8
1952	Viktor Chukarin (U.S.S.R.) 115.70 pts.	Grant Shaginyan (U.S.S.R.) 114.95	Josef Stalder (SWITZ.) 114.75
1956	Viktor Chukarin (U.S.S.R.) 114.25 pts.	Takashi Ono (JAPAN) 114.20	Yuriy Titov (U.S.S.R.) 113.80

GOLD	SILVER	BRONZE
1960 Boris Shakhlin (U.S.S.R.) 115.95 pts.	Takashi Ono (JAPAN) 115.90	Yuriy Titov (U.S.S.R.) 115.60
1964 Yukio Endo (JAPAN) 115.95 pts.	Shuji Tsurumi (JAPAN) 115.40	Boris Shakhlin (U.S.S.R.) Victor Libitsky (U.S.S.R.) 115.40
1968 Sawao Kato (JAPAN) 115.90 pts.	Mikhail Voronin (U.S.S.R.) 115.85	Akinori Nakayama (JAPAN) 115.65
1972		

COMBINED EXERCISES (TEAM)

1896–1920   Event not held

1924[1] ITALY 839.058 pts.	FRANCE 820.528	SWITZ. 816.66
Fernando Mandrini	Jean Gounot	August Güttinger
Mario Lertora	Delsarte	Jean Gutweniger
Vittorio Lucchetti	A. Séguin	Hans Grieder
Franco Martino	Cordonnier	Georges Miez
Luigi Cambiaso	F. Gangloff	Josef Wilhelm
Giuseppe Paris	Hermann	Otto Pfister
Giorgio Zampori	A. Hingelin	Carl Widmer
Luigi Maiocco	Huber	Antoine Rebetez
1928 SWITZ. 1,718.625 pts.	CZECHO. 1,712.5	YUGO. 1,648.5
Georges Miez	Ladislav Vácha	Leon Skutelj
Hermann Hänggi	E. Löffler	Josip Primozic
Eugen Mack	Jan Gajdos	Eduard Antosiewicz
M. Wezel	J. Effenberger	Boris Grekorka
Edi Steinemann	Bedrich Supcik	Anton Malej
August Güttinger	V. Vesely	Ivan Perenta
Hans Grieder	Jan Koutny	Stane Drganc
Otto Pfister	L. Tikal	Dragutin Ciotti
		Vladimir Orel
1932 ITALY 541.850 pts.	U.S. 522.275	FINLAND 509.995
Romeo Neri	Frank Haubold	Heikki Savolainen
Mario Lertora	Frederick Meyer	Mauri Noroma
Savino Guglielmetti	Alfred Jochim	Einari Teräsvirta
Oreste Capuzzo	Frank Cumiskey	Veikkö Pakarinen
Franco Tognini	Michael Schuler	Martti Uosikinnen
1936 GERMANY 657.430 pts.	SWITZ. 654.802	FINLAND 638.468
Franz Beckert	Walter Bach	Martti Uosikinnen
Konrad Frey	Albert Bachmann	Heikki Savolainen
Karl Schwarzmann	Eugen Mack	Mauri Noroma
Willi Stadel	Georges Miez	Aleksanteri Saarvala
Walter Steffens	Michael Reusch	Esa Seeste
Matthias Volz	Edi Steinemann	Veikkö Pakarinen
1948 FINLAND 1,358.3 pts.	SWITZ. 1,356.7	HUNGARY 1,330.35
Veikkö Huhtanen	Walter Lehmann	Lajos Tóth
Paavo Aaltonen	Josef Stalder	Lajos Sántha
Heikki Savolainen	Christian Kipfer	László Baranyai
Olavi Rove	Emil Studer	Ferenc Pataki
Einari Teräsvirta	Robert Lucy	János Mogyorosi
Aleksanteri Saarvala	Michael Reusch	Ferenc Várköi
Kalevi Laitinen	Melchior Thalmann	József Fekete
Sulo Salmi	Karl Frei	Győző Mogyorósi

There were various team events in the Olympic Games since 1896, as follows:—
1896: Separate team events in parallel bars and horizontal bar exercises, both won by GERMANY.
1904: Team event in combined competition (horizontal bar, parallel bars, pommelled horse, 100 yds., long jump, shot putt), won by U.S.
1908: Swedish gymnastics team event (as many as 60 individuals in a team), won by SWEDEN.
1912: Swedish gymnastics team event, won by SWEDEN; optional and free exercises event, won by ITALY; optional exercises event, won by NORWAY.
1920: European gymnastics team event (24-a-side), won by ITALY; Swedish gymnastics event, won by SWEDEN; optional exercises event, won by DENMARK.

	GOLD	SILVER	BRONZE
1952	U.S.S.R. 574.4 pts. Viktor Chukarin Grant Shaginyan Valentin Muratov Yevgeniy Korolkov Vladimir Belyakov Yosif Berdiyev Mikhail Perelman Dimitriy Leonkin	SWITZ. 567.5 Josef Stalder Hans Eugster Jean Tschabold Jack Günthard Melchior Thalmann Ernst Gebendinger Hans Schwarzentruber Ernst Fivian	FINLAND 564.2 Onni Lappalainen Berndt Lindfors Paavo Aaltonen Kaino Lempinen Heikki Savolainen Kalevi Laitinen Kalevi Viskari Olavi Rove
1956	U.S.S.R. 568.25 pts. Viktor Chukarin Valentin Muratov Boris Shakhlin Albert Azaryan Yuriy Titov Pavel Stolbov	JAPAN 566.40 Takashi Ono Masao Takemoto Akira Kono Nobuyuki Aihara Shinsaku Tsukawaki Masami Kubota	FINLAND 555.95 Raimo Heinonen Onni Lappalainen Olavi Leimuvirta Berndt Lindfors Martti Mansikka Kalevi Suoniemi
1960	JAPAN 575.20 pts. Takashi Ono Shuji Tsurumi Yukio Endo Masao Takemoto Nobuyuki Aihara Takashi Mitsukuri	U.S.S.R. 572.70 Boris Shakhlin Yuriy Titov Albert Azaryan Vladimir Portnoi Valeriy Kerdemilidi Nikolay Miligulo	ITALY 559.05 Franco Menichelli Giovanni Carminucci Gianfranco Marzolla Angelo Vicardi Orlando Polmonari Pasquale Carminucci
1964	JAPAN 577.95 pts. Yukio Endo Shuji Tsurumi Haruhiro Yamashita Takashi Mitsukuri Takuji Hayata Takashi Ono	U.S.S.R. 575.45 Yury Tsapenko Boris Shakhlin Victor Leontyev Victor Lisitsky Sergey Diomidor Yuriy Titov	GERMANY 565.10 Siegfried Fulle Klaus Koste Erwin Koppe Peter Weber Philipp Furst Gunter Lyhs
1968	JAPAN 575.90 pts. Sawao Kato Akinori Nakayama Eizo Kenmotsu Takeshi Kato Yukio Endo Mitsuo Tsukahara	U.S.S.R. 571.10 Mikhail Voronin Sergyi Diomidov Vladimir Klimenko Valeryi Karasyev Victor Lisitsky Valeryi Iljinykh	E. GERMANY 557.15 Matthias Brehme Klaus Koste Siegfried Fulle Peter Weber Gerhard Dietrich Gunter Beier
1972			

FLOOR EXERCISES

	GOLD	SILVER	BRONZE
1896–1928	Event not held		
1932	István Pelle (HUNGARY) 28.8 pts.	Georges Miez (SWITZ.) 28.4	Mario Lertora (ITALY) 27.7
1936	Georges Miez (SWITZ.) 18.666 pts.	Josef Walter (SWITZ.) 18.5	Konrad Frey (GERMANY) 18.466 Eugen Mack (SWITZ.) 18.466[1]
1948	Ferenc Pataki (HUNGARY) 38.7 pts.	János Mogyorósi (HUNGARY) 38.4	Zdenek Ruzicka (CZECHO.) 38.1
1952	Karl Thoresson (SWEDEN) 19.25 pts.	Tado Uesako (JAPAN) 19.15 Jerzy Jokiel (POLAND) 19.15[2]	—
1956	Valentin Muratov (U.S.S.R.) 19.20 pts.	Nobuyuki Aihara (JAPAN) 19.10 William Thoresson (SWEDEN) 19.10 Viktor Chukarin[2] (U.S.S.R.) 19.10	—

---

[1] Tie for third place.
[2] Tie for second place.

	GOLD	SILVER	BRONZE
1960	Nobuyuki Aihara (JAPAN) 19.45 pts.	Yuriy Titov (U.S.S.R.) 19.32	Franco Menichelli (ITALY) 19.27
1964	Franco Menicelli (ITALY) 19.45 pts.	Victor Lisitsky (U.S.S.R.) 19.35	Yukio Endo (JAPAN) 19.35
1968	Sawao Kato (JAPAN) 19.475	Akinori Nakayama (JAPAN) 19.400	Takeshi Kato (JAPAN) 19.275
1972			

HORIZONTAL BAR

1896	Hermann Weingärtner (GERMANY)	Alfred Flatow (GERMANY)	Petmĕsas (GREECE)
1900	Event not held		
1904	Anton Heida (U.S.) 40 pts. Edward Hennig[1] (U.S.) 40 pts.	—	George Eyser (U.S.) 39
1908–12–20	Event not held		
1924	Leon Stukelj (YUGO.) 19.73 pts.	Jean Gutweniger (SWITZ.) 19.236	A. Higelin (FRANCE) 19.163
1928	Georges Miez (SWITZ.) 19.17 pts.	Romeo Neri (ITALY) 19.00	Eugen Mack (SWITZ.) 18.92
1932	Dallas Bixler (U.S.) 18.33 pts.	Heikki Savolainen (FINLAND) 18.07	Einari Teräsvirta (FINLAND) 18.07[2]
1936	Aleksanteri Saarvala (FINLAND) 19.433 pts.	Konrad Frey (GERMANY) 19.267	Karl Schwarzmann (GERMANY) 19.233
1948	Josef Stalder (SWITZ.) 39.7 pts.	Walter Lehmann (SWITZ.) 39.4	Veikkö Huhtanen (FINLAND) 39.2
1952	Jack Günthard (SWITZ.) 19.55 pts.	Josef Stalder (SWITZ.) 19.50 Karl Schwarzmann (GERMANY) 19.50[3]	—
1956	Takashi Ono (JAPAN) 19.60 pts.	Yuriy Titov (U.S.S.R.) 19.40	Masao Takemoto (JAPAN) 19.30
1960	Takashi Ono (JAPAN) 19.60 pts.	Masao Takemoto (JAPAN) 19.52	Boris Shakhlin (U.S.S.R.) 19.47
1964	Boris Shakhlin (U.S.S.R.) 19.625 pts.	Yuriy Titov (U.S.S.R.) 19.55	Miroslav Cerar (YUGOSLAVIA) 19.50
1968	Mikhail Voronin (U.S.S.R.) 19.550 pts. Akinori Nakayama (JAPAN) 19.550		Eizo Kenmotsu (JAPAN) 19.375
1972			

---

[1] Tie for first place.
[2] Teräsvirta conceded second place to Savolainen.
[3] Tie for second place.

PARALLEL BARS

1896	Alfred Flatow (GERMANY)	Hermann Weingärtner (GERMANY)	Louis Zutter (SWITZ.)
1900	Event not held		
1904	George Eyser (U.S.) 44 pts.	Anton Heida (U.S.) 43	John Duha (U.S.) 40
1908–12–20	Event not held		
1924	August Güttinger (SWITZ.) 21.63 pts.	Robert Prazak (CZECHO.) 21.61	Giorgio Zampori (ITALY) 21.45
1928	Ladislav Vácha (CZECHO.) 18.83 pts.	Josip Primozic (YUGO.) 18.50	Hermann Hänggi (SWITZ.) 18.08
1932	Romeo Neri (ITALY) 18.97 pts.	István Pelle (HUNGARY) 18.60	Heikki Savolainen (FINLAND) 18.27
1936	Konrad Frey (GERMANY)19.067pts.	Michael Reusch (SWITZ.) 19.034	Karl Schwarzmann (GERMANY) 18.967

Olympic champion of the rings in both 1956 and 1960 was Albert Azaryan of Russia.

	GOLD	SILVER	BRONZE
1948	Michael Reusch (SWITZ.) 39.5 pts.	Veikkö Huhtanen (FINLAND) 39.3	Christian Kipfer (SWITZ.) 39.1 Josef Stalder (SWITZ.) 39.1[1]
1952	Hans Eugster (SWITZ.) 19.65 pts.	Viktor Chukarin (U.S.S.R.) 19.60	Josef Stalder (SWITZ.) 19.50
1956	Viktor Chukarin (U.S.S.R.) 19.20 pts.	Masami Kubota (JAPAN) 19.15	Takashi Ono (JAPAN) 19.10 Masao Takemoto (JAPAN) 19.10[1]
1960	Boris Shakhlin (U.S.S.R.) 19.40 pts.	Giovanni Carminucci (ITALY) 19.37	Takashi Ono (JAPAN) 19.35
1964	Yukio Endo (JAPAN) 19.675 pts.	Shuji Tsurumi (JAPAN) 19.45	Franco Menicelli (ITALY) 19.35
1968	Akinori Nakayama (JAPAN) 19.475 pts.	Mikhail Voronin (U.S.S.R.) 19.425	Vladimir Klimenko (U.S.S.R.) 19.225
1972			

[1] Tie for third place.

POMMELLED HORSE
(first held 1896)

	GOLD	SILVER	BRONZE
1896	Louis Zutter (SWITZ.)	Hermann Weingärtner (GERMANY)	Gyula Kokas (HUNGARY)
1900	Event not held		
1904	Anton Heida (U.S.) 42 pts.	George Eyser (U.S.) 33	W. A. Merz (U.S.) 29
1908–12–20	Event not held		
1924	Josef Wilhelm (SWITZ.) 21.23 pts.	Jean Gutweniger (SWITZ.) 21.13	Antoine Rebetez (SWITZ.) 20.73
1928	Hermann Hänggi (SWITZ.) 19.75 pts.	Georges Miez (SWITZ.) 19.25	Heikki Savolainen (FINLAND) 18.83
1932	István Pelle (HUNGARY) 19.07 pts.	Omero Bonoli (ITALY) 18.87	Frank Haubold (U.S.) 18.57
1936	Konrad Frey (GERMANY)19.333pts.	Eugen Mack (SWITZ.) 19.167	Albert Bachmann (SWITZ.) 19.067
1948	Paavo Aaltonen, Veikkö Huhtanen, Heikki Savolainen (all FINLAND) tied for first place, each 38.7 pts.		
1952	Viktor Chukarin (U.S.S.R.) 19.50 pts.	Yevgeniy Korolkov (U.S.S.R.) 19.40 Grant Shaginyan (U.S.S.R.) 19.40[1]	—
1956	Boris Shakhlin (U.S.S.R.) 19.25 pts.	Takashi Ono (JAPAN) 19.20	Viktor Chukarin (U.S.S.R.) 19.10
1960	Eugen Ekman (FINLAND) 19.37 pts. Boris Shakhlin (U.S.S.R.) 19.37 pts.[2]	—	Shuji Tsurumi (JAPAN) 19.15
1964	Miroslav Cerar (YUGOSLAVIA) 19.525 pts.	Shuji Tsurumi (JAPAN) 19.325	Yury Tsapenko (U.S.S.R.) 19.20
1968	Miroslav Cerar (YUGOSLAVIA) 19.325 pts.	Olli Laiho (FINLAND) 19.225	Mikhail Veronin (U.S.S.R.) 19.200
1972			

[1] Tie for second place.
[2] Tie for first place.

LONG HORSE VAULT

1896	Karl Schumann (GERMANY)	Louis Zutter (SWITZ.)	—
1900	Event not held		
1904	Anton Heida (U.S.) 36 pts. George Eyser (U.S.) 36 pts.[1]	—	W. A. Merz (U.S.) 31
1908–12–20	Event not held		
1924	Frank Kriz (U.S.) 9.98 pts.	Jan Koutny (CZECHO.) 9.97	Bohumil Morkovsky (CZECHO.) 9.93
1928	Eugen Mack (SWITZ.) 9.58 pts.	Emanuel Löffler (CZECHO.) 9.50	Stane Derganc (YUGO.) 9.46
1932	Savino Guglielmetti (ITALY) 18.03 pts.	Alfred Jochim (GERMANY) 17.77	Edward Carmichael (U.S.) 17.53
1936	Karl Schwarzmann (GERMANY) 19.20 pts.	Eugen Mack (SWITZ.) 18.967	Matthias Volz (GERMANY) 18.467
1948	Paavo Aaltonen (FINLAND) 39.1 pts.	Olavi Rove (FINLAND) 39.0	János Mogyorósi (HUNGARY) 38.5 Ferenc Pataki (HUNGARY) 38.5 Leos Sotornik (CZECHO.) 38.5[2]
1952	Viktor Chukarin (U.S.S.R.) 19.20 pts.	Masao Takemoto (JAPAN) 19.15	Tadao Uesako (JAPAN) 19.05 Takashi Ono (JAPAN) 19.05[2]

	GOLD	SILVER	BRONZE
1956	Helmuth Bantz (GERMANY) 18.85 pts. Valentin Muratov (U.S.S.R.) 18.85 pts.[1]	—	Yuriy Titov (U.S.S.R.) 18.75
1960	Takashi Ono (JAPAN) 19.35 pts. Boris Shakhlin (U.S.S.R.) 19.35 pts.[1]	—	Vladimir Portnoi (U.S.S.R.) 19.22
1964	Haruhiro Yamashita (JAPAN) 19.660 pts	Victor Lisitsky (U.S.S.R.) 19.325	Hannu Rantakari (FINLAND) 19.30
1968	Mikhail Veronin (U.S.S.R.) 19.00 pts.	Yukio Endo (JAPAN) 18.950	Sergyi Diomidov (U.S.S.R.) 18.925
1972			

---

[1] Tie for first place.
[2] Tie for third place.

RINGS

	GOLD	SILVER	BRONZE
1896	Jean Mitropoulos (GREECE)	Hermann Weingärtner (GERMANY)	Persakis (GREECE)
1900	Event not held		
1904	Herman Glass (U.S.) 45 pts.	W. A. Merz (U.S.) 35	E. Voight (U.S.) 32
1908–12–20	Event not held		
1924	Francesco Martino (ITALY) 21.553 pts.	Robert Prazak (CZECHO.) 21.483	Ladislav Vácha (CZECHO.) 21.43
1928	Leon Skutelj (YUGO.) 19.25 pts.	Ladislav Vácha (CZECHO.) 19.17	Emanuel Löffler (CZECHO.) 18.83
1932	George Gulack (U.S.) 18.97 pts.	William Denton (U.S.) 18.60	Giovanni Lattuada (ITALY) 18.50
1936	Alois Hudec (CZECHO.) 19.433 pts.	Leon Skutelj (YUGO.) 18.87	Matthias Volz (GERMANY) 18.67
1948	Karl Frei (SWITZ.) 39.6 pts.	Michael Reusch (SWITZ.) 39.1	Zdenek Ruzicka (CZECHO.) 38.5
1952	Grant Shaginyan (U.S.S.R.) 19.75 pts.	Viktor Chukarin (U.S.S.R.) 19.55	Hans Eugster (SWITZ.) 19.40 Dimitriy Leonkin (U.S.S.R.) 19.40[1]
1956	Albert Azaryan (U.S.S.R.) 19.35 pts.	Valentin Muratov (U.S.S.R.) 19.15	Masao Takemoto (JAPAN) 19.10 Masami Kubota (JAPAN) 19.10[1]
1960	Albert Azaryan (U.S.S.R.) 19.72 pts.	Boris Shakhlin (U.S.S.R.) 19.50	Velik Kapsazov (BULGARIA) 19.42 Takashi Ono (JAPAN) 19.42[1]
1964	Takuji Hayata (JAPAN) 19.475 pts.	Franco Menicelli (ITALY) 19.425	Boris Shakhlin (U.S.S.R.) 19.40
1968	Akinori Nakayama (JAPAN) 19.450 pts.	Mikhail Voronin (U.S.S.R.) 19.325	Sawao Kato (JAPAN) 19.225
1972			

---

[1] Tie for third place.

9b. Gymnastics (Women)

COMBINED EXERCISES (INDIVIDUAL)

	GOLD	SILVER	BRONZE
1896–1948	Event not held		
1952	Maria Gorokhovskaya (U.S.S.R.) 76.78 pts.	Nina Bocharyova (U.S.S.R.) 75.94	Margit Korondi (HUNGARY) 75.8

Vera Caslavska (Czechoslovakia) was the gymnastic star of the 1964 and 1968 Games. Her total tally is six golds and four silvers.

	GOLD	SILVER	BRONZE
1956	Larisa Latynina (U.S.S.R.) 74.93 pts.	Agnes Keleti (HUNGARY) 74.63	Sofia Muratova (U.S.S.R.) 74.46
1960	Larisa Latynina (U.S.S.R.) 77.03 pts.	Sofia Muratova (U.S.S.R.) 76.69	Polina Astakhova (U.S.S.R.) 76.16
1964	Vera Caslavska (CZECHO.) 77.564 pts.	Larisa Latynina (U.S.S.R.) 76.998	Polina Astakhova (U.S.S.R.) 76.965
1968	Vera Caslavska (CZECHO) 78.25 pts.	Zinaida Veronina (U.S.S.R.) 76.85	Natalya Kuchinskaya (U.S.S.R.) 76.75

COMBINED EXERCISES (TEAM)

GOLD	SILVER	BRONZE
1896–1924 Event not held		
1928 NETHS. 316.75 pts.	ITALY 289.00	G.B. 258.25
van Radwijk	Bianca Ambrosetti	Margaret Hartley
van der Berg	Lavinia Gianoni	Carrie Pickles
Polak	Gino Grevi	Annie Broadbent
Nordheim	Germana Malabarba	Amy Jagger
van der Bos	Clara Marangoni	Ada Smith
van Rumst	Luigina Perversi	Lucy Desmond
van der Vegt	Diana Pizzavini	Doris Woods
Burgerhof	Anna Tanzini	Queenie Kite
Simons	Carolina Tronconi	Jessie Judd
de Levie	Ines Vercesi	Midge Moreman
Stelma	Rina Vittadini	Ethel Seymour
Agsteribbe		Hilda Smith
1932 Event not held		
1936 GERMANY 506.50 pts.	CZECHO. 503.50	HUNGARY 499
Anita Bärwirth	Vlasta Dekanova	Margit Csillik
Erna Bürger	Bozena Dobesova	Gabriella Mészáros
Isolde Frölian	Vlasta Foltova	Judit Tóth
Paula Pöhlsen	Anna Hrebinova	Margit Nagy
Käthe Sohnemann	Mathylda Pálfyova	Olga Törös
Trudi Meyer	Zdenka Vermirovska	Eszter Voigt
Friedl Iby	Vetrovska	Madary
Julie Schmitt	Bayerova	Kalocsai
1948 CZECHO. 445.45 pts.	HUNGARY 440.55	U.S. 422.63
Z. Honsova	Edit Vásárhelyi	Helen Schifano
M. Misakova	Mária Kövi	Clara Schroth
V. Ruzickova	Irén Karcsics	Meta Elste
Bozena Srncova	Erzsébet Gulyás	Marian Barone
M. Mullerova	Agnes Keleti	Laddie Bakanie
Zdenka Vermirovska	Olga Tass	Consetta Lenz
O. Silhanova	Anna Fehér	Anita Simonis
M. Kovarova	Mária Sándor	Dorothy Dalton
1952 U.S.S.R. 527.03 pts.	HUNGARY 520.96	CZECHO. 503.32
Maria Gorokhovskaya	Margit Korondi	Eva Vechtova
Nina Bocharyova	Agnes Keleti	Alena Chadimova
Galina Minaycheva	Edit Perényi	Jana Rabascova
Galina Urbanovich	Olga Tass	Bozena Srncova
Pelageya Danilova	Erzsébet Gulyás	Hana Bobkova
Galina Shamray	Mária Zalai	Mathylda Sinova
Medeya Dshugeli	Andrea Bodó	Vera Vancuorva
Yekaterina Kalinchuk	Irén Daruházi	Alena Reichova
1956 U.S.S.R. 444.80 pts.	HUNGARY 443.50	RUMANIA 438.20
Larisa Latynina	Agnes Keleti	Elena Leusteanu
Sofia Muratova	Olga Tass	Sonia Inovan
Tamara Manina	Margit Korondi	Emilia Vatasoiu
Lyudmila Egorova	Andrea Bodó	Georgeta Hurmuzachi
Polina Astakhova	Alice Kertész	Elena Margarit
Lydia Kalinina	Károlyné Gulyás	Elena Sacalici
1960 U.S.S.R. 382.32 pts.	CZECHO. 373.32	RUMANIA 372.05
Larisa Latynina	Vera Caslavska	Sonia Inovan
Sofia Muratova	Eva Bosakova	Elena Leusteanu
Polina Astakhova	Ludmila Svedova	Antanasia Ionescu
Marganita Nikolayeva	Adolfina Tkacikova	Uta Poreceanu
Lydia Ivanova	Mathydla Matouskova	Emilia Lita
Tamara Lyukhina	Hana Ruzickova	Elena Niculescu
1964 U.S.S.R. 380.890 pts.	CZECHO. 379.989	JAPAN 377.889
Larisa Latynina	Vera Caslavska	Keiko Ikeda
Elena Volchetskaya	Hana Ruzickova	Toshiko Aihara
Polina Astakhova	Jaroslava Sedlackova	Kiyoko Ono
Tamara Zamotailova	Adolfina Tkacikova	Taniko Nakamura
Tamara Manina	Marie Krajcirova	Hiroko Tsuji
Ludmila Gromova	Jana Posnerova	Ginko Chiba

	GOLD	SILVER	BRONZE
1968	U.S.S.R. 382.85 pts.	CZECHO. 382.20	E. GERMANY 379.10
	Zinaida Voronina	Vera Caslavaska	Erika Zuchold
	Natalya Kuchinskaya	Bohumila Rimnacova	Karin Janz
	Larissa Petrik	Miroslava Sklenickova	Maritta Bauerschmidt
	Olga Kharlova	Mariana Krajcirova	Ute Starke
	Liudmila Turisheva	Hana Liskova	Marianne Noack
	Ljubov Burda	Jana Kubickova	Magdalena Schmidt
1972			

BEAM

	GOLD	SILVER	BRONZE
1896–1948	Event not held		
1952	Nina Bocharyova	Maria Gorokhovskaya	Margit Korondi
	(U.S.S.R.) 19.22 pts.	(U.S.S.R.) 19.13	(HUNGARY) 19.02
1956	Agnes Keleti	Eva Bosakova	—
	(HUNGARY) 18.80 pts.	(CZECHO.) 18.63	
		Tamara Manina	
		(U.S.S.R.) 18.63[1]	
1960	Eva Bosakova	Larisa Latynina	Sofia Muratova
	(CZECHO.) 19.28 pts.	(U.S.S.R.) 19.233	(U.S.S.R.) 19.232
1964	Vera Caslavska	Tamara Manina	Larisa Latynina
	(CZECHO.) 19.449 pts.	(U.S.S.R.) 19.399	(U.S.S.R.) 19.382
1968	Natalya Kuchinskaya	Vera Caslavska	Larissa Petrik
	(U.S.S.R.) 19.650 pts.	(CZECHO.) 19.575	(U.S.S.R.) 19.250
1972			

[1] Tie for second place.

ASYMMETRIC BARS

	GOLD	SILVER	BRONZE
1896–1948	Event not held		
1952	Margit Korondi	Maria Gorokhovskaya	Agnes Keleti
	(HUNGARY) 19.40 pts.	(U.S.S.R.) 19.26	(HUNGARY) 19.16
1956	Agnes Keleti	Larisa Latynina	Sofia Muratova
	(HUNGARY) 18.96 pts.	(U.S.S.R.) 18.83	(U.S.S.R.) 18.80
1960	Polina Astakhova	Larisa Latynina	Tamara Lyukhina
	(U.S.S.R.) 19.61 pts.	(U.S.S.R.) 19.41	(U.S.S.R.) 19.39
1964	Polina Astakhova	Katalin Makray	Larisa Latynina
	(U.S.S.R.) 19.332 pts.	(HUNGARY) 19.216	(U.S.S.R.) 19.199
1968	Vera Caslavska	Karin Janz	Zinaida Voronina
	(CZECHO.) 19.650 pts.	(E. GERMANY) 19.500	(U.S.S.R.) 19.425
1972			

HORSE VAULT

	GOLD	SILVER	BRONZE
1896–1948	Event not held		
1952	Yekaterina Kalinchuk	Maria Gorokhovskaya	Galina Minaycheva
	(U.S.S.R.) 19.20 pts.	(U.S.S.R.) 19.19	(U.S.S.R.) 19.16
1956	Larisa Latynina	Tamara Manina	Ann-Sofi Colling
	(U.S.S.R.) 18.83 pts.	(U.S.S.R.) 18.80	(SWEDEN) 18.73
			Olga Tass
			(HUNGARY) 18.73[1]
1960	Margarita Nikolayeva	Sofia Muratova	Larisa Latynina
	(U.S.S.R.) 19.31 pts.	(U.S.S.R.) 19.04	(U.S.S.R.) 19.01
1964	Vera Caslavska	Larisa Latynina[2]	Birgit Radochla[2]
	(CZECHO.) 19.483 pts.	(U.S.S.R.) 19.283	(GERMANY) 19.283
1968	Vera Caslavska	Erika Zuchold	Zinaida Voronina
	(CZECHO.) 19.775 pts.	(E. GERMANY) 19.625	(U.S.S.R.) 19.425
1972			

Tie for third place.
Shared Silver medal.

FLOOR EXERCISES

	GOLD	SILVER	BRONZE
1896–1948	Event not held		
1952	Agnes Keleti (HUNGARY) 19.36 pts.	Maria Gorokhovskaya (U.S.S.R.) 19.20	Margit Korondi (HUNGARY) 19.00
1956	Larisa Latynina (U.S.S.R.) 18.73 pts. Agnes Keleti (HUNGARY) 18.73 pts.[1]	—	Elena Leusteanu (RUMANIA) 18.70
1960	Larisa Latynina (U.S.S.R.) 19.58 pts.	Polina Astakhova (U.S.S.R.) 19.53	Tamara Lyukhina (U.S.S.R.) 19.44
1964	Larisa Latynina (U.S.S.R.) 19.599 pts.	Polina Astakhova (U.S.S.R.) 19.50	Ducza Janosi (HUNGARY) 19.30
1968	Larissa Petrik (U.S.S.R.) 19.675 pts.	Vera Caslavska (CZECHO.) 19.675	Natalya Kuchinskaya (U.S.S.R.) 19.650
1972			

---

[1] Tie for first place.

10. Handball

1896–1932	Event not held		
1936	GERMANY* 6 pts. Heinz Körvers Arthur Knautz Willy Bandholz Hans Keiter Walter Brinkmann Georg Dascher Erich Herrmann Hans Theiling Helmut Berthold Alfred Klingler Fritz Fromm	AUSTRIA 4 pts. Alois Schnabel Johann Tauscher Franz Bartl Leopold Wohlrab Emil Juracka Otto Licha Anton Perwein Ferdinand Kieffler Ludwig Schubert Alfred Schmalzer Jaroslaw Volak	SWITZERLAND 2 pts. Willy Gysi Erland Herkenrath Erich Schmitt Rolf Fass Max Streib Robert Studer Werner Meyer Ernst Hufschmied Georg Mischon Rudolf Würz
1948–1968	Event not held		
1972			

---

* GERMANY bt AUSTRIA 10–6. SWITZERLAND lost to GERMANY 6–16 and to AUSTRIA 6–11.

11. Judo

No limit class (any body weight)

1964	Anton Geesink (NETH.)	Akio Kaminaga (JAPAN)	Theodore Boronovskis (AUSTRIA) Klaus Glahn (GERMANY)
1972			

Heavyweight

1964	Isao Inokuma (JAPAN)	Alfred Rogers (CANADA)	Parnauz Chikviladze (U.S.S.R.) Anzor Kiknadze (U.S.S.R.)
1972			

	GOLD	SILVER	BRONZE

Middle-heavyweight (new event)

1972

Middleweight

1964	Isao Okano (JAPAN)	Wolfgang Hofmann (GERMANY)	James Bregman (U.S.) Eui Tae Kim (S. KOREA)
1972			

Welterweight (new event)

1972

Lightweight

1964	Takehide Nakatani (JAPAN)	Eric Haenni (SWITZ.)	Oleg Styepanov (U.S.S.R.) Aron Bogulubov (U.S.S.R.)
1972			

12. Modern Pentathlon[1]

1896–1908	Event not held		
1912	Gustaf Lilliehöök (SWEDEN) 27 pts.[2]	Gösta Asbrink (SWEDEN) 28	Georg de Laval (SWEDEN) 30
1920	Gustaf Dryssen (SWEDEN) 18 pts.	Erik de Laval (SWEDEN) 23	Gösta Rüno (SWEDEN) 27
1924	Bo Lindman (SWEDEN) 18 pts.	Gustaf Dryssen (SWEDEN) 39	Bertil Uggla (SWEDEN) 45
1928	Sven Thofelt (SWEDEN) 47 pts.	Bo Lindman (SWEDEN) 50	Helmuth Kahl (GERMANY) 52
1932	Johan Gabriel Oxenstierna (SWEDEN) 32 pts.	Bo Lindman (SWEDEN) 35.5	Richard Mayo (U.S.) 38.5
1936	Gotthardt Handrick (GERMANY) 31.5 pts.	Charles Leonard (U.S.) 39.5	Silvano Abba (ITALY) 45.5
1948	William Grut (SWEDEN) 16 pts.[3]	George Moore (U.S.) 47	Gösta Gardin (SWEDEN) 49
1952[4]	Lars Hall (SWEDEN) 32 pts.	Gábor Benedek (HUNGARY) 39	István Szondi (HUNGARY) 41
Teams—	HUNGARY 166pts. Gábor Benedek István Szondi Aladár Kovácsi	SWEDEN 182 pts. Lars Hall Torsten Lindqvist Cläes Egnell	FINLAND 213 pts. Olavi Mannonen Lauri Vilkko Olavi Rokka
1956	Lars Hall (SWEDEN) 4,833 pts.[5]	Olavi Mannonen (FINLAND) 4,774.5 pts.	Väinö Korhonen (FINLAND) 4,750 pts.
Teams—	U.S.S.R. 13,609.5 pts. Igor Novikov Aleksandr Tarasov Ivan Deryugin	U.S. 13,482 pts. George Lambert William Andre Jack Daniels	FINLAND 13,185.5 pts. Olavi Mannonen Väinö Korhonen Berndt Katter
1960	Ferenc Nemeth (HUNGARY) 5,024 pts.	Imre Nagy (HUNGARY) 4,988 pts.	Robert Beck (U.S.) 4,981 pts.
Teams—	HUNGARY 14,863 pts. Ferenc Nemeth Imre Nagy András Balczo	U.S.S.R. 14,309 pts. Igor Novikov Nikolay Tatarinov Khanno Selg	U.S. 14,192 pts. Robert Beck Jack Daniels George Lambert

	GOLD	SILVER	BRONZE
1964	Ferenc Török	Igor Novikov	Albert Mokeyev
	(HUNGARY) 5,116 pts.	(U.S.S.R.) 5,067 pts.	(U.S.S.R.) 5,039 pts.
Teams—	U.S.S.R. 14,961 pts.	U.S. 14,189 pts.	HUNGARY 14,173 pts.
	Igor Novikov	James Moore	Ferenc Török
	Albert Mokeyev	David Kirkwood	Imre Nagy
	Victor Mineyev	Paul Pesthy	Otto Toerek
1968	Bjorn Ferm	András Balczo	Pavel Lednyev
	(SWEDEN) 4,964 pts.	(HUNGARY) 4,953 pts.	(U.S.S.R.) 4,795 pts.
Teams—			
	HUNGARY 14,325 pts.	U.S.S.R. 14,248 pts.	FRANCE 14,188 pts.
	András Balczo	Boris Onishenko	Raoul Gueguen
	István Mona	Pavel Lednyev	Lucien Guiguet
	Ferenc Török	Stasis Shaparnis	Jean-Pierre Giudicelli
1972			

---

[1] Five events: shooting; swimming; fencing; horse-riding; cross-country running.
[2] From 1912 to 1952 points-scoring system was one for first place, two for second, three for third, etc. in each event.
[3] Grut won the horse-riding, fencing and swimming events, and was fifth in shooting and eighth in cross-country.
[4] Team event held for first time.
[5] International system of graduated scoring adopted.

13. Rowing

SINGLE SCULLS

1896	Event not held		
1900	Henri Barrelet	Gaudin	George St. Ashe
	(FRANCE) 7m 35.6s	(FRANCE) 7m 41.6s	(G.B.) 8m 15.6s
1904[1]	Frank Greer	James Juvenal	Constance Titus
	(U.S.) 10m 08.5s	(U.S.) 2 lengths	(U.S.) 1 length
1908[2]	Harry Blackstaffe	Alexander McCulloch	Bernhard von Gaza
	(G.B.) 9m 26.0s	(G.B.) 1¼ lengths	(GERMANY) d.n.a.
1912[3]	William Kinnear	Polydore Veirman	Everett Butler
	(G.B.) 7m 47.6s	(BELGIUM) 7m 56.0s	(CANADA) d.n.a.
1920[3]	John Kelly	Jack Beresford	ClarenceHadfieldd'Arcy
	(U.S.) 7m 35.0s	(G.B.) 7m 36.0s	(N.Z.) 7m 48.0s
1924	Jack Beresford	William Garrett-Gilmore	Josef Schneider
	(G.B.) 7m 49.2s	(U.S.) 7m 54.0s	(SWITZ.) 8m 01.0s
1928[3]	Henry Pearce	Kenneth Myers	T. David Collet
	(AUSTRALIA) 7m 11.0s	(U.S.) 7m 20.8s	(G.B.) 7m 19.8s[4]
1932	Henry Pearce	William Miller	Guillermo Douglas
	(AUSTRALIA) 7m 44.4s	(U.S.) 7m 45.2s	(URUGUAY) 8m 13.6s
1936	Gustav Schäfer	Josef Hasenohrl	Daniel Barrow
	(GERMANY) 8m 21.5s	(AUSTRIA) 8m 25.8s	(U.S.) 8m 28.0s
1948[5]	Mervyn Wood	Eduardo Risso	Romolo Catasta
	(AUSTRALIA) 7m 24.4s	(URUGUAY) 7m 38.2s	(ITALY) 7m 51.4s
1952	Yuri Tyukalov	Mervyn Wood	Teodor Kocerka
	(U.S.S.R.) 8m 12.8s	(AUSTRALIA) 8m 14.5s	(POLAND) 8m 19.4s
1956	Vyacheslav Ivanov	Stuart Mackenzie	John B. Kelly
	(U.S.S.R.) 8m 02.5s	(AUSTRALIA) 8m 07.7s	(U.S.) 8m 11.8s
1960	Vyacheslav Ivanov	Achim Hill	Teodor Kocerka
	(U.S.S.R.) 7m 13.96s	(GERMANY) 7m 20.21s	(POLAND) 7m 21.26s
1964	Vyacheslav Ivanov	Achim Hill	Gottfried Kottman
	(U.S.S.R.) 8m 22.51s	(GERMANY) 8m 26.34s	(SWITZ.) 8m 29.68s

One of only three
oarsmen to take three
gold medals, Jack
Beresford of Great
Britain won rowing
events in 1924, 1932 and
1936.

	GOLD	SILVER	BRONZE
1968	Henri Jan Wienese (NETHS.) 7m 47.80s	Jochen Meissner (W. GERMANY) 7m 52.00s	Alberto Demiddi (ARGENTINA) 7m 57.19s
1972			

[1] Course of 2 miles.
[2] Course of 1½ miles.
[3] Course of 2,000 metres (1 mile 427 yards).
[4] Third place decided in separate race.
[5] Course of 1,929 metres (1 mile 350 yards).

DOUBLE SCULLS

1896–1900	Event not held		
1904[1]	U.S. 10m 03.2s	U.S.	U.S.
	John Mulcahy	John Hobsen	John Wells
	William Varley	James McLoughlin	Joseph Rauanack
1908–1912	Event not held		
1920[2]	U.S. 7m 09.0s	ITALY 7m 19.0s	FRANCE 7m 21.0s
	John Kelly	Erminio Dones	Alfred Plé
	Paul Costello	Pietro Anoni	Gaston Giran
1924	U.S. 7m 45.0s	FRANCE 7m 54.8s	SWITZ. d.n.a.
	John Kelly	Jean-Pierre Stock	Rudolf Bosshard
	Paul Costello	Marc Detton	Heini Thoma
1928[2]	U.S. 6m 41.4s	CANADA 6m 51.0s	AUSTRIA 6m 48.8s[3]
	Charles McIlvaine	Jack Guest	Viktor Flessl
	Paul Costello	Joseph Wright	Leo Losert
1932	U.S. 7m 17.4s	GERMANY 7m 22.8s	CANADA 7m 27.6s
	William Garrett-Gilmore	Gerhard Boetzelen	Noel de Mille
	Kenneth Myers	Herbert Buhtz	Charles Pratt
1936	G.B. 7m 20.8s	GERMANY 7m 26.2s	POLAND 7m 36.2s
	Leslie Southwood	Joachim Pirsch	Jerzy Ustupski
	Jack Beresford	Willy Kaidel	Roger Verey
1948[4]	G.B. 6m 51.3s	DENMARK 6m 55.3s	URUGUAY 7m 12.4s
	B. Herbert Bushnell	Aage Larsen	Juan Rodriguez
	Richard Burnell	Ebbe Parsner	W. Jones
1952	ARGENTINA 7m 32.2s	U.S.S.R. 7m 38.3s	URUGUAY 7m 43.7s
	Tranquilino Copozzo	Georgiy Zhilin	Miguel Seijas
	Eduardo Guerrero	Igor Emchuk	Juan Rodriguez

	GOLD	SILVER	BRONZE
1956	U.S.S.R. 7m 24.0s Aleksandr Berkutov Yuriy Tyukalov	U.S. 7m 42.2s Bernard Costello James Gardiner	AUSTRALIA 7m 37.4s Murray Riley Mervyn Wood
1960	CZECHO. 6m 47.50s Vaclav Kozak Pavel Schmidt	U.S.S.R. 6m 50.48s Aleksandr Berkutov Yuriy Tyukalov	SWITZ. 6m 50.59s Ernst Huerlimann Rolf Larcher
1964	U.S.S.R. 7m 10.66s Oleg Tyurin Boris Dubrovsky	U.S. 7m 13.16s Seymour Cromwell James Storm	CZECHO. 7m 14.23s Vladimir Andrs Pavel Hofman
1968	U.S.S.R. 6m 51.52s Anatoly Sass Alexander Timoshinin	NETHS. 6m 52.80s Henricus Droog Leendert van Dis	U.S. 6m 54.21s John Nunn William Maher
1972			

[1] Course of 2 miles.
[2] Course of 2,000 metres (1 mile 427 yards).
[3] Third place decided in separate race.
[4] Course of 1,929 metres (1 mile 350 yards).

COXSWAINLESS PAIRS

1896	Event not held		
1900	BELGIUM I d.n.a. Van Crombuge De Sonville	BELGIUM II d.n.a. Delattre Delattre	FRANCE d.n.a. Tellier Beauchamps
1904	U.S. 10m 57.0s (Seawanhaka C.)	U.S. d.n.a. (Atalanta B.C.)	U.S. d.n.a. (Western R.C.)
1908[1]	G.B. 9m 41.0s (Leander I) J. R. K. Fenning Gordon Thomson	G.B. 2½ lengths (Leander II) George Fairbairn Philip Verdon	CANADA d.n.a. F. P. Toms N. B. Jackes
1912	Event not held		
1920[2]	ITALY 7m 56.0s Ercole Olgeni Giovanni Scatturin	FRANCE 7m 57.0s Gabriel Poix Maurice Bouton	SWITZ. d.n.a. Eduard Candeveau Alfred Felber [3]
1924	NETHS. 8m 19.4s W. Rosingh A. Beynen	FRANCE 8m 21.6s Maurice Bouton Georges Piot	
1928[2]	GERMANY 7m 06.4s Bruno Muller Kurt Moeschter	G.B. 7m 08.8s R. Archibald Nisbet Terence O'Brien	U.S. 7m 20.4s John Schmitt Paul McDowell
1932	G.B. 8m 00.0s H. R. Arthur Edwards Lewis Clive	N.Z. 8m 02.4s Frederick Thompson Cyril Stiles	POLAND 8m 08.2s Janusz Mikolajezyk Henryk Budzynski
1936	GERMANY 8m 16.1s Hugo Strauss Willi Eichhorn	DENMARK 8m 19.2s Harry Larsen Richard Olsen	ARGENTINA 8m 23.0s J. Curatella H. Podestá
1948[4]	G.B. 7m 21.1s John Wilson W. Stanley Laurie	SWITZ. 7m 23.9s Josef Kalt Hans Kalt	ITALY 7m 31.5s Bruno Boni Felice Fanetti
1952	U.S. 8m 20.7s Charles Logg Thomas Price	BELGIUM 8m 23.5s Michel Knuysen Robert Baetens	SWITZ. 8m 32.7s Kurt Schmid Hans Kalt
1956	U.S. 7m 55.4s James Fifer Duvall Hecht	U.S.S.R. 8m 03.9s Igor Buldakov Vyacheslav Ivanov	AUSTRIA 8m 11.8s Josef Kloimstein Alfred Sageder
1960	U.S.S.R. 7m 02.01s Valentin Boreyko Olyeg Golovanov	AUSTRIA 7m 03.69s Josef Kloimstein Alfred Sageder	FINLAND 7m 03.80s Veli Lehtelä Toimi Pitkänen

[1] Course of 1½ miles.
[2] Course of 2,000 metres (1 mile 427 yards).
[3] G.B. did not take part in the final.
[4] Course of 1,929 metres (1 mile 350 yards).

John B. Kelly of Philadelphia, winner of the bronze medal in the 1956 single sculls at Melbourne, is the brother of Princess Grace of Monaco, and the son of the Olympic winner of 3 gold medals—in single sculls (1920) and double sculls (1920 and 1924).

	GOLD	SILVER	BRONZE
1964	CANADA 7m 32.94s G. Hungerford R. Jackson	NETHS. 7m 33.40s S. Blaisse E. Veenemans	GERMANY 7m 38.63s M. Schwan W. Hottenrott
1968	E. GERMANY 7m 26.56s Jorg Lucke Heinz-Jurgen Bothe	U.S. 7m 26.71s Lawrence Hough Philip Johnson	DENMARK 7m 31.84s Peter Christiansen Ib Ivan Larsen
1972			

COXED PAIRS

1896	Event not held		
1900	NETHS. 7m 34.2s (Minerva, Amsterdam)	FRANCE I 7m 34.4s (Soc. de la Marne)	FRANCE II 7m 57.2s (Rowing Club de Castillon)
1904–1920	Event not held		
1924	SWITZ. 8m 39.0s Eduard Candeveau Alfred Felber Emil Lachapelle (cox)	ITALY 8m 39.1s Ercole Olgeni Giovanni Scatturin Gino Sopracordevole(cox)	U.S. d.n.a. Leon Butler Edward Jennings (cox)
1928[1]	SWITZ. 7m 42.6s Hans Schochlin Karl Schochlin H. Bourquin (cox)	FRANCE 7m 48.4s Armand Marcelle Edouard Marcelle H. Préaux (cox)	BELGIUM 7m 59.4s L. Flament F. de Coninck M. Degroef (cox)
1932	U.S. 8m 25.8s Charles Kieffer Joseph Schauers Edward Jennings (cox)	POLAND 8m 31.2s Janusz Slazak Jerzy Braun Jerzy Skolimowski (cox)	FRANCE 8m 41.2s Andre Giriat Anselme Brusa Pierre Brunet (cox)
1936	GERMANY 8m 36.9s Herbert Adamski Gerhard Gustmann Dieter Arend (cox)	ITALY 8m 49.7s Guido Santin Almiro Bergamo Luciano Negrini (cox)	FRANCE 8m 54.0s Georges Tapie M. Fourcade Noel Vandernotte (cox)
1948[2]	DENMARK 8m 05.0s Tage Henriksen Finn Pedersen Carl Ebbe Andersen (cox)	ITALY 8m 12.2s Aldo Tarlao Giovanni Steffe Alberto Radi (cox)	HUNGARY 8m 25.2s Bela Zsitnik Antal Szendey Robert Zimonyi (cox)

	GOLD	SILVER	BRONZE
1952	FRANCE 8m 28.6s	GERMANY 8m 32.1s	DENMARK 8m 34.9s
	Raymond Salles	Heinz Manchen	Svend Petersen
	Gaston Mercier	Helmut Heinhold	Paul Svendsen
	Bernard Malivoire (cox)	Helmut Noll (cox)	Jorgen Frandsen (cox)
1956	U.S. 8m 26.1s	GERMANY 8m 29.2s	U.S.S.R. 8m 31.0s
	Arthur Ayrault	Karl von Groddeck	Igor Emchuk
	F. Conn Findlay	Horst Arndt	Georgiy Zhilin
	Kurt Seiffert (cox)	Rainer Borkowsky (cox)	Vladimir Petrov (cox)
1960	GERMANY 7m 29.14s	U.S.S.R. 7m 30.17s	U.S. 7m 34.58s
	Bernhard Knubel	Antonas Bogdanovichus	F. Conn Findlay
	Heinz Renneberg	Zigmas Yukna	Richard Draeger
	Klaus Zerta (cox)	Igor Rudakov (cox)	Kent Mitchell (cox)
1964	U.S. 8m 21.33s	FRANCE 8m 23.15s	NETHS. 8m 23.42s
	E. Ferry	G. Morel	J. Bos
	C. Findlay	J. Morel	H. Rouwe
	K. Mitchell (cox)	J. Darouy (cox)	F. Hartsuiker (cox)
1968	ITALY 8m 04.81s	NETHS. 8m 06.80s	DENMARK 8m 08.07s
	Primo Baran	Herman Suselbeek	Jorn Krab
	Renzo Sambo	Hadriaan van Nes	Harry Jorgensen
	Bruno Cipolla	Roderick Rijnders	Preben Krab
1972			

---

[1] Course of 2,000 metres (1 mile 427 yards).
[2] Course of 1,929 metres (1 mile 350 yards).

COXSWAINLESS FOURS

	GOLD	SILVER	BRONZE
1896	Event not held		
1900	FRANCE I 7m 11.0s	FRANCE II 7m 18.0s	GERMANY 7m 18.2s
	(Roubaix)	(Lyon)	(Fav. Hammonia, Hamburg)
1904[1]	U.S. 9m 53.8s	U.S. d.n.a.	U.S. d.n.a.
	(Century B.C., St. Louis)	(Western R.C.)	(Independent R.C., New Orleans)
	A. M. Stockhoff	Fred Sverig	
	A. C. Erker	Martin Fromanack	
	George Dietz	Charles Aman	
	Albert Nasse	M. Begley	
1908[2]	G.B. 8m 34.0s	G.B. 1½ lengths	d.n.a.
	(Magdalene B.C., Oxford)	(Leander)	
	Robert Cudmore	Philip Filleul	
	James Gillan	Harold Barker	
	Duncan McKinnon	J. R. K. Fenning	
	John Somers-Smith	Gordon Thomson	
1912–1920	Event not held		
1924	G.B. 7m 08.6s	CANADA 1¼ lengths	SWITZ. d.n.a.
	(Trinity B.C., Cambridge)		
	Charles Eley	Archibald Black	Emile Albrecht
	James McNabb	Colin Finlayson	Alfred Probst
	Robert Morrison	George McKay	Eugen Sigg
	Robert Sanders	William Wood	Hans Walter
1928[3]	G.B. 6m 36.0s	U.S. 6m 37.0s	ITALY 6m 37.0s
	(Trinity B.C., Cambridge)		
	Edward Bevan	Charles Karle	Cesare Rossi
	Richard Beesly	William Miller	Pietro Freschi
	M. Humphrey Warriner	George Healis	Umberto Bonade
	John Lander	Ernest Bayer	Paolo Gennari
1932	G.B. 6m 58.2s	GERMANY 7m 03.0s	ITALY 7m 04.0s
	Rowland George	Hans Maier	Antonio Provenzani
	Jack Beresford	Walter Flinsch	Giliante d'Este
	Hugh Edwards	Ernst Gaber	Francesco Cossu
	John Badcock	Karl Aletter	Antonio Ghiardello

	GOLD	SILVER	BRONZE
1936	GERMANY 7m 01.8s	G.B. 7m 06.5s	SWITZ. 7m 10.6s
	Wilhelm Menne	Thomas Bristow	Karl Schmid
	Martin Karl	Alan Barrett	Alex Homberger
	Anton Romm	Peter Jackson	Hans Homberger
	Rudolf Eckstein	John Sturrock	Hermann Betschart
1948[4]	ITALY 7m 15.0s	DENMARK 7m 43.5s	U.S. 7m 47.7s
	Franco Faggi	Storm Larsen	Robert Perew
	Giovanni Invernizzi	Helge Schroeder	Gregory Gates
	Elio Morille	Bonde Hansen	Stuart Griffing
	Giuseppe Moioli	Helge Halkjaer	John Kingsbury
1952	YUGOSLAVIA 7m 16.0s	FRANCE 7m 18.9s	FINLAND 7m 23.3s
	Duje Bonacic	Pierre Blondiaux	Veikko Lommi
	Velimir Valenta	Jacques Guissart	Kauko Wahlsten
	Mate Trojanovic	Marc Bovissou	Oiva Lommi
	Petar Segvic	Roger Gautier	Lauri Nevalainen
1956	CANADA 7m 08.8s	U.S. 7m 18.4s	FRANCE 7m 20.9s
	Archibald McKinnon	John Welchli	Guy Guillabert
	Lorne Loomer	John McKinlay	Gaston Mercier
	I. Walter d'Hondt	Arthur McKinlay	Yves Delacour
	Donald Arnold	James McIntosh	René Guissart
1960	U.S. 6m 26.26s	ITALY 6m 28.78s	U.S.S.R. 6m 29.62s
	Arthur Ayrault	Tullio Baraglia	Igor Akhremchik
	Theodore Nash	Renato Bosatta	Yuriy Bakhurov
	John Sayre	Giancarlo Crosta	Valentin Morkovkin
	Richard Wailes	Giuseppe Galante	Anatoliy Tarabrin
1964	DENMARK 6m 59.30s	U.S. 7m 00.47s	U.S. 7m 01.37s
	John Orsted Hansen	John Russel	Geoffrey Picard
	Bjorn Haslov	Hugh Wardell-Yerburgh	Richard Lyon
	Erik Petersen	William Barry	Theodore Mittet
	Kurt Helmut	John James	Ted Nash
1968	E. GERMANY 6m 39.18s	HUNGARY 6m 41.64s	ITALY 6m 44.01s
	Frank Forberger	Zoltan Melis	Renato Bosatta
	Dieter Grahn	Gyorgy Sarlos	Tullio Baraglia
	Frank Ruhle	Jozsef Csermely	Pier Angelo Conti Manzini
	Dieter Schubert	Antal Melis	Abramo Albini
1972			

[1] Course of 2 miles.
[2] Course of 1½ miles.
[3] Course of 2,000 metres (1 mile 427 yards).
[4] Course of 1,929 metres (1 mile 350 yards).

COXED FOURS

1896	Event not held		
1900	GERMANY 5m 59.0s	NETHS. 6m 33.0s	GERMANY 6m 35.0s
	(Germania, Hamburg)	(Minerva, Amsterdam)	(Ruderverein,
	Oskar Gossler		Ludwigshafen)
	Katzenstein		
	Tietgens		
	G. Gossler		
	C. Gossler (cox)		
1904–1908	Event not held		
1912[1]	GERMANY 6m 58.0s	G.B. 2½ lengths	NORWAY d.n.a.
	(Ludwigshafen)	(Thames R.C.)	(Christiania R.C.)
	Albert Arnheiter	Julius Beresford	Henry Larsen
	Otto Fickeisen	Charles Rought	Matias Torstensen
	Rudolf Fickeisen	Bruce Logan	Theodor Klem
	Herman Wilker	Charles Vernon	Haakon Tonsager
	Karl Leister (cox)	Geoffrey Carr (cox)	Ejnar Tonsager (cox)

	GOLD	SILVER	BRONZE
1920[1]	SWITZ. 6m 54.0s Hans Walther Max Rudolf Willy Bruderlein Paul Rudolf d.n.a.	U.S. 6m 58.0s Kenneth Myers Karl Klose Franz Federschmidt Hans Federschmidt Clark (cox)	NORWAY 7m 01.0s Henry Larsen Per Gulbrandsen Theodor Klem Birgir Var Thoralf Hagen (cox)
1924	SWITZ. 7m 18.4s Hans Walter Alfred Probst Emile Albrecht Eugen Sigg Walter Loosli (cox)	FRANCE 7m 21.6s L. Gressier G. Lacointe R. Talleux E. Barberolle Constant (cox)	U.S. d.n.a. Robert Gerhardt Sidney Jelinek Edward Mitchell Henry Welsford John Kennedy (cox)
1928[1]	ITALY 6m 47.8s Valerio Perentin Giliante d'Este Nicolo Vittori Giovanni Delise Renato Petronio (cox)	SWITZ. 7m 03.4s E. Haas J. Meyer O. Bucher K. Schwegler F. Boesch (cox)	POLAND 7m 12.8s F. Vronikowski E. Janskowski L. Birkholz Ormanowski B. Drewek (cox)
1932	GERMANY 7m 19.0s Joachim Spemberg Walter Meyer Horst Hoeck Hans Eller Karl Neumann (cox)	ITALY 7m 19.2s Bruno Parovel Riccardo Divora Giovanni Plazzer Bruno Vattovaz Giovanni Scherl (cox)	POLAND 7m 26.8s Edward Kobylinski Stanislaw Urban Janusz Slazak Jerzy Braun Jerzy Skolimowski (cox)
1936	GERMANY 7m 16.4s Paul Söllner Ernst Gaber Walter Volle Hans Maier Fritz Bauer (cox)	SWITZ. 7m 24.3s Karl Schmid Hans Homberger Alex Homberger Hermann Betschart R. Spring (cox)	FRANCE 7m 33.3s Fernand Vandernotte Marcel Vandernotte Marcel Cosmat Marcel Chauvigne Noel Vandernotte (cox)
1948[2]	U.S. 6m 50.3s Gordon Giovanelli Robert Will Robert Martin Warren Westlund Allen Morgan (cox)	SWITZ. 6m 53.3s Pierre Stebler E. Schriever Emile Knecht R. Reichling A. Moccard (cox)	DENMARK 6m 58.6s Harry Knudsen Henry Larsen Borge Nielsen Erik Larsen Ib Olsen (cox)
1952	CZECHO. 7m 33.4s Karel Mejta Jiri Havlis Jan Jindra Stanislav Lusk Miroslav Koranda (cox)	SWITZ. 7m 36.5s Enrico Bianchi Karl Weidmann Heinrich Scheller Emile Ess Walter Leiser (cox)	U.S. 7m 37.0s Carl Lovested Alvin Ulbrickson Richard Wahlström Mathew Leanderson Albert Rossi (cox)
1956	ITALY 7m 19.4s Alberto Winkler Romano Sgheiz Angelo Vanzin Franco Trincavelli Ivo Stefanoni (cox)	SWEDEN 7m 22.4s Olof Larsson Gösta Eriksson Ivar Aronsson Sven Gunnarsson Bertil Göransson (cox)	FINLAND 7m 30.9s Kauko Hanninen Reino Poutanen Veikko Lehtelä Toimi Pitkänen Matti Niemi (cox)
1960	GERMANY 6m 39.12s Gerd Cintl Horst Effertz Jürgen Litz Klaus Riekemann Michael Obst (cox)	FRANCE 6m 41.62s Robert Dumontois Claude Martin Jacques Morel Guy Nosbaum Jean Klein (cox)	ITALY 6m 43.12s Fulvio Balatti Romano Sgheiz Franco Trincavelli Giovanni Zucchi Ivo Stefanoni (cox)
1964	GERMANY 7m 00.44s Peter Neusal Bernhard Britting Joachim Werner Egbert Hirschfelder Jürgen Oelke (cox)	ITALY 7m 02.84s Renato Bosatta Emilio Trivini Giuseppe Galante Franco de Pedrina Giovanni Spinola (cox)	NETHS. 7m 06.46s Alex Mullink Jan van der Graaf F. R. van der Graaf Robert van der Graaf M. Klumperbeck (cox)
1968	N. ZEALAND 6m 45.62s Richard Joyce Dudley Storey Warren Cole Ross Collinge Simon Dickie	E. GERMANY 6m 48.20s Peter Kremtz Roland Gohler Klaus Jacob Manfred Gelpke Dieter Semetzky	SWITZ. 6m 49.04s Denis Oswald Hugo Waser Jakob Grob Peter Bolliger Gottlieb Frohlich

GOLD	SILVER	BRONZE

1972

---

[1] Course of 2,000 metres (1 mile 427 yards).
[2] Course of 1,929 metres (1 mile 350 yards).

EIGHTS

GOLD	SILVER	BRONZE
1896 Event not held		
1900 U.S. 6m 09.8s	BELGIUM 6m 13.8s	NETHS. 6m 23.0s
(Vesper B.C., Philadelphia)	(Club Nautique de Ghent)	(Minerva, Amsterdam)
A. C. Lockwood		
Edward Marsh		
Edward Hedley		
William Carr		
J. E. Geiger		
James Juvenal		
Harry Debaecke		
J. N. Exley		
L. G. Abell		
1904[1] U.S. 7m 50.0s	CANADA d.n.a.	—
(Vesper B.C., Philadelphia)	(Argonaut, Toronto)	
Fred Gresser		
M. D. Gleason		
Frank Schell		
J. S. Flanagan		
C. E. Armstrong		
H. H. Lott		
J. F. Demisey		
J. N. Exley		
L. G. Abell		
1908[2] G.B. 7m 56.0s	BELGIUM 2 lengths	G.B. II
(Leander)	(Club Nautique de Ghent)	(Cambridge University B.C.)
Albert Gladstone	Oscar Taelman	F. Jerwood
Frederick Kelly	Marcel Morimont	E. W. Powell
Banner Johnstone	Remi Orban	O. A. Carver
Guy Nickalls	Georges Mys	E. G. Williams
Charles Burnell	Francois Vergucht	H. M. Goldsmith
Ronald Sanderson	Polydore Veirman	H. E. Kitching
Raymond Etherington-Smith	Oscar de Somville	J. S. Burn
Henry Bucknall	Rodolphe Poma	D. C. R. Stuart
Gilchrist Maclagen (cox)	Alfred Vanlandeghem (cox)	R. F. Boyle (cox)
1912[3] G.B. 6m 15.0s	G.B. 6m 19.0s	GERMANY d.n.a.
(Leander Club)	(New College, Oxford)	(Berliner Ruder-Gesellschaft)
Sidney Swann	Sir William Parker	Otto Liebing
Leslie Wormald	William Fison	Max Broeske
Ewart Horsfall	Thomas Gillespie	Max Vetter
James Gillan	Beaufort Burdekin	Wilhelm Bartholoma
Arthur Garton	Frederick Pitman	Fritz Bartholoma
Alister Kirby	Arthur Wiggins	Werner Dehn
Philip Fleming	Charles Littlejohn	Rudolf Reichelt
E. R. Burgess	Robert Bourne	Hans Mathiar
Henry Wells (cox)	John Walker (cox)	Kurt Runge (cox)

Course of 2 miles.
Course of 1½ miles.
Course of 2,000 metres (1 mile 427 yards).

	GOLD	SILVER	BRONZE
1920[2]	U.S. 6m 05.0s	G.B. 6m 05.8s	NORWAY 6m 36.0s
	(Navy)	(Leander Club)	
	Virgil Jacomini	Rev. Sidney Swann	Theodor Nag
	Edwin Graves	Ralph Shove	Conrad Olsen
	William Jordan	Sebastian Earl	Adolf Nilsen
	Edward Moore	John Campbell	Haakon Ellingsen
	Allen Sanborn	Walter James	Thore Michelsen
	Donald Johnston	Richard Lucas	Arne Mortensen
	Vincent Gallacher	Guy Nickalls	Käre Nag
	Clyde King	Ewart Horsfall	Tollef Tollefsen
	Sherman Clark (cox)	Robin Johnstone (cox)	Thoralf Hagen (cox)
1924	U.S. 6m 33.4s	CANADA 6m 49.0s	ITALY d.n.a.
	(Yale) B.C.	(Toronto B.C.)	(Zara R.C.)
	L. G. Carpentier	Arthur Bell	Antonio Cattalinich
	H. T. Kingsbury	Robert Hunter	Francesco Cattalinich
	A. M. Wilson	William Langford	Simeone Cattalinich
	J. D. Lindley	Boyd Little	Giuseppe Crivelli
	J. L. Miller	Jack Smith	Latino Galasso
	J. S. Rockefeller	Warren Snyder	Pietro Ivanov
	F. Sheffield	Norman Taylor	Bruno Sorich
	B. M. Spock	William Wallace	Carlo Toniatti
	L. R. Stoddard (cox)	Ivor Campbell (cox)	Vittorio Gliubich (cox)
1928[3]	U.S. 6m 03.2s	G.B. 6m 05.6s	CANADA 6m 03.8s[4]
	(Univ. of California)	(Thames R.C.)	
	Marvin Stalder	Harold West	Frederick Hodges
	John Brinck	Jack Beresford	Frank Fiddes
	Francis Frederick	Gordon Killick	Jack Hand
	Walter Thompson	Harold Lane	Herbert Richardson
	William Dally	Donald Gollan	Jack Murdock
	James Workman	John Badcock	Athol Meech
	Hubert Caldwell	Guy Nickalls	Edgar Norns
	Peter Donlon	James Hamilton	William Ross
	Donald Blessing (cox)	Arthur Sulley (cox)	Jack Donelly
1932	U.S. 6m 37.6s	ITALY 6m 37.8s	CANADA 6m 40.4s
	(Univ. of California)		
	Winslow Hall	Renato Barbieri	Albert Taylor
	Harold Tower	Enrico Garzelli	Donald Boal
	Charles Chandler	Guglielmo del Bimbo	William Thoburn
	Burton Jastram	Roberto Vestrini	Cedric Liddell
	David Dunlap	Dino Barsotti	Harry Fry
	Duncan Gregg	Renato Bracci	Stanley Stanyar
	James Blair	Mario Balleri	Joseph Harris
	Edwin Salisbury	Vittorio Cioni	Earl Eastwood
	Norris Graham (cox)	Cesare Milani (cox)	Geo. MacDonald (cox)
1936	U.S. 6m 25.8s	ITALY 6m 26.0s	GERMANY 6m 26.4s
	(Washington Univ.)		
	Donald Hume	Guglielmo del Bimbo	Herbert Schmidt
	Joseph Rantz	Dino Barsotti	Hans Hannemann
	George Hunt	Oreste Grossi	Werner Loeckle
	James McMillin	Enzo Bartolini	Gerd Völs
	John White	Mario Checcacci	Heinz Kaufmann
	Gordon Adam	Dante Secchi	Hans Kuschke
	Charles Day	Ottorino Quaglierini	Helmut Radach
	Herbert Morris	Enrico Garzelli	Alfred Rieck
	Robert Moch (cox)	Cezare Milani (cox)	Wilhelm Mahlow (cox)
1948[5]	U.S. 5m 56.7s	G.B. 6m 06.9s	NORWAY 6m 10.3s
	(Univ. of California)		
	John Stack	Andrew Mellows	Carl Monssen
	Justus Smith	David Meyrick	Thor Pedersen
	David Brown	Brian Lloyd	Leif Naess
	Lloyd Butler	Paul Massey	Harald Krakenes
	George Ahlgreen	E. A. Paul Bircher	Halfdan Gran-Olsen
	James Hardy	Guy Richardson	Hans Hansen
	David Turner	Maurice Lapage	Thorstein Krakenes
	Ian Turner	Christopher Barton	Kristoffer Lepsoe
	Ralph Purchase (cox)	Jack Dearlove (cox)	Sigurd Monssen (cox)

---

[2] Course of 1½ miles.
[3] Course of 2,000 metres (1 mile 427 yards).

In Stockholm in 1912 the Swedish eight (shown here) despite the advantage of home water, failed to beat Leander (G.B.), New College, Oxford (G.B.) and the Berliner Ruder-Gesellschaft (Germany) eights.

	GOLD	SILVER	BRONZE
1952	U.S. 6m 25.9s (Navy)	U.S.S.R. 6m 31.2s	AUSTRALIA 6m 33.1s
	Frank Shakespeare	Yevgeniy Brago	Robert Tinning
	William Fields	Vladimir Rodimushkin	Ernest Chapman
	James Dunbar	Aleksey Komarov	Nimrod Greenwood
	Richard Murphy	Igor Borisov	Mervyn Finlay
	Robert Detweiler	Slava Amiragov	Edward Pain
	Henry Proctor	Leonid Gissen	Phillip Cayzer
	Wayne Frye	Yevgeniy Samsonov	Thomas Chessel
	Edward Stevens	Vladimir Kryukov	David Anderson
	Charles Manring (cox)	Igor Polyakov (cox)	Geoffrey Williamson (cox)
1956	U.S. 6m 35.2s (Yale Univ.)	CANADA 6m 37.1s	AUSTRALIA 6m 39.2s
	Thomas Charlton	Philip Kueber	Michael Aikman
	David Wight	Richard McClure	David Boykett
	John Cooke	Robert Wilson	Angus Benfield
	Donald Beer	David Helliwell	James Howden
	Caldwell Esselstyn	Donald Pretty	Garth Manton
	Charles Grimes	William McKerlich	Walter Howell
	Richard Wailes	Douglas McDonald	Adrian Monger
	Robert Morey	Lawrence West	Brian Doyle
	William Becklean (cox)	Carlton Ogawa (cox)	Harold Hewitt (cox)
60	GERMANY 5m 57.18s	CANADA 6m 01.52s	CZECHO. 6m 04.84s
	Klaus Bittner	Donald Arnold	Josef Ventus
	Karl-Heinz Hopp	I. Walter d'Hondt	Bohumil Janousek
	Hans Lenk	Nelson Kuhn	Jan Jindra
	Manfred Rulffs	John Lecky	Jiri Lundak
	Frank Schepke	Lorne Loomer	Stanislav Lusk
	Kraft Schepke	Archibald McKinnon	Vaclav Pavkovic
	Walter Schröder	William McKerlich	Ludek Pojezny
	Karl von Groddeck	Glen Mervyn	Jan Sveda
	Willi Padge (cox)	Sohen Biln (cox)	Miroslav Konicek (cox)

Third place decided in separate race.
Course of 1,929 metres (1 mile 350 yards).

GOLD	SILVER	BRONZE
1964 U.S. 6m 18.23s	GERMANY 6m 23.29s	CZECHO. 6m 25.11s
Joseph Amlong	Klaus Aeffko	Petr Carmak
Thomas Amlong	Klaus Bittner	Jiri Lundak
Harold Budd	Karl von Groddock	Jan Mrvik
Emory Clark	Hans-Jürgen Wallbrecht	Julnis Tocek
Stanley Cwikluiski	Klaus Behrens	Josef Ventus
Hugh Foley	Jürgen Schroeder	Ludek Pojezny
William Knecht	Jürgen Plagemann	Richard Novy
William Stowe	Horst Meyer	Bohumil Janousek
Robert Zimonvi (cox)	Thomas Ahrens (cox)	Miroslav Konicek (cox)
1968 W. GERMANY	AUSTRALIA	U.S.S.R. 6m 09.11s
6m 07.00s	6m 07.98s	
Horst Meyer	Alfred Duval	Zugmas Jukna
Dirk Schreyer	Michael Morgan	Antanas Bagdonavichus
Ruediger Henning	Joseph Fazio	Vladimir Sterlik
Lutz Ulbricht	Peter Dickson	Iozapas Yagelavichus
Wolfgang Hottenrott	David Douglas	Alexander Matryshkin
Egbert Hirschfelder	John Ranch	Vitautas Briedis
Joerg Siebert	Gary Pearce	Valentin Kravchuk
Roland Bose	Robert Shirlaw	Victor Suslin
Gunther Thiersch	Alan Grover	Yury Lorentsson
1972		

14. Shooting

* indicates present Olympic record.

FREE PISTOL[1]

GOLD	SILVER	BRONZE
1896 Sommer Paine (U.S.) 442 pts.	Vigo Jensen (DENMARK)	Holger Nielsen (DENMARK)
1900 Karl Röderer (SWITZ.) 503 pts.	Konrad Staeheli (SWITZ.) 453 pts.	Louis Richardet (SWITZ.) 448 pts.
1904–1908 Event not held		
1912 Alfred Lane (U.S.) 499 pts.	P. J. Dolfen (U.S.) 474 pts.	G. E. Stewart (G.B.) 470 pts.
1920 Carl Frederick (U.S.) 496 pts.	Afranio da Costa (BRAZIL) 489 pts.	Alfred Lane (U.S.) 481 pts.
1924–1932 Event not held		
1936 Thorsten Ullmann (SWEDEN) 559 pts.	Erich Krempel (GERMANY) 544 pts.	Charles des Jammonière (FRANCE) 540 pts.
1948 Edwin Vazquez (PERU) 545 pts.	Rudolf Schnyder (SWITZ.) 539 pts.	Thorsten Ullmann (SWEDEN) 539 pts.
1952 Huelet Benner (U.S.) 553 pts.	Angel Leon (SPAIN) 550 pts.	Ambrus Balogh (HUNGARY) 549 pts
1956 Pentti Linnosvuo (FINLAND) 556 pts.	Makhmoud Oumarov (U.S.S.R.) 556 pts.	Offutt Pinion (U.S.) 551 pts.
1960 Aleksey Gushchin (U.S.S.R.) 560 pts.	Makhmoud Oumarov (U.S.S.R.) 552 pts.	Yoshihisa Yoshikawa (JAPAN) 552 pts.
1964 Vaino Markkanen (FINLAND) 560 pts.	Franklin Green (U.S.) 557 pts.	Yoshihisa Yoshikawa (JAPAN) 554 pts.
1968 Grigory Kosykh (U.S.S.R.) 562 pts.*	Heinz Mertel (GERMANY) 562 pts.*	Harald Vollmar (E. GERMANY) 560 pts.
1972		

---

[1] Range 50 metres.

RAPID-FIRE PISTOL[1]

	GOLD	SILVER	BRONZE
1896–1920	Event not held		
1924	H. N. Bailey (U.S.) 18 pts.	Vilhelm Carlberg (SWEDEN) 18 pts.	Lennart Hannelius (FINLAND) 18 pts.
1928	Event not held		
1932	Renzo Morigi (ITALY) 42 pts.	Heinrich Hax (GERMANY) 40 pts.	Domenico Matteucci (ITALY) 39 pts.
1936	Cornelius van Oyen (GERMANY) 36 pts.	Heinrich Hax (GERMANY) 35 pts.	Thorsten Ullmann (SWEDEN) 34 pts.
1948	Károly Takács (HUNGARY) 580 pts.	Enrique Diaz Saenz Valiente (ARGENTINA) 571 pts.	S. Lundquist (SWEDEN) 569 pts.
1952	Károly Takács (HUNGARY) 579 pts.	Szilard Kun (HUNGARY) 578 pts.	Gheorghe Lichiardopol (RUMANIA) 578 pts.
1956	Stefan Petrescu (RUMANIA) 587 pts.	Evgeniy Shcherkasov (U.S.S.R.) 585 pts.	Gheorghe Lichiardopol (RUMANIA) 581 pts.
1960	William McMillan (U.S.) 587 pts.	Pentti Linnosvuo (FINLAND) 587 pts.	Aleksandr Zabelin (U.S.S.R.) 587 pts.
1964	Pentti Linnosvuop (FINLAND) 592 pts.	Ion Tripsa (RUMANIA) 591 pts.	Lubomi Nacovsky (CZECHO.) 590 pts.
1968	Jozef Zapedzki (POLAND) 593 pts.*	Marcel Rosca (RUMANIA) 591 pts.	Renart Suleimanov (U.S.S.R.) 591 pts.
1972			

[1] Range 25 metres.

FREE RIFLE[1]

	GOLD	SILVER	BRONZE
1896–1904	Event not held		
1908	Albert Helgerud (NORWAY) 909 pts.	A. H. Simon (U.S.) 887 pts.	Ole Saether (NORWAY) 883 pts.
1912	Paul Colas (FRANCE) 987 pts.	Lars Jörgen Madsen (DENMARK) 981 pts.	Niels Larsen (DENMARK) 962 pts.
1920	Morris Fisher (U.S.) 997 pts.	Niels Larsen (DENMARK) 985 pts.	Osten Ostensen (NORWAY) 980 pts.
1924[2]	Morris Fisher (U.S.) 95 pts.	Carl Osburn (U.S.) 95 pts.	Niels Larsen (DENMARK) 93 pts.
1928–1936	Event not held		
1948	Emil Grünig (SWITZ.) 1,120 pts.	Pauli Janhonen (FINLAND) 1,114 pts.	Willy Rögeberg (NORWAY) 1,112 pts.
1952	Anatoliy Bogdanov (U.S.S.R.) 1,123 pts.	Robert Bürchler (SWITZ.) 1,120 pts.	Lev Vainshtein (U.S.S.R.) 1,109 pts.
1956	Vasiliy Borisov (U.S.S.R.) 1,138 pts.	Allan Erdman (U.S.S.R.) 1,137 pts.	Vilho Ylönen (FINLAND) 1,128 pts.
1960	Hubert Hammerer (AUSTRIA) 1,129 pts.	Hansrüdi Spillmann (SWITZ.) 1,127 pts.	Vasiliy Borisov (U.S.S.R.) 1,127 pts.
1964	Gary Anderson (U.S.) 1,153 pts.	Shota Kveliashvili (U.S.S.R.) 1,144 pts.	Martin Gunnarson (U.S.) 1,136 pts.
1968	Gary Anderson (U.S.) 1,157 pts.*	Valentin Kornev (U.S.S.R.) 1,151 pts.	Kurt Muller (SWITZ.) 1,148 pts.
1972			

Range 300 metres.
Range 400–800 metres.

Lones Wigger (U.S.) receiving his gold medal in small-bore rifle shooting at Tokyo in 1964.

SMALL-BORE RIFLES—PRONE[1]

	GOLD	SILVER	BRONZE
1896–1904	Event not held		
1908[2]	A. A. Carnell (G.B.) 387 pts.	H. R. Humby (G.B.) 386 pts.	G. Barnes (G.B.) 385 pts.
1912	Frederick Hird (U.S.) 194 pts.	W. Milne (G.B.) 193 pts.	H. Burt (G.B.) 192 pts.
1920	Lawrence Nuesslein (U.S.) 391 pts.	Arthur Rothrock (U.S.) 386 pts.	Dennis Fenton (U.S.) 385 pts.
1924	Charles Coquelin de Lisle (FRANCE) 398 pts.	M. W. Dinwiddie (U.S.) 396 pts.	Josias Hartmann (SWITZ.) 394 pts.
1928	Event not held		
1932	Bartil Rönmark (SWEDEN) 294 pts.	Gustavo Huest (MEXICO) 294 pts.	Zoltan Hradetsky-Soos (HUNGARY) 293 pts
1936	Willy Rögeberg (NORWAY) 300 pts.	Ralph Berzsenyi (HUNGARY) 296 pts.	Wladyslaw Karas (POLAND) 296 pts.
1948	Arthur Cook (U.S.) 599 pts.	Walter Tomsen (U.S.) 599 pts.	Jonas Jonsson (SWEDEN) 597 pts.
1952	Iosif Sarbu (RUMANIA) 400 pts.	Boris Andreyev (U.S.S.R.) 400 pts.	Arthur Jackson (U.S.) 399 pts.
1956	Gerald Quellette (CANADA) 600 pts.	Vasiliy Borisov (U.S.S.R.) 599 pts.	Gilmour Boa (CANADA) 598 pts.
1960	Peter Kohnke (GERMANY) 590 pts.	James Hill (U.S.) 589 pts.	Enrico Forcella (VENEZUELA) 587 p
1964	Laszlo Hammerl (HUNGARY) 597 pts.	Lones Wigger (U.S.) 597 pts.	Tommy Pool (U.S.) 596 pts.
1968	Jan Kurka (CZECHO.) 598 pts.*	Laszlo Hammerl (HUNGARY) 598 pts.*	Ian Ballinger (N. ZEALAND)
1972			597 pts.

[1] Range 50 metres.
[2] Range 50 and 100 yards, 40 shots.

SMALL-BORE RIFLE—THREE POSITIONS[1]

	GOLD	SILVER	BRONZE
1896–1948	Event not held		
1952	Erling Kongshaug (NORWAY) 1,164 pts.	Vilho Ylönen (FINLAND) 1,164 pts.	Boris Andreyev (U.S.S.R.) 1,163 pts.
1956	Anatoliy Bogdanov (U.S.S.R.) 1,172 pts.*	Otto Horinek (CZECHO.) 1,172 pts.	Nils Sundberg (SWEDEN) 1,167 pts.
1960	Viktor Shamburkin (U.S.S.R.) 1,149 pts.	Marat Nyesov (U.S.S.R.) 1,145 pts.	Klaus Zaehriger (GERMANY) 1,139 pts.
1964	Lones Wigger (U.S.) 1,164 pts.	Velitchko Hustov (BULGARIA) 1,152 pts.	Laszlo Hammerl (HUNGARY) 1,151 pts.
1968	Bernd Klingner (GERMANY) 1,157 pts.	John Writer (U.S.) 1,156 pts.	Vitaly Parkhimovich (U.S.S.R.) 1,154 pts.
1972			

[1] Range 50 metres, standing, kneeling, prone.

CLAY PIGEON[4] (OLYMPIC TRENCH)

	GOLD	SILVER	BRONZE
1896	Event not held		
1900	W. H. Ewing (CANADA) d.n.a.	R. de Barbarin (FRANCE)	Guyot (FRANCE)
1904	Event not held		
1908[5]	W. H. Ewing (CANADA) 72 pts.	G. Beattie (CANADA) 60 pts.	Alexander Maunder (G.B.) 57 pts. Anastassios Metaxas (GREECE) 57 pts.
1912	James Graham (U.S.) 96 pts.	Alfred Goeldel (GERMANY) 94 pts.	Harry Blau (RUSSIA) 91 pts.
1920	Mark Arie (U.S.) 95 pts.	Frank Troeh (U.S.) 93 pts.	Frank Wright (U.S.) 87 pts.
1924	Gyula Halasy (HUNGARY) 98 pts.	Konrad Hubert (FINLAND) 98 pts.	Frank Hughes (U.S.) 97 pts.
1928–1948	Event not held		
1952	George Généreux (CANADA) 192 pts.	Knut Holmqvist (SWEDEN) 191 pts.	Hans Liljedahl (SWEDEN) 190 pts.
1956	Galliano Rossini (ITALY) 195 pts.	Adam Smelczynski (POLAND) 190 pts.	Alessandro Ciceri (ITALY) 188 pts.
1960	Ion Dumitrescu (RUMANIA) 192 pts.	Galliano Rossini (ITALY) 191 pts.	Sergey Kalinin (U.S.S.R.) 190 pts.
1964	Ennio Mattarelli (ITALY) 198 pts.*	Pavel Senichev (U.S.S.R.) 194 pts.	William Morris (U.S.) 194 pts.
1968	John Braithwaite (G.B.) 198 pts.*	Thomas Garrigus (U.S.) 196 pts.	Kurt Czekalla (E. GERMANY) 196 pts.
1972			

200 pigeons.
80 pigeons.

SKEET

	GOLD	SILVER	BRONZE
1896–1964	Event not held		
1968	Evgeny Petrov (U.S.S.R.) 198 pts.*	Romano Garagnani (ITALY) 198 pts.*	Konrad Wirnhier (W. GERMANY) 198 pts.*
1972			

15. Soccer

GOLD	SILVER	BRONZE
1896–1904 Event not held[1]		
1908 G.B.[2]	DENMARK	NETHS.
Harold Bailey	Ludwig Drescher	Reinier Breuwkes
William Corbett	Charles Buchwald	Karel Heijting
Herbert Smith	Harald Hansen	Lou Otten
Kenneth Hunt	Harald Bohr	Johan Sol
Frederick Chapman	Christian Middelboe	J. M. de Korver
Robert Hawkes	Nils Middelboe	Emil Mundt
Arthur Berry	Oscar Nielsen	J. H. Welcker
Vivian Woodward	August Lindgreen	Edu Snethlage
Hubert Stapley	Sophus Nielsen	G. S. Reeman
Claude Purnell	Vilhelm Wolfhagen	Johannes Thomee
Harold Hardman	Björn Rasmussen	G. F. de Bruijnkops
	Marius Andersen	
	Johannes Gandil	
1912 G.B.[3]	DENMARK	NETHS.
Ronald Brebner	Sophus Hansen	M. J. Göbel
Thomas Burn	Nils Middelboe	D. Wijnfeldt
Arthur Knight	Harald Hansen	P. Bouman
Douglas McWhirter	Charles Buchwald	G. Fortgens
Horace Littlewort	Emil Jörgensen	C. W. Feith
James Dines	Paul Berth	N. de Wolff
Arthur Berry	Oscar Nielsen	D. N. Lotsy
Vivian Woodward	Axel Thufvason	J. W. Boutmy
Harold Walden	Anton Olsen	J. G. van Bredakolff
Gordon Hoare	Sophus Nielsen	H. F. de Groot
Ivan Sharpe	Vilhelm Wolfhagen	C. H. ten Cate
E. Hanney	A. M. Petersen	J. van der Sluis
H. Stamper	Christoffersen	J. Vos
E. G. D. Wright	Poul Nielsen	N. J. Bouvy
		J. M. de Korver
1920 BELGIUM[4]	SPAIN	NETHS.
Jan de Bie	Ricardo Zamora	R. McNeill
Armand Swartenbroeks	Pedro Valana	H. L. B. Denis
Oscar Verbeek	Mariano Arrate	L. F. G. Bosschart
Joseph Musch	Juan Antola	F. C. Kuipers
Emile Hanse	Agustin Sancho	H. H. Steeman
André Fierens	Ramón Equiazabal	J. D. de Natris
Louis van Hege	Francisco	J. E. Bulder
Robert Coppée	Pagazaurtundua	B. Groosjohan
Mathieu Bragard	Felix Sesumaga	J. van Dort
Henri Larnoe	José Belausteguigoitia	C. van Rappard
Désiré Bastin	Patricio Arbolaza	H. C. von Heyden
Fernand Nizot	Rafael Moreno	
Georges Hebdin	Domingo Acedo	
Félix Balyu	José Samitier	
1924 URUGUAY[5]	SWITZ.	SWEDEN
Mazzali	Hans Pulver	Sigge Lindberg
José Nasazzi	Adolphe Raymond	Axel Alfredsson
Arispe	Rudolf Ramseyer	Fritjof Hillen
José Andrade	August Oberhauser	Sven Friberg
Vidal	Paul Schmiedlin	Gustaf Carlsson
Ghierra	Aron Pollitz	Harry Sundberg
A. Urdinarán	Karl Ehrenbolger	Charles Bromesson
Hector Scarone	Robert Pache	Sven Rydell
Pedro Petrone	Walter Dietrich	Per Kaufeldt
Pedro Céa	Max Abbeglen	Albin Dahl
Romano	Paul Fässler	Rudolf Kock
Tomasina	Paul Sturzenegger	
Naya	Evert Lundquist	
Zibechi	Sten Mellgren	
S. Urdinarán	Gunnar Holmberg	
	Tore Keller	
	Edmond Kramer	

[1] There were unofficial competitions as follows: 1900, G.B. bt FRANCE 4–
1904, CANADA (Galt) bt U.S. (St. Rose of St. Louis) 4–0.

GOLD	SILVER	BRONZE
1928 URUGUAY[6]	**ARGENTINA**	**ITALY**
Mazzali	Angel Bossio	Giampiero Combi
José Nasazzi	Fernando Paternoster	Delfo Bellini
Arispe	Bidoglio	Umberto Caligaris
José Andrade	Juan Evaristo	Alfredo Pitto
Lorenzo Fernández	Luigi Monti	Fulvio Bernardini
Alvaro Gestido	Medici	Pietro Genovesi
S. Urdinarán	Raimundo Orsi	Adolfo Baloncieri
Castro	Gainzarain	Elvio Banchero
Pedro Petrone	Manuel Ferreira	Angelo Schiavo
Pedro Céa	Tarasconi	Mario Magnozzi
Hector Scarone	Carricaberri	Virgilio Levratto
Campolo	Perduca	Giovanni de Pra
Aremón	Calandra	Antonio Janni
Borjas	Cherro	Silvio Pietroboni
Piriz	Orlandini	Enrico Rivolta
Canavesi	Diaz	Virginio Rosetta
Figueroa		Gino Rossetti
1932 Event not held		
1936 ITALY[7]	**AUSTRIA**	**NORWAY**
Bruno Venturini	Eduard Kainberger	Henry Johansen
Alfredo Foni	Ernst Künz	Nils Eriksen
Pietro Rava	Martin Kargl	Olvind Holmsen
Giuseppe Baldo	Anton Krenn	Fritjof Ulleberg
Achille Piccini	Karl Wahlmüller	Jörgen Juve
Ugo Locatelli	Max Hofmeister	Rolf Holberg
Annibale Frossi	Walter Werginz	Magdalon Monsen
Libero Marchini	Adolf Laudon	Reidar Kvammen
Sergio Bertoni	Klement Steinmetz	Alf Martinsen
Carlo Biagi	Karl Kainberger	Odd Frantzen
Francesco Gabriotti	Franz Fuchsberger	Arne Brustad
Luigi Scarabello	Josef Kitzmüller	
Giulio Cappelli	Franz Mandl	
Alfonso Negro		
1948 SWEDEN[8]	**YUGOSLAVIA**	**DENMARK**
Torsten Lindberg	Ljubomir Lovric	Ejgil Nielsen
Knut Nordahl	Meho Brozovic	Viggo Jensen
Erik Nilsson	Branko Stankovic	Knud Overgaard
Birger Rosengren	Zlatko Cajkovski	Axel Pülmark
Bertil Nordahl	Miodrag Jovanovic	Dion Ornvold
Sune Andersson	Aleksandar Atanakovic	Ivan Jensen
Kjell Rosén	Zvonko Cimermancic	Johannes Plöger
Gunnar Grén	Rajko Mitic	Knud Lundberg
Gunnar Nordahl	Stejpan Bobek	Carl Praest
Henry Carlsson	Zeljko Cajkovski	Jörgen Hansen
Nils Liedholm	Bernard Vukas	Jörn Sörensen
Börje Leander	Franjo Sostaric	Holger Seebach
Garvis Carlsson	Prvoslav Mihajlovic	Karl Aage Hansen
Rune Emanuelsson	Franjo Völfl	
Stellan Nilsson		
Stig Nyström		
Karl Svensson		

---

[2] Semi-finals: DENMARK bt FRANCE 17–1; G.B. bt NETHS. 4–0. Final: G.B. bt DENMARK 2–0. Third place: NETHS. bt SWEDEN 2–0.

[3] Semi-finals: G.B. bt FINLAND 4–0; DENMARK bt NETHS. 4–1; Final: G.B. bt DENMARK 4–2. Third place: NETHS. bt FINLAND 9–0.

[4] Semi-finals: BELGIUM bt NETHS. 3–0; CZECHOSLOVAKIA bt FRANCE 4–1. Final abandoned in BELGIUM'S favor when they were leading 2–0. CZECHO. player was sent off and rest of team left field in protest.

[5] Semi-finals: SWITZERLAND bt SWEDEN 2–1; URUGUAY bt NETHS. 2–1. Final: URUGUAY bt SWITZ. 3–0. Third place: SWEDEN bt NETHS. 3–1, after 1–1 draw.

[6] Semi-finals: URUGUAY bt ITALY 3–2: ARGENTINA bt EGYPT 6–0. Final: URUGUAY bt ARGENTINA 2–1, after 1–1 draw.

[7] Semi-finals: AUSTRIA bt POLAND 3–1; ITALY bt NORWAY 2–1. Final: ITALY bt AUSTRIA 2–1. Third place: NORWAY bt POLAND 3–2.

Italy vs. U.S. in soccer at Helsinki, 1952. Hungary won more soccer titles than any other nation—3 out of 12 Olympics.

	GOLD	SILVER	BRONZE
1952	HUNGARY[9]	YUGOSLAVIA	SWEDEN
	Gyula Grosics	Vladimir Beara	Karl Svensson
	Jenö Buzánszky	Branko Stankovic	Lennart Samuelsson
	Gyula Lóránt	Tomislav Crnkovic	Erik Nilsson
	Mihály Lantos	Zlatko Cajkovski	Olle Ahlund
	József Bozsik	Ivan Horvat	Bengt Gustavsson
	Nándor Hidegkuti	Vujadin Boskov	Gösta Lindh
	Sándor Kocsis	Tihomir Ognjanov	Sylve Bengtsson
	Pétér Palotás	Rajko Mitic	Gösta Löfgren
	Ferenc Puskás	Bernard Vukas	Ingvar Rydell
	Zoltán Csibor	Stjepan Bobek	Yngve Brodd
	Sándor Gellér	Branko Zebec	Gösta Sandberg
	János Börzsei		Holger Hansson
	Jenö Dalnoki		
	Imre Kovács		
	Ferenc Szojka		
	László Budai		
	Lajos Csordás		
1956	U.S.S.R.[10]	YUGOSLAVIA	BULGARIA
	Lev Yashin	Petar Radenkovic	Georgi Naydenov
	Boris Kuznyetsov	Mladen Koscak	Kiril Rakarov
	Mikhail Ogognikov	Nikola Radovic	Georgi Nikolov
	Aleksey Paramanov	Ivan Santek	Stefan Stefanov
	Anatoliy Bashashkin	Ljubisa Spajic	Manol Manolov
	Igor Netto	Dobrosav Krstic	Nikola Kovatchev
	Boris Tatushin	Dragoslav Sekularac	Dimitar Stoyanov
	Anatoliy Isayev	Zlatko Papec	Miltcho Nikolov
	Edouard Streltsov	Sava Antic	Panayot Panayotov
	Sergey Salnikov	Todor Veselinovic	Ivan Kolev
	Anatoliy Ilin	Muhamed Mujic	Kroum Yanev
	Anatoliy Maslenkin	Blagoje Vidinic	Yordan Yordanov
	Nikita Simonian	Ibrahim Biogradlic	Thodor Diev
	Nikolay Tyshenko	Luka Liposinovic	
	Vladimir Rykkin		
	Iosif Betsa		

---

[8] Semi-finals: SWEDEN bt DENMARK 4–2; YUGOSLAVIA bt G.B. 3–1. Final: SWEDEN bt YUGOSLAVIA 3–1. Third place: DENMARK bt G.B. 5–3.

[9] Semi-finals: HUNGARY bt SWEDEN 6–0; YUGOSLAVIA bt GERMANY 3–1. Final: HUNGARY bt YUGOSLAVIA 2–0. Third place: SWEDEN bt GERMANY 2–0.

[10] Semi-finals: U.S.S.R. bt. BULGARIA 2–1; YUGOSLAVIA bt. INDIA 4–1 Final: U.S.S.R. bt. YUGOSLAVIA 1–0. Third place: BULGARIA bt INDIA 3–0.

	GOLD	SILVER	BRONZE
1960	YUGOSLAVIA[11]	DENMARK	HUNGARY
	Blagoje Vidinic	Paul Andersen	Gabor Török
	Vladimir Djurkovic	Paul Jensen	Zoltán Dudas
	Fahrudin Jusufi	Bent Hansen	Jenö Dalnoki
	Ante Zanetic	Hans Nielsen	Ernö Sölymösi
	Novak Roganovic	Flemming Nielsen	Pal Varmidi
	Zelijko Perusic	Paul Pedersen	Ferenc Kovács
	Andreja Ankovic	Tommy Troelsan	Imre Satori
	Zelijko Maius	Harald Nielsen	János Göröcs
	Milan Galic	Henning Enoksen	Florian Albert
	Tomislav Knez	Jörn Sörensen	Pal Orosz
	Borivoje Kostic	Henry Fröm	János Dunai
	Velimir Sombolac	John Danielsen	Dezsö Novak
	Alexsandar Kozlina	Jörgen Hansen	Oszkar Vilezsal
	Dusan Maravic		Gyula Rakosi
	Silvester Takac		Lajos Farago
	Milutin Soskic[12]		
1964	HUNGARY[13]	CZECHO.	GERMANY
	Antal Szentmihalyi	Anton Urban	Hans Heinsch
	Dezso Novak	Karel Picman	Peter Rock
	Kalman Ihasz	Josef Vojta	Manfred Geisler
	Arpad Orban	Vladimir Weiss	Herbert Pankau
	Ferenc Nogradi	Jan Geleta	Manfred Watter
	Janos Farkas	Jan Bramovsky	Gerhard Koerner
	Tibor Csernai	Ivan Miaz	Hermann Stoeker
	Ferenc Bene	Karel Lichtnegl	Otto Fraessdorf
	Imre Komora	Vojtech Masny	Henning Frenzel
	Gustav Szepesi	Frantisek Valosek	Jurgen Noeldner
	Sandor Katona	Anton Svajlen[12]	Eberhard Vogel
	Jozsef Gelei[12]	Karel Knesl[12]	Horst Weigang[12]
	Karoly Palotai[12]	Stefan Matlak[12]	Klaus Urbanczyk[12]
	Zoltan Varga[12]	Karel Nepomucky[12]	Klaus-Dieter Seehaus[12]
		Ludevit Cvetter[12]	Werner Unger[12]
		Frantisek Knebat[12]	Dieter Engelhardt[12]
			Wolfgang Bartels[12]
			Bernd Bauchspiess[12]
			Klaus Liesiewicz[12]
1968	HUNGARY[14]	BULGARIA	JAPAN
	Karoly Fater	Stoyan Yordanov	Kenzo Yokoyama
	Dezso Novak	Atanasse Guerov	Hiroshi Katayama
	Lajos Drestyak Dunai	Gueorgui Christakiev	Yoshitada Yamaguchi
	Miklos Pancsics	Milko Gaidarski	Mitsuo Kamata
	Ivan Menczel	Kiril Ivkov	Takaji Mori
	Lajos Sjucs	Ivailo Gueorguiev	Aritatsu Ogi
	Laszlo Fazekas	Tzvetan Dimitrov	Teruki Miyamoto
	Antal Dunai	Evgueni Yantchovski	Masashi Watanabe
	Laszlo Nagy	Petar Jekov	Kunishige Kamamoto
	Erno Nosko	Atanasse Christov	Ikuo Matsumoto
	Istvan Juhasz	Asparoukh Donev	Ryuichi Sugiyama
	Zoltan Varga	Gueorgui Vassilev	Masakatsu Miyamoto
	Lajos Kocsis	Atanasse Christov	Ryozo Suzuki
	Laszlo Keglovich	Mikhail Guionine	Kiyoshi Tomizawa
	Bertalan Bicskei	Yantcho Dimitrov	Eizo Yuguchi
	Miklos Szalai	Gueorgui Ivanov	Shigeo Yaegashi
	Gabor Sarközi	Ivan Zafirov	Yasuyuki Kuwahara
	Istvan Basti	Mitiu Monev	Masahiro Hamazaki
	Zoltan Szarka	Todor Nikolov	Shunichiro Okano

[11] Semi-finals: YUGOSLAVIA drew with ITALY 1–1, after extra-time, and qualified for final by winning toss of coin; DENMARK bt. HUNGARY 2–0. Final:YUGOSLAVIA bt DENMARK 3–1. Third place: HUNGARY bt ITALY 2–1.

[12] Lists of team-members include, where known, names of all who played in preliminaries as well as finals.

[3] Semi-finals: CZECHO. beat GERMANY 2–1; HUNGARY beat U.A.R. 6–0. Final: HUNGARY beat CZECHO. 2–1. Third place: GERMANY beat U.A.R. 3–1.

[4] Semi-finals: HUNGARY beat JAPAN 5–0; BULGARIA beat MEXICO 3–2. Final: HUNGARY beat BULGARIA 4–1. Third place: JAPAN beat MEXICO 2–0.

Two of the greatest swimmers of Olympic fame: Johnny Weismuller (left) and Duke Kahanamoku, both of the U.S., at the Paris Olympics in 1924. In the 100 metre freestyle in 1912, the Duke became the first Hawaiian gold medal winner and set an Olympic record of 1m 02.4s which he could not break in 1920 when he again won the event. In 1924, Weismuller beat the Duke, set a new record of 59.0s, and also won the 400 metre contest. Again in 1928 he took the gold medal in the 100 metres—for a total of 5 gold medals, more than anyone else in swimming. Later Weismuller attained even greater renown as a Tarzan of the movies.

16a. Swimming and Diving (Men)

* indicates Olympic record

100 METRES FREE-STYLE (109 yds. 1 ft.)

	GOLD	SILVER	BRONZE
1896	Alfred Hajós[1] (HUNGARY) 1m 22.2s*	Gardrez Williams[2] (U.S.) 1m 23.0s	Otto Herschmann (AUSTRIA) d.n.a.
1900	Event not held		
1904[3]	Zoltán Halmay (HUNGARY) 1m 02.8s	Charles Daniels (U.S.) d.n.a.	Scott Leary (U.S.) d.n.a.
1908	Charles Daniels (U.S.) 1m 05.6s*	Zóltan Halmay (HUNGARY) 1m 06.2s	Harald Julin (SWEDEN) 1m 08.0s
1912	Duke Kahanamoku (U.S.) 1m 03.4s[4]	Cecil Healy (AUSTRALASIA) 1m 04.6s	Kenneth Huszagh (U.S.) 1m 05.6s
1920	Duke Kahanamoku (U.S.) 1m 00.4s*	Pua Kealoha (U.S.) 1m 02.2s	William Harris (U.S.) 1m 03.2s
1924	Johnny Weismuller (U.S.) 59.0s	Duke Kahanamoku (U.S.) 1m 01.4s	Samuel Kahanamoku (U.S.) 1m 01.8s

[1] Pseudonym assumed in sports contests; actual name was Guttman, though he later changed it to Hajós.
[2] All reports except one list Korphas (Greece) as second, but Hajós has categorically stated that Williams was second.
[3] Race actually 100 yds. (91.44 metres).
[4] Set O.R. of 1m 02.6s and 1m 02.4s in preliminaries.

	GOLD	SILVER	BRONZE
1928	Johnny Weismuller (U.S.) 58.6s*	István Bárány (HUNGARY) 59.8s	Katsuo Takaishi (JAPAN) 1m 00.0s
1932	Yasuji Miyazaki (JAPAN) 58.2s[5]	Tatsugo Kawaishi (JAPAN) 58.6s	Albert Schwartz (U.S.) 58.8s
1936	Ferenc Csik (HUNGARY) 57.6s[6]	Masanori Yusa (JAPAN) 57.9s	Shigeo Arai (JAPAN) 58.0s
1948	Walter Ris (U.S.) 57.3s*	Alan Ford (U.S.) 57.8s	Géza Kádas (HUNGARY) 58.1s
1952	C. Clarke Scholes (U.S.) 57.4s[7]	Hiroshi Suzuki (JAPAN) 57.4s	Goran Larsson (SWEDEN) 58.2s
1956	Jon Henricks (AUSTRALIA) 55.4s*	John Devitt (AUSTRALIA) 55.8s	Gary Chapman (AUSTRALIA) 56.7s
1960	John Devitt (AUSTRALIA) 55.2s*	Lance Larson (U.S.) 55.2s*	Manoel dos Santos (BRAZIL) 55.4s
1964	Donald Schollander (U.S.) 53.4s*	Robert McGregor (G.B.) 53.5s	Hans Klein (GERMANY) 54.0s
1968	Michael Wenden (AUSTRALIA) 52.2s*	Kenneth Walsh (U.S.) 52.8s	Mark Spitz (U.S.) 53.0s
1972			

---

[5] Set O.R. of 58.0s in preliminaries.
[6] O.R. of 57.5s set in preliminaries by Masaharu Taguchi (JAPAN) and equalled by Yusa.
[7] Set O.R. of 57.1s in preliminaries.

200 METRES FREE-STYLE (218 yds. 2 ft.)

1896	Event not held		
1900	Frederick Lane (AUSTRALIA) 2m 25.2s	Zoltán Halmay (HUNGARY) 2m 31.0s	Karl Ruberl (AUSTRIA) 2m 32.0s
1904-1964	Event not held		

In winning the 100 metres free-style in 1968, Michael Wenden (Australia) set a world record of 4.285 m.p.h.

	GOLD	SILVER	BRONZE
1968	Michael Wenden (AUSTRALIA) 1m 55.2s*	Donald Schollander (U.S.) 1m 55.8s	John Nelson (U.S.) 1m 58.1s
1972			

400 METRES FREE-STYLE (437 yds. 1 ft.)

1896–1900	Event not held		
1904[1]	Charles Daniels (U.S.) 6m 16.2s	Francis Gailey (U.S.) 6m 22.0s	Otto Wahle (AUSTRIA) 6m 39.0s
1908[2]	Henry Taylor (G.B.) 5m 36.8s*	Frank Beaurepaire (AUSTRALASIA) 5m 44.2s	Otto Scheff (AUSTRIA) 5m 46.0s
1912	George Hodgson (CANADA) 5m 24.4s*	John Hatfield (G.B.) 5m 25.8s	Harold Hardwick (AUSTRALASIA) 5m 31.2s
1920	Norman Ross (U.S.) 5m 26.8s	Ludy Langer (U.S.) 5m 29.2s	George Vernot (CANADA) 5m 29.8s
1924	Johnny Weismuller (U.S.) 5m 04.2s*	Arne Borg (SWEDEN) 5m 05.6s	Andrew Charlton (AUSTRALIA) 5m 06.6s
1928	Alberto Zorilla (ARGENTINA) 5m 01.6s*	Andrew Charlton (AUSTRALIA) 5m 03.6s	Arne Borg (SWEDEN) 5m 04.6s
1932	Clarence Crabbe (U.S.) 4m 48.4s*	Jean Taris (FRANCE) 4m 48.5s	Tsutoma Oyokota (JAPAN) 4m 52.3s
1936	Jack Medica (U.S.) 4m 44.5s*	Shumpei Uto (JAPAN) 4m 45.6s	Shozo Makino (JAPAN) 4m 48.1s

---

[1] Race actually 440 yds. (402.34 metres).
[2] O.R. in preliminaries set by Thomas Battersby (G.B.) 5m 48.8s; Taylor 5m 42.2s; Scheff 5m 40.6s.

Three of the swimmers, who dominated the 1956 and 1960 Olympics in the 400 metres and 1,500 metre free-style: above, left to right, George Breen (U.S.), Murray Rose (Australia), and Tsuyoshi Yamanaka (Japan).

Donald Schollander (U.S.), in 1964 became the only man to win four swimming gold medals at one Olympic Games.

	GOLD	SILVER	BRONZE
1948	William Smith (U.S.) 4m 41.0s*	James McLane (U.S.) 4m 43.4s	John Marshall (AUSTRALIA) 4m 47.7s
1952	Jean Boiteux (FRANCE) 4m 30.7s*	Ford Konno (U.S.) 4m 31.3s	Per-Olof Ostrand (SWEDEN) 4m 35.2s
1956	Murray Rose (AUSTRALIA) 4m 27.3s*	Tsuyoshi Yamanaka (JAPAN) 4m 30.4s	George Breen (U.S.) 4m 32.5s
1960	Murray Rose (AUSTRALIA) 4m 18.3s*	Tsuyoshi Yamanaka (JAPAN) 4m 21.4s	Jon Konrads (AUSTRALIA) 4m 21.8s
1964	Donald Schollander (U.S.) 4m 12.2s*	Frank Wiegand (GERMANY) 4m 14.9s	Allan Wood (AUSTRALIA) 4m 15.1s
1968	Michael Burton (U.S.) 4m 09.0s*	Ralph Hutton (CANADA) 4m 11.7s	Alain Mosconi (FRANCE) 4m 13.3s
1972			

1,500 METRES FREE-STYLE (1,640 yds. 1 ft.)

	GOLD	SILVER	BRONZE
1896–1900	Event not held		
1904[1]	Emil Rausch (GERMANY) 27m 18.2s	Géza Kiss (HUNGARY) 28m 28.2s	Francis Gailey (U.S.) 28m 54.0s
1908[2]	Henry Taylor (G.B.) 22m 48.4s*	Thomas Battersby (G.B.) 22m 51.2s	Frank Beaurepaire (AUSTRALASIA) 22m 56.2s
1912	George Hodgson (CANADA) 22m 00.0s*	John Hatfield (G.B.) 22m 39.0s	Harold Hardwick (AUSTRALASIA) 23m 15.4s
1920	Norman Ross (U.S.) 22m 23.2s	George Vernot (CANADA) 22m 36.4s	Frank Beaurepaire (AUSTRALIA) 23m 04.0s
1924[3]	Andrew Charlton (AUSTRALIA) 20m 06.6s*	Arne Borg (SWEDEN) 20m 41.4s	Frank Beaurepaire (AUSTRALIA) 20m 48.4s
1928	Arne Borg (SWEDEN) 19m 51.8s*	Andrew Charlton (AUSTRALIA) 20m 02.6s	Clarence Crabbe (U.S.) 20m 28.8s
1932[4]	Kusuo Kitamura (JAPAN) 19m 12.4s*	Shozo Makino (JAPAN) 19m 14.1s	James Christy (U.S.) 19m 39.5s
1936	Noboru Terada (JAPAN) 19m 13.7s	Jack Medica (U.S.) 19m 34.0s	Shumpei Uto (JAPAN) 19m 34.5s
1948	James McLane (U.S.) 19m 18.5s	John Marshall (AUSTRALIA) 19m 31.3s	György Mitró (HUNGARY) 19m 43.2s
1952	Ford Konno (U.S.) 18m 30.0s*	Shiro Hashizume (JAPAN) 18m 41.4s	Tetsuo Okamoto (BRAZIL) 18m 51.3s
1956[5]	Murray Rose (AUSTRALIA) 17m 58.9s	Tsuyoshi Yamanaka (JAPAN) 18m 00.3s	George Breen (U.S.) 18m 08.2s
1960	Jon Konrads (AUSTRALIA) 17m 19.6s*	Murray Rose (AUSTRALIA) 17m 21.7s	George Breen (U.S.) 17m 30.6s

---

[1] Race actually 1 mile (1,609 metres).
[2] O.R. set in preliminaries by Paul Radmilovic (G.B.) 27m 15.4s; Beaurepaire 23m 45.8s; Battersby 23m 42.8s; Taylor 23m 24.4s; Battersby 23m 22.0s.
[3] O.R. set in preliminaries by Charlton 21m 20.4s; Borg 21m 11.4s.
[4] O.R. set in preliminaries by Kitamura 19m 51.6s; Makino 19m 38.7s.
[5] O.R. of 17m 52.9s in preliminaries set by Breen.

	GOLD	SILVER	BRONZE
1964	Robert Windle (AUSTRALIA) 17m 01.7s*	John Nelson (U.S.) 17m 03.0s	Allan Wood (AUSTRALIA) 17m 07.7s
1968	Michael Burton (U.S.) 16m 38.9s*	John Kinsella (U.S.) 16m 57.3s	Gregory Brough (AUSTRALIA) 17m 04.7s
1972			

100 METRES BREAST STROKE (109 yds. 1 ft.)

	GOLD	SILVER	BRONZE
1896–1964	Event not held		
1968	Donald McKenzie (U.S.) 1m 07.7s*	Vladimir Kosinsky (U.S.S.R.) 1m 08.0s	Nickolay Pankin (U.S.S.R.) 1m 08.0s
1972			

200 METRES BREAST STROKE (218 yds. 2 ft.)

	GOLD	SILVER	BRONZE
1896–1904	Event not held		
1908	Frederick Holman[1] (G.B.) 3m 09.2s*	W. W. Robinson (G.B.) 3m 12.8s	Pontus Hansson (SWEDEN) 3m 14.6s
1912	Walter Bathe (GERMANY) 3m 01.8s*	Wilhelm Lützow (GERMANY) 3m 05.0s	Paul Malisch (GERMANY) 3m 08.0s
1920	Håkan Malmroth (SWEDEN) 3m 04.4s	Thor Henning (SWEDEN) 3m 09.2s	Arvo Aaltonen (FINLAND) 3m 12.2s
1924	Robert Skelton (U.S.) 2m 56.6s*	Joseph de Combe (BELGIUM) 2m 59.2s	William Kirschbaum (U.S.) 3m 01.0s
1928	Yoshiyuki Tsuruta (JAPAN) 2m 48.8s*	Erich Rademacher (GERMANY) 2m 50.6s	Teofilo Yldefonso (PHILIPPINES) 2m 56.4s
1932	Yoshiyuki Tsuruta (JAPAN) 2m 45.4s*	Reizo Koike (JAPAN) 2m 46.4s[2]	Teofilo Yldefonso (PHILIPPINES) 2m 47.1s
1936	Tetsuo Hamuro (JAPAN) 2m 42.5s*	Erwin Sietas (GERMANY) 2m 42.9s	Reizo Koike (JAPAN) 2m 44.2s
1948	Joseph Verdeur (U.S.) 2m 39.3s*	Keith Carter (U.S.) 2m 40.2s	Robert Sohl (U.S.) 2m 43.9s
1952	John Davies (AUSTRALIA) 2m 34.4s*	Bowen Stassforth (U.S.) 2m 34.7s	Herbert Klein (GERMANY) 2m 35.9s
1956	Masura Furukawa (JAPAN) 2m 34.7s[3]	Masahiro Yoshimura (JAPAN) 2m 36.7s	Kharis Yunishev (U.S.S.R.) 2m 36.8s
1960	William Mulliken (U.S.) 2m 37.4s[4]	Yoshihiko Ohsaki (JAPAN) 2m 38.0s	Wieger Mensonides (NETHS.) 2m 39.7s
1964	Ian O'Brien (AUSTRALIA) 2m 27.8s*	Georgy Prokopenko (U.S.S.R.) 2m 28.2s	Chester Jastremski (U.S.) 2m 29.6s
1968	Felipe Munox (MEXICO) 2m 28.7s	Vladimir Kosinsky (U.S.S.R.) 2m 29.2s	Brian Job (U.S.) 2m 29.9s
1972			

---

[1] Set O.R. of 3m 10.6s in preliminaries.
[2] Set O.R. of 2m 44.9s in preliminaries.
[3] Recognized as new O.R. when butterfly stroke—until then permitted in breast-stroke races—was established as separate event. Previous fastest time using orthodox breast stroke was 2m 41.5s by Hamuro in 1936.
[4] Time of 2m 37.2s set by Mulliken in preliminaries recognized as new O.R. as underwater swimming is no longer allowed.

Mike Burton (U.S.) took the 400 metres and 1500 metres free-style double at Mexico City and, despite the thin air, set new Olympic records for both events.

100 METRES BUTTERFLY (109 yds. 1 ft.)

	GOLD	SILVER	BRONZE
1896–1964	Event not held		
1968	Douglas Russell (U.S.) 55.9s*[1]	Mark Spitz (U.S.) 56.4s	Ross Wales (U.S.) 57.2s
1972			

---

[1] Also achieved O.R. of 55.9s in semi-finals.

200 METRES BUTTERFLY (218 yds. 2 ft.)

	GOLD	SILVER	BRONZE
1896–1952	Event not held		
1956	William Yorzyk (U.S.) 2m 19.3s[1]	Takashi Ishimoto (JAPAN) 2m 23.8s	György Tumpek (HUNGARY) 2m 23.9s
1960	Michael Troy (U.S.) 2m 12.8s*	Neville Hayes (AUSTRALIA) 2m 14.6s	J. David Gillanders (U.S.) 2m 15.3s
1964	Kevin Berry (AUSTRALIA) 2m 06.6s*	Carl Robie[2] (U.S.) 2m 07.5s	Fred Schmidt (U.S.) 2m 09.3s
1968	Carl Robie (U.S.) 2m 08.7s	Martyn Woodroffe (G.B.) 2m 09.0s	John Ferris (U.S.) 2m 09.3s
1972			

Set O.R. of 2m 18.6s in preliminaries. Time of 2m 34.4s set by John Davies (Australia) in winning 1952 200m breast stroke title, using the butterfly action, was recognized as inaugural O.R.
Set O.R. of 2m 10.0s in preliminaries and 2m 09.3s in Semi-finals.

100 METRES BACK STROKE (109 yds. 1 ft.)

	GOLD	SILVER	BRONZE
1896–1904	Event not held		
1908	Arno Bieberstein (GERMANY) 1m 24.6s*	Ludvig Dam (DENMARK) 1m 26.6s	Herbert Haresnape (G.B.) 1m 27.0s
1912	Harry Hebner[1] (U.S.) 1m 21.2s	Otto Fahr (GERMANY) 1m 22.4s	Paul Kellner (GERMANY) 1m 24.0s
1920	Warren Kealoha (U.S.) 1m 15.2s*	Ray Kegeris (U.S.) 1m 16.2s	Gerald Blitz (BELGIUM) 1m 19.0s
1924	Warren Kealoha (U.S.) 1m 13.2s*	Paul Wyatt (U.S.) 1m 15.4s	Károly Bartha (HUNGARY) 1m 17.8s
1928	George Kojac (U.S.) 1m 08.2s*	Walter Laufer (U.S.) 1m 10.0s	Paul Wyatt (U.S.) 1m 12.0s
1932	Masaji Kiyokawa (JAPAN) 1m 08.6s	Toshio Irie (JAPAN) 1m 09.8s	Kentaro Kawatsu (JAPAN) 1m 10.0s
1936	Adolf Kiefer (U.S.) 1m 05.9s*	Albert Van de Weghe (U.S.) 1m 07.7s	Masaji Kiyokawa (JAPAN) 1m 08.4s
1948	Allen Stack (U.S.) 1m 06.4s	Robert Cowell (U.S.) 1m 06.5s	Georges Vallerey (FRANCE) 1m 07.8s
1952	Yoshio Oyakawa (U.S.) 1m 05.4s*	Gilbert Bozon (FRANCE) 1m 06.2s	Jack Taylor (U.S.) 1m 06.4s
1956	David Thiele (AUSTRALIA) 1m 02.2s*	John Monckton (AUSTRALIA) 1m 03.2s	Frank McKinney (U.S.) 1m 04.5s
1960	David Thiele (AUSTRALIA) 1m 01.9s*	Frank McKinney (U,S.) 1m 02.1s	Robert Bennett (U.S.) 1m 02.3s
1964	Event not held		
1968	Roland Matthes (E. GERMANY) 58.7s*	Charles Hickcox (U.S.) 1m 00.2s	Ronnie Mills (U.S.) 1m 00.5s
1972			

[1] Set O.R. of 1m 20.8s in semi-final.

200 METRES BACK STROKE (218 yds. 2 ft.)

1900	Ernst Hoppenberg (GERMANY) 2m 47.0s*	Karl Ruberl (AUSTRIA) 2m 56.0s	F. Dooxt (NETHS.) 3m 01.0s
1964	Jed Graef (U.S.) 2m 10.3s*	Gary Dilley (U.S.) 2m 10.5s[1]	Robert Bennett (U.S.) 2m 13.1s[2]
1968	Roland Matthes (E. GERMANY) 2m 09.6s*	Mitchell Ivey (U.S.) 2m 10.6s	Jack Horsley (U.S.) 2m 10.9s
1972			

[1] Set O.R. of 2m 14.2s in preliminaries, and 2m 13.8s in semi-finals.
[2] Set O.R. of 2m 16.1s in preliminaries.

200 METRES INDIVIDUAL MEDLEY (218 yds. 2 ft.)

1896–1964	Event not held		
1968	Charles Hickcox (U.S.) 2m 12.0s	Gregory Buckingham (U.S.) 2m 13.0s	John Ferris (U.S.) 2m 13.3s
1972			

400 METRES INDIVIDUAL MEDLEY

1896–1960	Event not held		
1964	Richard Roth (U.S.) 4m 45.4s*	Roy Saari (U.S.) 4m 47.1s	Gerhard Hetz (GERMANY) 2m 51.

	GOLD	SILVER	BRONZE
1968	Charles Hickcox (U.S.) 4m 48.4s	Gary Hall (U.S.) 4m 48.7s	Michael Holthaus (W. GERMANY) 4m 51.4s
1972			

4 × 100 METRES FREE-STYLE RELAY

1896–1960	Event not held		
1964	U.S. 3m 33.2s*	GERMANY 3m 37.2s	AUSTRALIA 3m 39.1s
	Stephen Clark	Horst Loffler	David Dickson
	Michael Austin	Frank Wiegand	Peter Doak
	Gary Ilman	Uwe Jacobsen	John Ryan
	Donald Schollander	Hans Klein	Robert Windle
1968	U.S. 3m 31.7s*	U.S.S.R. 3m 34.2s	AUSTRALIA 3m 34.7s
	Zachary Zorn	Semyon Belits-Geiman	Gregory Rogers
	Stephen Rerych	Victor Mazanov	Robert Cusack
	Mark Spitz	Leonid Ilyichev	Robert Windle
	Kenneth Walsh	Georgy Kulikov	Michael Wenden
1972			

4 × 200 METRES FREE-STYLE RELAY

1896–1904	Event not held		
1908	G.B. 10m 55.6s*[1]	HUNGARY 10m 59.0s	U.S. 11m 02.8s
	John Derbyshire	József Munk	Harry Hebner
	Paul Radmilovic	Imre Zachár	Budd Goodwin
	Willie Foster	Béla Las Torres	Charles Daniels
	Henry Taylor	Zoltán Halmay	L. G. Rich
1912	AUSTRALASIA 10m 11.2s*	U.S. 10m 20.2s	G.B. 10m 28.2s
	Cecil Healy	Perry McGillivray	Willie Foster
	Malcolm Champion[2]	Harry Hebner	Thomas Battersby
	Leslie Boardman	Kenneth Huszagh	John Hatfield
	Harold Hardwick	Duke Kahanamoku	Henry Taylor
1920	U.S. 10m 04.4s*	AUSTRALIA 10m 25.4s	G.B. 10m 37.2s
	Perry McGillivray	William Herald	L. Savage
	Pua Kealoha	Ivan Stedman	Henry Taylor
	Norman Ross	Keit Kirkland	H. E. Annison
	Duke Kahanamoku	Frank Beaurepaire	E. P. Peter
1924	U.S. 9m 53.4s*[3]	AUSTRALIA 10m 02.2s	SWEDEN 10m 06.8s
	Wallace O'Connor	Andrew Charlton	Georg Werner
	Harry Glancy	Frank Beaurepaire	Orvar Trolle
	Ralph Breyer	Maurice Christie	Ake Borg
	Johnny Weismuller	Ernest Henry	Arne Borg
1928	U.S. 9m 36.2s*[4]	JAPAN 9m 41.4s	CANADA 9m 47.8s
	Austin Clapp	H. Yoneyama	Bourne
	Walter Laufer	Shigeo Arai	Thompson
	George Kojac	T. Sata	Ault
	Johnny Weissmuller	Katsuo Takaishi	Spence
1932	JAPAN 8m 58.4s*	U.S. 9m 10.5s	HUNGARY 9m 31.4s
	Yasuji Miyazaki	Frank Booth	András Wannie
	Takashi Yokoyama	Maiola Kalili	László Szabados
	Masanori Yusa	George Fissler	András Székely
	Hisakichi Toyoda	Manuella Kalili	István Bárány

---

[1] O.R. set in preliminaries by AUSTRALIA (Frank Beaurepaire, F. W. Springfield, R. L. Baker, T. B. Tartakover) 11m 35.0s; GREAT BRITAIN 10m 53.4s.
[2] A New Zealander; the other three members of the team were Australians. The two countries entered a composite team in the Olympic Games until 1920.
[3] O.R. of 9m 59.4s in preliminaries.
[4] O.R. of 9m 30.8s in preliminaries.

	GOLD	SILVER	BRONZE
1936	JAPAN 8m 51.5s*	U.S. 9m 03.0s	HUNGARY 9m 12.3s
	Masanori Yusa	Ralph Flanagan	Odön Gróf
	Shigeo Sugiura	John Macionis	Arpád Lengyel
	Masaharu Taguchi	Paul Wolf	Oszkár Abay-Nemes
	Shigeo Arai	Jack Medica	Ferenc Csik
1948	U.S. 8m 46.0s*	HUNGARY 8m 48.4s	FRANCE 9m 08.0s
	Walter Ris	Imre Nyéki	Henri Padou
	Wallace Wolf	György Mitró	R. Cornu
	James McLane	Elemér Szatmári	Joseph Bernardo
	William Smith	Géza Kádas	Alexandre Jany
1952	U.S. 8m 31.1s*	JAPAN 8m 33.5s	FRANCE 8m 45.9s
	Wayne Moore	Hiroshi Suzuki	Joseph Bernardo
	William Woolsey	Yoshihiro Hamaguchi	Aldo Eminente
	Ford Konno	Toru Goto	Alexandre Jany
	James McLane	Teijiro Tanikawa	Jean Boiteux
1956	AUSTRALIA 8m 23.6s*	U.S. 8m 31.5s	U.S.S.R. 8m 34.7s
	Kevin O'Halloran	Richard Hanley	Vitaliy Sorokin
	John Devitt	George Breen	Vladimir Struyanov
	Murray Rose	William Woolsey	Gennadiy Nikolayev
	Jon Henricks	Ford Konno	Boris Nikitin
1960	U.S. 8m 10.2s*[1]	JAPAN 8m 13.2s	AUSTRALIA 8m 13.8s
	George Harrison	Makoto Fukui	David Dickson
	Richard Blick	Hiroshi Ishii	John Devitt
	Michael Troy	Tsuyoshi Yamanaka	Murray Rose
	F. Jeffrey Farrell	Tatsuo Fujimoto	John Konrads
1964	U.S. 7m 52.1s	GERMANY 7m 59.3s[2]	JAPAN 8m 03.8s
	Stephen Clark	Horst Gregor	Makoto Fukui
	Roy Saari	Gerhard Hetz	Kunihiro Iwasaki
	Gary Ilman	Frank Wiegand	Toshio Shoji
	Don Schollander	Hans Klein	Yukiabi Okabe
1968	U.S. 7m 52.3s	AUSTRALIA 7m 53.7s	U.S.S.R. 8m 01.6s
	John Nelson	Gregory Rogers	Vladimir Bure
	Stephen Rerych	Graham White	Semyon Belits-Geiman
	Mark Spitz	Robert Windle	Georgy Kulikov
	Donald Schollander	Michael Wenden	Leonid Ilyichev
1972			

------

[1] In the preliminaries JAPAN also set O.R. at 8m 17.1s and U.S. team, containing three reserves, recorded 8m 18.0s.
[2] Germany set up O.R. of 8m 09.17s in preliminaries, while the U.S. team, with a reserve team recorded 8m 09.0s.

4 × 100 METRES MEDLEY RELAY

1896–1956   Event not held

	GOLD	SILVER	BRONZE
1960[1]	U.S. 4m 05.4s*	AUSTRALIA 4m 12.0s.	JAPAN 4m 12.2s
	Frank McKinney	David Theile	Kazuo Tomita
	Paul Hait	Terry Gathercole	Koichi Hirakida
	Lance Larson	Neville Hayes	Yoshihiko Ohsaki
	F. Jeffrey Farrell	Gary Shipton	Keigo Shimizu
1964	U.S. 3m 58.4s*[2]	GERMANY 4m 01.6s	AUSTRALIA 4m 02.3s
	Harold Mann	Ernst Kneppers	Peter Reynolds
	William Craig	Egon Henninger	Ian O'Brien
	Fred Schmidt	Horst Gregor	Kevin Berry
	Stephen Clark	Hans Klein	David Dickson

GOLD	SILVER	BRONZE
1968 U.S. 3m 54.9s*	E. GERMANY	U.S.S.R. 4m 00.7s
Charles Hickcox	3m 57.5s	Yuri Gromak
Donald McKenzie	Roland Matthes	Vladimir Kosinsky
Douglas Russell	Egon Henninger	Vladimir Nemshilov
Kenneth Walsh	Horst-Gunter Gregor	Leonid Ilyichev
	Frank Wiegand	
1972		

[1] Order of strokes: back-stroke, breast-stroke, butterfly, free-style. Decision of whether to use McKinney or Robert Bennett on the back-stroke leg was made by toss of a coin. In the preliminaries U.S. team of Bennett, Hait, J. David Gillanders and Steve Clark recorded 5m 08.2s, beating existing world record by one second.

[2] U.S. set up O.R. of 4m 05.1s in preliminaries with a reserve team.

PLATFORM DIVING

1896–1904 Event not held[1]		
1908 Hjalmar Johansson (SWEDEN) 83.75 pts.	K. Malmström (SWEDEN) 78.73	A. Spangberg (SWEDEN) 74
1912[2] Erik Adlerz (SWEDEN) 73.94 pts.	Albert Zürner (GERMANY) 72.60	Gustaf Blomgren (SWEDEN) 69.56
1920[3] Clarence Pinkston (U.S.) 100.67 pts.	Erik Adlerz (SWEDEN) 99.08	Harry Prieste (U.S.) 93.73
1924[4] Albert White (U.S.) 97.46 pts.	David Fall (U.S.) 97.30	Clarence Pinkston (U.S.) 94.60
1928 Peter Desjardins (U.S.) 98.74 pts.	Farid Simaika (EGYPT) 98.58	Michael Galitzen (U.S.) 92.34
1932 Harold Smith (U.S.) 124.80 pts.	Michael Galitzen (U.S.) 124.28	Frank Kurtz (U.S.) 121.98
1936 Marshall Wayne (U.S.) 113.58 pts.	Elbert Root (U.S.) 110.60	Hermann Stork (GERMANY) 110.31
1948 Samuel Lee (U.S.) 130.05 pts.	Bruce Harlan (U.S.) 122.30	Joaquin Capilla (MEXICO) 113.52
1952 Samuel Lee (U.S.) 156.28 pts.	Joaquin Capilla (MEXICO) 145.21	Günther Haase (GERMANY) 141.31
1956 Joaquin Capilla[5] (MEXICO) 152.44 pts.	Gary Tobian (U.S.) 152.41	Richard Connor (U.S.) 149.79
1960 Robert Webster (U.S.) 165.56 pts.	Gary Tobian (U.S.) 165.25	Brian Phelps (G.B.) 157.13
1964 Robert Webster (U.S.) 148.58 pts.	Klaus Dibiasi (ITALY) 147.54	Tom Gompf (U.S.) 146.57
1968 Klaus Dibiasi (ITALY) 164.18 pts.	Alvaro Gaxiola (MEXICO) 154.49	Edwin Young (U.S.) 153.93
1972		

[1] There was a combined platform and springboard event in 1904, won by G. E. Sheldon (U.S.), with 12.75 pts. from Georg Hoffmann (GERMANY), 11.33, and Frank Kehoe (U.S.) and A. Braunschweiger (GERMANY), who tied for third place, also with 11.33.

[2] There was also an event from 5-metre and 10-metre boards, won by Adlerz from Hjalmar Johansson and John Jansson (both SWEDEN).

[3] There was also an event from 5-metre and 10-metre boards, won by Arvid Wallman, from Nils Skoglund and John Jansson (all SWEDEN).

[4] There was also a "direct" event, won by Richmond Eve (AUSTRALIA), from John Jansson (SWEDEN), and Harold Clarke (G.B.).

[5] This was the first occasion on which the U.S. had failed to win an Olympic diving event, for men or women, since 1920.

SPRINGBOARD DIVING

GOLD	SILVER	BRONZE
1896–1904 Event not held		
1908 Albert Zürner (GERMANY) 85.5 pts.	Kurt Behrens (GERMANY) 85.3	George Gaidzik (U.S.) 80.8 Gottlob Walz (GERMANY) 80.8[1]
1912 Paul Günther (GERMANY) 79.23 pts.	Hans Luber (GERMANY) 76.78	Kurt Behrens (GERMANY) 73.73
1920 Louis Kuehn (U.S.) 675 pts.	Clarence Pinkston (U.S.) 655.3	Louis Balbach (U.S.) 649.5
1924 Albert White (U.S.) 696.4 pts.	Peter Desjardins (U.S.) 693.2	Clarence Pinkston (U.S.) 653
1928 Peter Desjardins (U.S.) 185.04 pts.	Michael Galitzen (U.S.) 174.06	Farid Simaika (Egypt) 172.46
1932 Michael Galitzen (U.S.) 161.38 pts.	Harold Smith (U.S.) 158.54	Richard Degener (U.S.) 151.82
1936 Richard Degener (U.S.) 163.57 pts.	Marshall Wayne (U.S.) 159.56	Al Greene (U.S.) 146.29
1948 Bruce Harlan (U.S.) 163.64 pts.	Miller Anderson (U.S.) 157.29	Samuel Lee (U.S.) 145.52
1952 David Browning (U.S.) 205.29 pts.	Miller Anderson (U.S.) 199.84	Robert Clotworthy (U.S.) 184.92
1956 Robert Clotworthy (U.S.) 159.56 pts.	Donald Harper (U.S.) 156.23	Joaquin Capilla (MEXICO) 150.69
1960 Gary Tobian (U.S.) 170.00 pts.	Samuel Hall (U.S.) 167.08	Juan Botella (MEXICO) 162.30
1964 Ken Sitzberger (U.S.) 159.90 pts.	Frank Gorman (U.S.) 157.63	Larry Andreasen (U.S.) 143.77
1968 Bernard Wrightson (U.S.) 170.15 pts.	Klaus Dibiasi (ITALY) 159.74	James Henry (U.S.) 158.09
1972		

---

[1] Tie for third place.

16b. Swimming and Diving (Women)

100 METRES FREE-STYLE (109 yds. 1 ft.)

GOLD	SILVER	BRONZE
1896–1908 Event not held		
1912 Fanny Durack (AUSTRALASIA) 1m 22.2s*	Wilhelmina Wylie (AUSTRALASIA) 1m 25.4s	Jennie Fletcher (G.B.) 1m 27.0s
1920 Ethelda Bleibtrey (U.S.) 1m 13.6s*	Irene Guest (U.S.) 1m 17.0s	Frances Schroth (U.S.) 1m 17.2s
1924 Ethel Lackie (U.S.) 1m 12.4s	Mariechen Wehselau[1] (U.S.) 1m 12.8s	Gertrude Ederle (U.S.) 1m 14.2s
1928 Albina Osipowich[2] (U.S.) 1m 11.0s*	Eleonora Garatti[3] (U.S.) 1m 11.4 s	Margaret Cooper (G.B.) 1m 13.6s
1932 Helene Madison[4] (U.S.) 1m 06.8s*	Willemijnte den Ouden (NETHS.) 1m 07.8s	Eleonora Saville[5] (U.S.) 1m 08.2s

---

[1] Set O.R. of 1m 12.2s in preliminaries.
[2] Set O.R. of 1m 12.2s in preliminaries.
[3] Set O.R. of 1m 11.4s in preliminaries.
[4] O.R. set in preliminaries by Margaret Cooper (G.B.) 1m 09.0s; Madison 1m 08.9s; Garatti 1m 08.5s; den Ouden 1m 07.6s.
[5] Formerly Garatti.

Dawn Fraser (Australia), holder of the world record in the 100 metres free-style, and winner of the event three times in the Olympics.

	GOLD	SILVER	BRONZE
1936	Hendrika Mastenbroek (NETHS.) 1m 05.9s*	Jeanette Campbell (ARGENTINA) 1m 06.4s	Gisela Arendt (GERMANY) 1m 06.6s
1948	Greta Andersen (DENMARK) 1m 06.3s[6]	Ann Curtis (U.S.) 1m 06.5s	Marie-Louise Vaessen (NETHS.) 1m 07.6s
1952	Katalin Szöke (HUNGARY) 1m 06.8s	Johanna Termeulen (NETHS.) 1m 07.0s	Judit Temes (HUNGARY) 1m 07.1s[7]
1956	Dawn Fraser (AUSTRALIA) 1m 02.0s*	Lorraine Crapp (AUSTRALIA) 1m 02.3s	Faith Leech (AUSTRALIA) 1m 05.1s
1960	Dawn Fraser (AUSTRALIA) 1m 01.2s[8]	Christine von Saltza (U.S.) 1m 02.8s	Natalie Steward (G.B.) 1m 03.1s
1964	Dawn Fraser (AUSTRALIA) 59.5s*	Sharon Stouder (U.S.) 59.9s	Kathleen Ellis (U.S. 1m 00.8s
1968	Jan Henne (U.S.) 1m 00.0s	Susan Pedersen (U.S.) 1m 00.3s	Linda Gustavson (U.S.) 1m 00.3s
1972			

[6] Equalled O.R. of 1m 05.9s in preliminaries.
[7] Set O.R. of 1m 05.5s in preliminaries.
[8] Set O.R. of 1m 00.6s on first leg of 4 × 100 metres free-style relay final.

200 METRES FREE-STYLE (218 yds. 2 ft.)

1896–1964 Event not held

1968	Debbie Meyer (U.S.) 2m 10.5s*	Jan Henne (U.S.) 2m 11.0s	Jane Barkman (U.S.) 2m 11.2s
1972			

400 METRES FREE-STYLE (437 yds. 1 ft.)

1896–1920 Event not held

1924	Martha Norelius (U.S.) 6m 02.2s*	Helen Wainwright (U.S.) 6m 03.8s	Gertrude Ederle[1] (U.S.) 6m 04.8s
1932	Helene Madison (U.S.) 5m 28.5s*	Lenore Kight (U.S.) 5m 28.6s[3]	Jennie Maakal (S. AFRICA) 5m 47.3s
1928	Martha Norelius[2] (U.S.) 5m 42.8s*	Marie Braun (NETHS.) 5m 57.8s	Josephine McKim (U.S.) 6m 00.2s

[1] Set O.R. of 6m 12.2s in preliminaries.
[2] Set O.R. of 5m 45.4s in preliminaries.
[3] Set O.R. of 5m 40.9s in preliminaries.

GOLD	SILVER	BRONZE
1936 Hendrika Mastenbroek (NETHS.) 5m 26.4s*	Ranghild Hveger (DENMARK) 5m 27.5s	Lenore Wingard[4] (U.S.) 5m 29.0s
1948 Ann Curtis (U.S.) 5m 17.8s*	Karen Harup (DENMARK) 5m 21.2s	Cathie Gibson (G.B.) 5m 22.5s
1952 Valéria Gyenge (HUNGARY) 5m 12.1s*	Eva Novák (HUNGARY) 5m 13.7s	Evelyn Kawamoto (U.S.) 5m 14.6s
1956 Lorraine Crapp (AUSTRALIA) 4m 54.6s*	Dawn Fraser (AUSTRALIA) 5m 02.5s	Sylvia Ruuska (U.S.) 5m 07.1s
1960 Christine von Saltza (U.S.) 4m 50.6s*	Jane Cederqvist (SWEDEN) 4m 53.9s	Tineke Lagerberg (NETHS.) 4m 56.9s
1964 Virginia Duenkel (U.S.) 4m 43.3s*	Marilyn Ramenofsky (U.S.) 4m 44.6s[5]	Terri Stickles (U.S.) 4m 47.2s
1968 Debbie Meyer (U.S.) 4m 31.8s	Linda Gustavson (U.S.) 4m 35.5s	Karen Moras (AUSTRALIA) 4m 37.0s
1972		

---

[4] Formerly Kight. Unofficial time; no official time taken.
[5] Set O.R. of 4m 47.7s in preliminaries.

800 METRES FREE-STYLE (874 yds. 2 ft.)

1896–1964 Event not held		
1968 Debbie Meyer (U.S.) 9m 24.0s*	Pam Kruse (U.S.) 9m 35.7s	Lidia Ramirez (MEXICO) 9m 38.5s
1972		

100 METRES BREAST STROKE (109 yds. 1 ft.)

1896–1964 Event not held		
1968 Djurdjica Bjedov (YUGOSLAVIA) 1m 15.8s*	Galina Prozumenshikova (U.S.S.R.) 1m 15.9s	Sharon Wichman (U.S.) 1m 16.1s
1972		

200 METRES BREAST STROKE (218 yds. 2 ft.)

1896–1920 Event not held		
1924 Lucy Morton (G.B.) 3m 33.2s*	Agnes Geraghty (U.S.) 3m 34.0s[1]	Gladys Carson (G.B.) 3m 35.4s
1928 Hilde Schrader (GERMANY) 3m 12.6s[2]	Marie Baron (NETHS.) 3m 15.2s	Lotte Mühe-Hildensheim (GERMANY) 3m 17.6s
1932 Clare Dennis (AUSTRALIA) 3m 06.3s*[3]	Hideko Maehata (JAPAN) 3m 06.4s	Else Jacobson (DENMARK) 3m 07.1s
1936 Hideko Maehata (JAPAN) 3m 03.6s[4]	Martha Genenger (GERMANY) 3m 04.2s	Inge Sörensen (DENMARK) 3m 07.8s
1948 Petronella van Vliet (NETHS.) 2m 57.2s[5]	Beatrice Lyons (AUSTRALIA)2m 57.7s	Eva Novák (HUNGARY) 3m 00.2s
1952 Eva Székely (HUNGARY) 2m 51.7s*	Eva Novák (HUNGARY) 2m 54.4s	Helen Gordon (G.B.) 2m 57.6s
1956 Ursula Happe (GERMANY) 2m 53.1s[6]	Eva Székely (HUNGARY) 2m 54.8s	Eva-Maria ten Elsen (GERMANY) 2m 55.1s

---

[1] Set O.R. of 3m 27.6s in preliminaries.
[2] Set O.R. of 3m 11.2s in preliminaries.
[3] Set O.R. of 3m 08.2s in preliminaries.
[4] Set O.R. of 3m 01.9s in preliminaries.
[5] Set O.R. of 2m 57.0s in preliminaries.

	GOLD	SILVER	BRONZE
1960	Anita Lonsbrough (G.B.) 2m 49.5s*	Wiltrud Urselmann (GERMANY) 2m 50.0s	Barbara Göbel (GERMANY) 2m 53.6s
1964	Galina Prozumenshchikova (U.S.S.R.) 2m 46.4s*	Claudia Kolb (U.S.) 2m 47.6s	Svetlana Babanena (U.S.S.R.) 2m 48.6s[7]
1968	Sharon Wichman (U.S.) 2m 44.4s*	Djurdjica Bjedov (YUGOSLAVIA) 2m 46.4s	Galina Prozumenshikova (U.S.S.R.) 2m 47.0s
1972			

---

[6] Recognized as new O.R. when butterfly was established as separate event. Previous fastest time using orthodox breast-stroke was 2m 54.0s by Novák in preliminaries in 1952.
[7] Set O.R. of 2m 48.3s in preliminaries.

Aagje (Ada) Kok (Netherlands) won the 200 metres butterfly in 1968 in record Olympic time, but did not break the world record she held in this event.

100 METRES BUTTERFLY (109 yds. 1 ft.)

	GOLD	SILVER	BRONZE
06–1952	Event not held		
56	Shelley Mann (U.S.) 1m 11.0s*	Nancy Jane Ramey (U.S.) 1m 11.9s	Mary Jane Sears (U.S.) 1m 14.4s
60	Carolyn Schuler (U.S.) 1m 09.5s*	Marian Heemskerk (NETHS.) 1m 10.4s	Janice Andrew (AUSTRALIA)1m12.2s

	GOLD	SILVER	BRONZE
1964	Sharon Stouder (U.S.) 1m 04.7s*	Aagje Kok (NETHS.) 1m 05.6s	Kathleen Ellis (U.S.) 1m 06.0s[1]
1968	Lynette McClements (AUSTRALIA) 1m 05.5s	Ellie Daniel (U.S.) 1m 05.8s	Susie Shields (U.S.) 1m 06.2s
1972			

_____

[1] Set O.R. of 1m 07.8s in preliminaries.

200 METRES BUTTERFLY (218 yds. 2 ft.)

1896–1964	Event not held		
1968	Aagje Kok (NETHS.) 2m 24.7s*	Helga Lindner (E. GERMANY) 2m 24.8s	Ellie Daniel (U.S.) 2m 25.9s
1972			

100 METRES BACK STROKE (109 yds. 1 ft.)

1896–1920	Event not held		
1924	Sybil Bauer (U.S.) 1m 23.2s*	Phyllis Harding (G.B.) 1m 27.4s	Aileen Riggin (U.S.) 1m 28.2s
1928	Marie Braun (NETHS.) 1m 22.0s[1]	Elizabeth King (G.B.) 1m 22.2s	Margaret Cooper (G.B.) 1m 22.8s
1932	Eleanor Holm (U.S.) 1m 19.4s[2]	Philomena Mealing (AUSTRALIA) 1m 21.3s	Elizabeth Davies (G.B.) 1m 22.5s
1936	Dina Senff (NETHS.) 1m 18.9s[3]	Hendrika Mastenbroek (NETHS.) 1m 19.2s	Alice Bridges (U.S.) 1m 19.4s
1948	Karen Harup (DENMARK) 1m 14.4s*	Suzanne Zimmermann (U.S.) 1m 16.0s	Judy Joy Davies (AUSTRALIA)1m16.7s
1952	Joan Harrison (S. AFRICA) 1m 14.3s*	Geertje Wielema (NETHS.) 1m 14.5s[4]	Jean Stewart (N.Z.) 1m 15.8s
1956	Judy Grinham (G.B.) 1m 12.9s*	Carin Cone (U.S.) 1m 12.9s	Margaret Edwards (G.B.) 1m 13.1s
1960	Lynn Burke (U.S.) 1m 09.3s[5]	Natalie Steward (G.B.) 1m 10.8s	Satoko Tanaká (JAPAN) 1m 11.4s
1964	Cathy Ferguson (U.S.) 1m 07.7s*	Christine Caron (FRANCE) 1m 07.9s[6]	Virginia Duenkel (U.S.) 1m 08.0s[7]
1968	Kaye Hall (U.S.) 1m 06.2s*	Elaine Tanner (CANADA) 1m 06.7s[8]	Jane Swagerty (U.S.) 1m 08.1s
1972			

_____

[1] Set O.R. of 1m 21.6s in preliminaries.
[2] Set O.R. of 1m 18.3s in preliminaries.
[3] Set O.R. of 1m 16.6s in preliminaries.
[4] Set O.R. of 1m 13.8s in preliminaries.
[5] Set O.R. of 1m 09.0s in 4 × 100 metres medley relay final.
[6] Set O.R. of 1m 08.5s in preliminaries.
[7] Set O.R. of 1m 08.9s in preliminaries.
[8] Set O.R. of 1m 07.6s and 1m 07.4s in preliminaries.

200 METRES BACK STROKE (218 yds. 2 ft.)

1896–1964	Event not held		
1968	Pokey Watson (U.S.) 2m 24.8s*	Elaine Tanner (CANADA) 2m 27.4s	Kaye Hall (U.S.) 2m 28.9s
1972			

200 METRES INDIVIDUAL MEDLEY (218 yds. 2 ft.)

	GOLD	SILVER	BRONZE
1896–1964	Event not held		
1968	Claudia Kolb (U.S.) 2m 24.7s*	Susan Pedersen (U.S.) 2m 28.8s	Jan Henne (U.S.) 2m 31.4s
1972			

400 METRES INDIVIDUAL MEDLEY

	GOLD	SILVER	BRONZE
1896–1960	Event not held		
1964	Donna de Varona (U.S.) 5m 18.7s*	Sharon Finneran (U.S.) 5m 24.1s	Martha Randall (U.S.) 5m 24.2s[1]
1968	Claudia Kolb (U.S.) 5m 08.5s*[2]	Lynn Vidali (U.S.) 5m 22.2s	Sabine Steinbach (E. GERMANY) 5m 25.3s
1972			

---

[1] Set O.R. of 5m 27.8s in preliminaries.
[2] Set O.R. of 5m 17.2s in preliminaries.

4 × 100 METRES FREE-STYLE RELAY

	GOLD	SILVER	BRONZE
1896–1908	Event not held		
1912	G.B. 5m 52.8s* Bella Moore Irene Steer Annie Speirs Jennie Fletcher	GERMANY 6m 04.6s Hermine Stindt Louise Otto Wally Dressel Grete Rosenberg	AUSTRIA 6m 17.0s Margarete Adler Klara Milch Berta Zahonrek Josephine Sticker
1920	U.S. 5m 11.6s* Ethelda Bleibtrey Frances Schroth Irene Guest Margaret Woodbridge	G.B. 5m 40.8s C. Radcliffe Hilda James G. McKenzie Constance Jeans	SWEDEN 5m 43.6s Emy Machnow Aina Berg Jane Gylling Karin Nilsson
1924	U.S. 4m 58.8s* Gertrude Ederle Mariechen Wehselau Ethel Lackie Euphrasia Donelly	G.B. 5m 17.0s G. McKenzie Constance Jeans Florence Barker Iris Tanner	SWEDEN 5m 35.8s Aina Berg Gulli Everlund Vivian Pettersson Hjördis Topel
1928	U.S. 4m 47.6s* Adelaide Lambert Albina Osipowich Eleonora Garatti Martha Norelius	G.B. 5m 02.8s Margaret Cooper S. Stewart Iris Tanner Elizabeth King	S. AFRICA 5m 13.4s Katharine Russel R. Rennie M. Bedford F. van der Goes
1932	U.S. 4m 38.0s* Josephine McKim Eleonora Saville[1] Helen Johns Helene Madison	NEHTS. 4m 46.5s Maria Vierdag Cornelia Ladde Maria Oversloot Willemijntje den Ouden	G.B. 4m 52.4s Elizabeth Davies Margaret Cooper Helen Varcoe Edna Hughes
1936	NETHS. 4m 36.0s* Johanna Selbach Catherina Wagner Willemijnte den Ouden Hendrika Mastenbroek	GERMANY 4m 36.8s Ruth Halbsgut Leni Lohmar Ingeborg Schmitz Gisela Arendt	U.S. 4m 40.2s Katherine Rawls Berenice Lapp Mavis Freeman Olive McKean
1948	U.S. 4m 29.2s* Marie Corridon Thelma Kalama Brenda Helser Ann Curtis	DENMARK 4m 29.6s Eva Riise Karen Harup Greta Andersen Fritzie Carstensen	NETHS. 4m 31.6s Irma Schuhmacher Margot Marsman Marie-Louise Vaessen Johanna Termeulen
1952	HUNGARY 4m 24.4s* Ilona Novák Judit Temes Eva Novák Katalin Szöke	NETHS. 4m 29.0s Marie-Louise Linssen[2] Koosje van Voorn Johanna Termeulen Irma Heyting[3]	U.S. 4m 30.1s Jacqueline Lavine Marilee Stepan Joan Alderson Evelyn Kawamoto

	GOLD	SILVER	BRONZE
1956	AUSTRALIA 4m 17.1s*	U.S. 4m 19.2s	S. AFRICA 4m 25.7s
	Dawn Fraser	Sylvia Ruuska	Natalie Myburgh
	Faith Leech	Shelley Mann	Susan Roberts
	Sandra Morgan	Nancy Simons	Moira Abernethy
	Lorraine Crapp	Joan Rosazza	Jeanette Myburgh
1960	U.S. 4m 08.9s*	AUSTRALIA 4m 11.3s	GERMANY 4m 19.7s
	Joan Spillane	Dawn Fraser	Christel Steffin
	Shirley Stobs	Ilsa Konrads	Heidi Pechstein
	Carolyn Wood	Lorraine Crapp	Gisella Weiss
	Christine von Saltza	Alva Colquhoun	Ursel Brunner
1964	U.S. 4m 03.8s*	AUSTRALIA 4m 06.9s	NETHS. 4m 12.0s
	Cathy Ferguson	Robyn Thorn	Paulina van der Wildt
	Cynthia Goyette	Janice Murphy	Catharina Beumer
	Sharon Stouder	Lynette Bell	W. Van Weerdenburg
	Kathleen Ellis	Dawn Fraser	Erica Terpstra
1968	U.S. 4m 02.5s*	E. GERMANY 4m 05.7s	CANADA 4m 07.2s
	Jane Barkman	Gabriele Wetzko	Angela Coughlan
	Linda Gustavson	Roswitha Krause	Marilyn Corson
	Susan Pedersen	Uta Schmuck	Elaine Tanner
	Jan Henne	Gabriele Perthes	Marion Lay
1972			

---

[1] Formerly Garatti.
[2] Formerly Vaessen.

4 × 100 METRES MEDLEY RELAY

1896–1956	Event not held		
1960[1]	U.S. 4m 41.1s*	AUSTRALIA 4m 45.9s	GERMANY 4m 47.6s
	Lynn Burke	Marilyn Wilson	Ingrid Schmidt
	Patty Kempner	Rosemary Lassig	Ursula Küper
	Carolyn Schuler	Janice Andrew	Barbara Fuhrmann
	Christine von Saltza	Dawn Fraser	Ursel Brunner
1964	U.S. 4m 33.9s*	NETHS. 4m 37.0s	U.S.S.R. 4m 39.2s[2]
	Sharon Stouder	Kornelia Winkel	Tatiana Savelieva
	Donna de Varona	Klena Bimolt	Svetlana Babanina
	Lilian Watson	Ada Kok	Tatiana Deviatova
	Kathleen Ellis	Erica Terpstra	Natalya Ustinova
1968	U.S. 4m 28.3s*	AUSTRALIA 4m 30.0s	GERMANY 4m 36.4s
	Kaye Hall	Lynette Watson	Regina Kraus
	Catie Ball	Lynette McClements	Uta Frommater
	Ellie Daniel	Judy Playfair	Heike Hustede
	Susan Pedersen	Janet Steinbeck	Heidi Reineck
1972			

---

[1] Order of strokes: back-stroke; breast stroke; butterfly; free-style.
[2] Set O.R. of 4m 39.1s in preliminaries.

PLATFORM DIVING

1896–1908	Event not held		
1912	Greta Johansson	Lisa Regnell	Isabelle White
	(SWEDEN) 39.9 pts.	(SWEDEN) 36	(G.B.) 34
1920	Stefani Fryland-Clausen	E. Armstrong	Eva Ollivier
	(DENMARK) 34.6 pts.	(G.B.) 33.3	(SWEDEN) 32.6
1924	Caroline Smith	Elizabeth Becker	Hjördis Topel
	(U.S.) 10.5, 166 pts.[1]	(U.S.) 11, 167	(SWEDEN) 15.5, 164

Milena Duchkova, the little Czech highboard diver, won her gold medal in 1968 with remarkable ease and with the full sympathy of the crowd in view of the then recent invasion of her country by the U.S.S.R.

	GOLD	SILVER	BRONZE
1928	Elizabeth Pinkston (U.S.) 31.6 pts.	Georgia Coleman (U.S.) 30.6	Lala Sjöquist (SWEDEN) 29.2
1932	Dorothy Poynton (U.S.) 40.26 pts.	Georgia Coleman (U.S.) 35.56	Marion Roper (U.S.) 35.22
1936	Dorothy Hill[2] (U.S.) 33.93 pts.	Velma Dunn (U.S.) 33.63	Käthe Köhler (GERMANY) 33.43
1948	Victoria Draves (U.S.) 68.87 pts.	Patricia Elsener (U.S.) 66.28	Birte Christoffersen (DENMARK) 66.04
1952	Patricia McCormick (U.S.) 79.37 pts.	Paula Jean Myers (U.S.) 71.63	Juno Irwin (U.S.) 70.49
1956	Patricia McCormick (U.S.) 84.85 pts.[3]	Juno Irwin[4] (U.S.) 81.64	Paula Jean Myers (U.S.) 81.58
1960	Ingrid Krämer (GERMANY) 91.28 pts.	Paula Jean Pope[5] (U.S.) 88.94	Ninel Krutova (U.S.S.R.) 86.99
1964	Lesley Bush (U.S.) 99.80 pts.	Ingrid Engel (GERMANY) 98.45	Galina Alekseyeva (U.S.S.R.) 97.60
1968	Milena Duchkova (CZECHO.) 109.59 pts.	Natalia Lobanova (U.S.S.R.) 105.14	Ann Peterson (U.S.) 101.11
1972			

---

[1] Figure before comma refers to place number.
[2] Formerly Poynton.
[3] This was Mrs. McCormick's fourth gold medal—a record in Olympic diving. Her husband, Glen, was chief coach to the U.S. swimming and diving team in the 1956 Games.
[4] A mother of three children, she was also 5th in 1948 and 4th in 1960.
[5] Formerly Myers.

SPRINGBOARD DIVING

	GOLD	SILVER	BRONZE
1896–1912	Event not held		
1920	Aileen Riggin (U.S.) 539.9 pts.	Helen Wainwright (U.S.) 534.8	Thelma Payne (U.S.) 534.1
1924	Elizabeth Becker (U.S.) 474.5 pts.	Aileen Riggin (U.S.) 460.4	Caroline Fletcher (U.S.) 434.4
1928	Helen Meany (U.S.) 78.62 pts.	Dorothy Poynton (U.S.) 75.62	Georgia Coleman (U.S.) 73.38
1932	Georgia Coleman (U.S.) 87.52 pts.	Katherine Rawls (U.S.) 82.56	Jane Fauntz (U.S.) 81.12
1936	Marjorie Gestring[1] (U.S.) 89.27 pts.	Katherine Rawls (U.S.) 88.35	Dorothy Hill[2] (U.S.) 82.36
1948	Victoria Draves (U.S.) 108.74 pts.	Zoe Ann Olsen (U.S.) 108.23	Patricia Elsener (U.S.) 101.30
1952	Patricia McCormick (U.S.) 147.30 pts.	Madeleine Moreau (FRANCE) 139.34	Zoe Ann Jensen[3] (U.S.) 127.57
1956	Patricia McCormick (U.S.) 142.36 pts.[4]	Jeanne Stunyo (U.S.) 125.89	Irene Macdonald (CANADA) 121.40
1960	Ingrid Krämer (GERMANY)155.81pts.	Paula Jean Pope (U.S.) 141.24	Elizabeth Ferris (G.B.) 139.09
1964	Ingrid Engel (GERMANY)145.00pts.	Jeanne Collier (U.S.) 138.36	Patsy Willard (U.S.) 138.18
1968	Sue Gossick (U.S.) 150.77 pts.	Tamara Pogozheva (U.S.S.R.) 145.30	Keala O'Sullivan (U.S.) 145.23
1972			

[1] Aged 13 at the time of her victory.
[2] Formerly Poynton.
[3] Formerly Olsen.
[4] Greatest winning margin in Olympic diving history.

(Left) Marjorie Gestring (U.S.), aged 13, the youngest-ever individual winner of an Olympic gold medal, in 1936 in Berlin. (Right) Mrs. Pat McCormick (U.S.) won first place in 1952 and 1956 in both platform and springboard diving, and her total of 4 gold medals is a record for any diver.

Jim Hines (U.S.) wins the 1968 Olympic 100 metres in the world record time of 9.9 seconds. High altitude helped sprinters because of reduced air resistance.

17a. Track and Field Athletics (Men)

100 METRES (109 yds. 1 ft.)

	GOLD	SILVER	BRONZE
1896	Thomas Burke[1] (U.S.) 12.0s	Fritz Hofmann (GERMANY) d.n.a.	Alajos Szokolyi (HUNGARY) d.n.a.
1900	Frank Jarvis[2] (U.S.) 11.0s	J. Walter Tewksbury[2] (U.S.) 1 ft.	Stanley Rowley (AUSTRALIA) inches
1904[3]	Archie Hahn (U.S.) 11.0s	Nathan Cartmell (U.S.) d.n.a.	William Hogensen (U.S.) d.n.a.
1908	Reginald Walker[4] (S. AFRICA) 10.8s*	James Rector[4] (U.S.) 2 ft.	Robert Kerr (CANADA) inches
1912	Ralph Craig (U.S.) 10.8s	Alvah Meyer (U.S.) 10.9s	Donald Lippincott[5] (U.S.) 10.9s
1920	Charles Paddock (U.S.) 10.8s	Morris Kirksey (U.S.) 1 ft.	Harry Edward (G.B.) d.n.a.
1924	Harold Abrahams[6] (G.B.) 10.6s*[7]	Jackson Scholz (U.S.) 2 ft.	Arthur Porritt (N.Z.) d.n.a.
1928	Percy Williams[8] (CANADA) 10.8s	Jack London[8] (G.B.) 2 ft.	Georg Lammers (GERMANY) inches
1932	Eddie Tolan[9] (U.S.) 10.3s*	Ralph Metcalfe (U.S.) 10.3s	Arthur Jonath (GERMANY) 10.4s
1936	Jesse Owens[10] (U.S.) 10.3s[11]	Ralph Metcalfe (U.S.) 10.4s	Martinus Osendarp (NETHS.) 10.5s

[1] Set O.R. of 11.8s in preliminaries.
[2] Set O.R. of 10.8s in preliminaries.
[3] 14 of the 15 competitors in this event were from U.S.
[4] Equalled O.R. of 10.8s in preliminaries.
[5] Set O.R. of 10.6s in preliminaries.
[6] Equalled O.R. of 10.6s in preliminaries.
[7] Electrical timing showed 10.52s.
[8] Equalled O.R. of 10.6s in preliminaries as also did Robert McAllister (U.S.)
[9] Set O.R. of 10.4s in preliminaries.
[10] Clocked 10.2s with wind assistance in preliminaries.
[11] Final was wind assisted, but equalled O.R. of 10.3s in preliminaries.

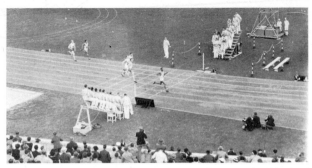

Jesse Owens (U.S.) setting an Olympic record in the 200 metre dash in 1936 in Berlin where he tied the record of 4 track and field gold medals in one celebration.

	GOLD	SILVER	BRONZE
1948	W. Harrison Dillard (U.S.) 10.3s*	H. Norwood Ewell (U.S.) 10.4s	Lloyd La Beach (PANAMA) 10.4s
1952	Lindy Remigino (U.S.) 10.4s	Herbert McKenley (JAMAICA) 10.4s	Emmanuel McDonald Bailey (G.B.) 10.4s
1956	Bobby-Joe Morrow[12] (U.S.) 10.5s[13]	W. Thane Baker (U.S.) 10.5s	Hector Hogan (AUSTRALIA) 10.6s
1960	Armin Hary[14] (GERMANY) 10.2s*	David Sime (U.S.) 10.2s*	Peter Radford (G.B.) 10.3s
1964	Robert Hayes (U.S.) 10.0s*	Enrique Figuerola (CUBA) 10.2s	Harold Jerome (CANADA) 10.2s
1968	James Hines (U.S.) 9.9s*	Lennox Miller (JAMAICA) 10.0s	Charles Greene (U.S.) 10.0s
1972			

[12] Equalled O.R. of 10.3s in preliminaries as also did Ira Murchison (U.S.)
[13] Run against a very strong wind.
[14] Set O.R. of 10.2s in preliminaries.

200 METRES (218 yds. 2 ft.)

1896	Event not held		
1900	J. Walter Tewksbury (U.S.) 22.2s*	Norman Pritchard (INDIA) 5 yds.	Stanley Rowley (AUSTRALIA) 1 yd.
1904	Archie Hahn (U.S.) 21.6s*[1]	Nathan Cartmell (U.S.) 2 yds.	William Hogensen (U.S.) d.n.a.
1908	Robert Kerr (CANADA) 22.6s	Robert Cloughen (U.S.) 1 ft.	Nathan Cartmell (U.S.) 1 ft.
1912	Ralph Craig (U.S.) 21.7s	Donald Lippincott (U.S.) 21.8s	William Applegarth (G.B.) 22.0s
1920	Allen Woodring (U.S.) 22.0s	Charles Paddock (U.S.) d.n.a.	Harry Edward (G.B.) d.n.a.
1924	Jackson Scholz (U.S.) 21.6s*	Charles Paddock (U.S.) ½ yd.	Eric Liddell (G.B.) 1½ yds.
1928	Percy Williams (CANADA) 21.8s	Walter Rangeley (G.B.) 2 ft.	Helmut Körnig[2] (GERMANY) 1 ft.
1932	Eddie Tolan[3] (U.S.) 21.2s*	George Simpson (U.S.) 21.4s	Ralph Metcalfe[3] (U.S.) 21.5s
1936	Jesse Owens[4] (U.S.) 20.7s*	Mack Robinson[4] (U.S.) 21.1s	Martinus Osendarp (NETHS.) 21.3s
1948	Melvin Patton (U.S.) 21.1s	H. Norwood Ewell (U.S.) 21.1s	Lloyd La Beach (PANAMA) 21.2s
1952	Andy Stanfield (U.S.) 20.7s*	W. Thane Baker (U.S.) 20.8s	James Gathers (U.S.) 20.8s
1956	Bobby Morrow (U.S.) 20.6s*	Andy Stanfield (U.S.) 20.7s	W. Thane Baker (U.S.) 20.9s

	GOLD	SILVER	BRONZE
1960	Livio Berutti[5] (ITALY) 20.5s*	Lester Carney (U.S.) 20.6s	Abdoulaye Seye (FRANCE) 20.7s
1964	Henry Carr (U.S.) 20.3s*	Paul Drayton (U.S.) 20.5s	Edwin Roberts (TRINIDAD) 20.6s
1968	Tommie Smith (U.S.) 19.8s*	Peter Norman (AUSTRALIA) 20.0s	John Carlos (U.S.) 20.0s
1972			

---

[1] Race run over straight course.
[2] Equalled O.R. of 21.6s in preliminaries.
[3] Set O.R. of 21.5s in preliminaries, but 21.4s (O.R.) clocked later by Carlos Luti (ARGENTINA) and Arthur Jonath (GERMANY).
[4] Set O.R. of 21.1s in preliminaries.
[5] Set O.R. of 20.5s in preliminaries.

400 METRES (437 yds. 1 ft.)

1896	Thomas Burke (U.S.) 54.2s*	Herbert Jameson (U.S.) 55.2s	Fritz Hofmann (GERMANY) 55.6s
1900[1]	Maxwell Long[2] (U.S.) 49.4s*	William Holland (U.S.) 1 yd.	Ernst Schultz (DENMARK) 15 yds.
1904[3]	Harry Hillman (U.S.) 49.2s*	Frank Waller (U.S.) 5 yds.	H. C. Groman (U.S.) 1 yd.
1908	Wyndham Halswell[4] (G.B.) 50.0s	No other competitors[5]	
1912	Charles Reidpath (U.S.) 48.2s*	Hanns Braun (GERMANY) 48.3s	Edward Lindberg (U.S.) 48.4s
1920	Bevil Rudd (S. AFRICA) 49.6s	Guy Butler (G.B.) d.n.a.	Nils Engdahl (SWEDEN) d.n.a.
1924	Eric Liddell (G.B.) 47.6s*	Horatio Fitch[6] (U.S.) 48.4s	Guy Butler (G.B.) 48.6s
1928	Raymond Barbuti (U.S.) 47.8s	James Ball (CANADA) 48.0s	Joachim Büchner (GERMANY) 48.2s

Ray Barbuti (U.S.) winner of the 400 metre dash in 1928, is shown here as anchor man of the relay team that won the gold medal in the 4 × 400 metres in 1928.

	GOLD	SILVER	BRONZE
1932	William Carr[7] (U.S.) 46.2s*	Benjamin Eastman (U.S.) 46.4s	Alex Wilson (CANADA) 47.4s
1936	Archie Williams (U.S.) 46.5s	A. Godfrey Brown (G.B.) 46.7s	James LuValle (U.S.) 46.8s
1948	Arthur Wint (JAMAICA) 46.2s*	Herbert McKenley (JAMAICA) 46.4s	Malvin Whitfield (U.S.) 46.6s
1952	George Rhoden (JAMAICA) 45.9s*	Herbert McKenley (JAMAICA) 45.9s*	Ollie Matson (U.S.) 46.8s
1956	Charles Jenkins (U.S.) 46.7s	Karl-Friedrich Haas (GERMANY) 46.8s	Voitto Hellsten[8] (FINLAND) 47.0s Ardalion Ignatyev (U.S.S.R.) 47.0s
1960	Otis Davis[9] (U.S.) 44.9s*	Carl Kaufmann (GERMANY) 44.9s*	Malcolm Spence (S. AFRICA) 45.5s
1964	Michael Larrabee (U.S.) 45.1s	Wendell Mottley (TRINIDAD) 45.2s	Andrzej Badenski (POLAND) 45.6s
1968	Lee Evans (U.S.) 43.8s*	Larry James (U.S.) 43.9s	Ronald Freeman (U.S.) 44.4s
1972			

[1] Final held on Sunday causing withdrawal of other three finalists—all Americans.
[2] Set O.R. of 50.4s in preliminaries.
[3] No preliminaries. Held as a final with 13 competitors.
[4] Set O.R. of 48.4s in preliminaries.
[5] Re-run ordered after J. C. Carpenter (U.S.) disqualified in original final. Only Halswell showed up and "walked over" for the title.
[6] Set O.R. of 47.8s in preliminaries bettering mark of 48.0s by Josef Imbach (SWITZERLAND) also made in preliminaries.
[7] Set O.R. of 47.2s in preliminaries.
[8] Only dead-heat for medal in Olympic track history.
[9] Set O.R. of 45.5s in preliminaries.

800 METRES (874 yds. 2 ft.)

	GOLD	SILVER	BRONZE
1896	Edwin Flack[1] (AUSTRALIA) 2m 11.0s	Nandor Dani (HUNGARY) 2m 11.8s	Demetrius Golemis (GREECE) d.n.a.
1900	Alfred Tysoe (G.B.) 2m 01.2s	John Cregan (U.S.) 1 yd.	David Hall[2] (U.S.) d.n.a.
1904	James Lightbody (U.S.) 1m 56.0s*	Howard Valentine (U.S.) 2 yds.	Emil Breitkreutz (U.S.) d.n.a.
1908	Melvin Sheppard (U.S.) 1m 52.8s*	Emilio Lunghi (ITALY) 1m 54.2s	Hanns Braun (GERMANY) 1m 55.4s
1912	James Meredith[3] (U.S.) 1m 51.9s*	Melvin Sheppard (U.S.) 1m 52.0s	Ira Davenport (U.S.) 1m 52.0s
1920	Albert Hill (G.B.) 1m 53.4s	Earl Eby (U.S.) 1 yd.	Bevil Rudd (S. AFRICA) d.n.a.
1924	Douglas Lowe (G.B.) 1m 52.4s	Paul Martin (SWITZ.) 1m 52.6s	Schuyler Enck (U.S.) 1m 53.0s
1928	Douglas Lowe (G.B.) 1m 51.8s*	Erik Byhlen (SWEDEN) 1m 52.8s	Hermann Engelhardt (GERMANY) 1m 53.2s
1932	Thomas Hampson (G.B.) 1m 49.7s*[4]	Alex Wilson (CANADA) 1m 49.9s[4]	Philip Edwards (CANADA) 1m 51.5s
1936	John Woodruff (U.S.) 1m 52.9s[5]	Mario Lanzi (ITALY) 1m 53.3s	Philip Edwards (CANADA) 1m 53.6s
1948	Malvin Whitfield (U.S.) 1m 49.2s*	Arthur Wint (JAMAICA) 1m 49.5s	Marcel Hansenne (FRANCE) 1m 49.8s
1952	Malvin Whitfield (U.S.) 1m 49.2s*	Arthur Wint (JAMAICA) 1m 49.4s	Heinz Ulzheimer (GERMANY) 1m 49.7s
1956	Thomas Courtney (U.S.) 1m 47.7s*	Derek Johnson (G.B.) 1m 47.8s	Audun Boysen (NORWAY) 1m 48.1s

[1] Set O.R. of 2m 10.0s in preliminaries.
[2] Set O.R. of 1m 59.0s in preliminaries.
[3] Carried on to break another tape at 880 yds. in 1m 52.5s for a double world record.
[4] According to the rules then in force times were rounded up to the nearest fifth of a second.
[5] Run in bad weather conditions.

Peter Snell (New Zealand), gold medal winner in the 1960 and 1964 Olympic Games, also set two world records for the fastest mile run.

Mel Sheppard (U.S.), winner in 1908 of the 800 metres run, is shown here in London, winning his second gold medal in the 1,500 metres event. Harold Wilson (G.B.) finished 2 seconds behind.

	GOLD	SILVER	BRONZE
1960	Peter Snell (N.Z.) 1m 46.3s*	Roger Moens (BELGIUM) 1m 46.5s	George Kerr[6] (JAMAICA) 1m 47.1s
1964	Peter Snell (N.Z.) 1m 45.1s*	William Crothers (CANADA) 1m 45.6s	Wilson Kiprugut[7] (KENYA) 1m 45.9s
1968	Ralph Doubell (AUSTRAL) 1m 44.3s*	Wilson Kiprugut (KENYA) 1m 44.5s	Thomas Farrell (U.S.) 1m 45.4s
1972			

[6] Set O.R. of 1m 47.1s in preliminaries.
[7] Set O.R. of 1m 46.1s in semi-final with George Kerr (JAMAICA) winning in the same time.

(Above) Abebe Bikila (Ethiopia), in the 1964 Games became the only runner in history to retain the Marathon championship he had won in the previous Olympics.

(Above) Kip Keino winning the 1500 metres by the remarkable margin of nearly 20 yards at Mexico City, 1968. Coming from a Kenyan people who have lived for generations at high altitude, he had a genetic advantage over lowlanders.

1500 METRES (1,640 yds. 1 ft.)

1896	Edwin Flack (AUSTRALIA) 4m 33.2s*	Arthur Blake (U.S.) 5 yds.	Albin Lermusiaux (FRANCE) 15 yds.
1900	Charles Bennett (G.B.) 4m 06.2s*	Henri Deloge (FRANCE) 2 yds.	John Bray (U.S.) d.n.a.
1904	James Lightbody (U.S.) 4m 05.4s*	Frank Verner (U.S.) d.n.a.	L. E. Hearn (U.S.) d.n.a.
1908	Melvin Sheppard (U.S.) 4m 03.4s*	Harold Wilson (G.B.) 4m 03.6s	Norman Hallows[1] (G.B.) 4m 04.0s
1912	Arnold Jackson (G.B.) 3m 56.8s*	Abel Kiviat (U.S.) 3m 56.9s	Norman Taber (U.S.) 3m 56.9s
1920	Albert Hill (G.B.) 4m 01.8s	Philip Baker (G.B.) 4m 02.4s	Lawrence Shields (U.S.) d.n.a.
1924	Paavo Nurmi (FINLAND) 3m 53.6s*	Willy Scherrer (SWITZ.) 3m 55.0s	Henry Stallard (G.B.) 3m 55.6s

	GOLD	SILVER	BRONZE
1928	Harri Larva	Jules Ladoumegue	Eino Purje
	(FINLAND) 3m 53.2s*	(FRANCE) 3m 53.8s	(FINLAND) 3m 56.4s
1932	Luigi Beccali	John Cornes	Philip Edwards
	(ITALY) 3m 51.2s*	(G.B.) 3m 52.6s	(CANADA) 3m 52.8s
1936	John Lovelock	Glenn Cunningham	Luigi Beccali
	(N.Z.) 3m 47.8s*	(U.S.) 3m 48.4s	(ITALY) 3m 49.2s
1948	Henry Eriksson	Lennart Strand	Willem Slykhuis
	(SWEDEN) 3m 49.8s	(SWEDEN) 3m 50.4s	(NETHS.) 3m 50.4s
1952	Josef Barthel	Robert McMillen	Werner Lueg
	(LUXEMBURG) 3m 45.1s*[2]	(U.S.) 3m 45.2s	(GERMANY) 3m 45.4s
1956	Ron Delany	Klaus Richtzenhain	John Landy
	(EIRE) 3m 41.2s*	(GERMANY) 3m 42.0s	(AUSTRALIA)3m42.0s
1960	Herbert Elliott	Michel Jazy	István Rozsavölgyi
	(AUSTRALIA) 3m 35.6s*	(FRANCE) 3m 38.4s	(HUNGARY) 3m 39.2s
1964	Peter Snell	Josef Odlozil	John Davies
	(N.Z.) 3m 38.1s	(CZECHO.) 3m 39.6s	(N.Z.) 3m 39.6s
1968	Kipchoge Keino	James Ryun	Bodo Tümmler
	(KENYA) 3m 34.9s*	(U.S.) 3m 37.8s	(W. GERMANY) 3m 39.0s
1972			

---

[1] Set O.R. of 4m 03.4s in preliminaries.
[2] According to rules then in force official time was rounded up to nearest fifth of a second.

5000 METRES (3 miles 188 yds.)

	GOLD	SILVER	BRONZE
1896–1908	Event not held		
1912	Hannes Kolehmainen	Jean Bouin	George Hutson
	(FINLAND) 14m 36.6s*	(FRANCE) 14m 36.7s	(G.B.) 15m 07.6s
1920	Joseph Guillemot	Paavo Nurmi	Eric Backman
	(FRANCE) 14m 55.6s	(FINLAND) 15m 00.0s	(SWEDEN) 15m 13.0s
1924	Paavo Nurmi[1]	Ville Ritola	Edvin Wide
	(FINLAND) 14m 31.2s*	(FINLAND) 14m 31.4s	(SWEDEN) 15m 01.8s
1928	Ville Ritola	Paavo Nurmi	Edvin Wide
	(FINLAND) 14m 38.0s	(FINLAND) 14m 40.0s	(SWEDEN) 14m 41.2s
1932	Lauri Lehtinen	Ralph Hill	Lauri Virtanen
	(FINLAND) 14m 30.0s*	(U.S.)14m 30.0s	(FINLAND) 14m 44.0s
1936	Gunnar Höckert	Lauri Lehtinen	Henry Jonsson
	(FINLAND) 14m 22.2s*	(FINLAND) 14m 25.8s	(SWEDEN) 14m 29.0s
1948	Gaston Reiff	Emil Zatopek	Willem Slykhuis
	(BELGIUM) 14m 17.6s*	(CZECHO.) 14m 17.8s	(NETHS.) 14m 26.8s
1952	Emil Zatopek	Alain Mimoun	Herbert Schade
	(CZECHO.) 14m 06.6s*	(FRANCE) 14m 07.4s	(GERMANY)14m08.6s
1956	Vladimir Kuts	D. A. Gordon Pirie	G. Derek Ibbotson
	(U.S.S.R.) 13m 39.6s*	(G.B.) 13m 50.6s	(G.B.) 13m 54.4s
1960	Murray Halberg	Hans Grodotzki	Kazimierz Zimny
	(N.Z.) 13m 43.4s	(GERMANY) 13m 44.6s	(POLAND) 13m 44.8s
1964	Robert Schul	Harold Norpoth	William Dellinger
	(U.S.) 13m 48.8s	(GERMANY) 13m 49.6s	(U.S.) 13m 49.8s
1968	Mohamed Gammoudi	Kipchoge Keino	Naftali Temu
	(TUNISIA) 14m 05.0s	(KENYA) 14m 05.2s	(KENYA) 14m 6.4s
1972			

Had won the 1500m gold medal only 1¼ hours before.

10,000 METRES (6 miles 376 yds.)

	GOLD	SILVER	BRONZE
1896–1904	Event not held		
1908[1]	Emil Voight	Edward Owen	John Svanberg
	(G.B.) 25m 11.2s	(G.B.) 25m 24.0s	(SWEDEN) 25m 37.2s
1912	Hannes Kolemainen	Lewis Tewanima	Albin Stenroos
	(FINLAND) 31m 20.8s*	(U.S.) 32m 06.6s	(FINLAND) 32m 21.8s

Dorando Pietri (Italy) in 1908 collapsed several times from exhaustion on the last lap of the marathon, but crossed the line first. Later, he was rightly, but sadly, disqualified for receiving assistance, and the gold medal went to John Hayes (see page 15). Pietri, however, received a special gold cup from Queen Alexandra as a consolation prize.

	GOLD	SILVER	BRONZE
1920	Paavo Nurmi (FINLAND) 31m 45.8s	Joseph Guillemot (FRANCE) 31m 47.2s	James Wilson (G.B.) 31m 50.8s
1924[2]	Ville Ritola (FINLAND) 30m 23.2s*	Edvin Wide (SWEDEN) 30m 55.2s	Eero Berg (FINLAND) 31m 43.0s
1928	Paavo Nurmi (FINLAND) 30m 18.8s*	Ville Ritola (FINLAND) 30m 19.4s	Edvin Wide (SWEDEN) 31m 00.8s
1932	Janusz Kusocinski (POLAND) 30m 11.4s*	Volmari Iso-Hollo (FINLAND) 30m 12.6s	Lauri Virtanen (FINLAND) 30m 35.0s
1936	Ilmari Salminen (FINLAND) 30m 15.4s	Arvo Askola (FINLAND) 30m 15.6s	Volmari Iso-Hollo (FINLAND) 30m 20.2s
1948	Emil Zatopek (CZECHO.) 29m 59.6s*	Alain Mimoun (FRANCE) 30m 47.4s	Bertil Albertsson (SWEDEN) 30m 53.6s
1952	Emil Zatopek (CZECHO.) 29m 17.0s*	Alain Mimoun (FRANCE) 29m 32.8s	Aleksandr Anufriuyev (U.S.S.R.) 29m 48.2s
1956	Vladimir Kuts[3] (U.S.S.R.) 28m 45.6s*	Jozsef Kovacs (HUNGARY) 28m 52.4s	Allan Lawrence (AUSTRALIA) 28m 53.6s
1960	Pyotr Bolotnikov (U.S.S.R.) 28m 32.2s*	Hans Grodotzki (GERMANY) 28m 37.0s	W. David Power (AUSTRALIA) 28m 38.2s
1964	William Mills (U.S.) 28m 24.4s*	Mohamed Gammoudi (TUNISIA) 28m 24.8s	Ronald Clarke (AUSTRALIA) 28m 25.8s
1968	Naftali Temu (KENYA) 29m 27.4s	Mamo Wolde (ETHIOPIA) 29m 28.0s	Mohamed Gammoudi (TUNISIA) 29m 34.2s
1972			

---

[1] Distance was only 5 miles (8046.7 metres).
[2] Prior to 1924 heats had been run in this event.
[3] The Russian's time at 5000m (half distance) was only 0.2s slower than the current Olympic Record for that event.

MARATHON (42,195 metres—26 miles 385 yds.)

	GOLD	SILVER	BRONZE
1896[1]	Spyridon Louis (GREECE) 2h 58m 50.0s	Charilaos Vasilakos (GREECE) 3h 06m 03.0s	Gyula Kellner[2] (HUNGARY) 3h 09m 35.0s
1900[3]	Michel Theato (FRANCE) 2h 59m 45.0s	Emile Champion (FRANCE) 3h 04m 17.0s	Ernst Fast (SWEDEN) 3h 37m 14.0s
1904[4]	Thomas Hicks (U.S.) 3h 28m 53.0s	Albert Corey (U.S.) 3h 34m 52.0s	Arthur Newton (U.S.) 3h 47m 33.0s
1908	John Hayes[5] (U.S.) 2h 55m 18.4s*	Charles Hefferon (S. AFRICA) 2h 56m 06.0s	Joseph Forshaw (U.S.) 2h 57m 10.4s
1912[6]	Kenneth McArthur (S. AFRICA) 2h 36m 54.8s	Christian Gitsham (S. AFRICA) 2h 37m 52.0s	Gaston Strobino (U.S.) 2h 38m 42.4s
1920[7]	Hannes Kolehmainen (FINLAND) 2h 32m 35.8s*[8]	Jüri Lossman (ESTONIA) 2h 32m 48.6s	Valerio Arri (ITALY) 2h 36m 32.8s
1924	Albin Stenroos (FINLAND) 2h 41m 22.6s	Romeo Bertini (ITALY) 2h 47m 19.6s	Clarence De Mar (U.S.) 2h 48m 14.0s
1928	El Ouafi (FRANCE) 2h 32m 57.0s	Miguel Plaza (CHILE) 2h 33m 23.0s	Martti Marttelin (FINLAND) 2h 35m 02.0s
1932	Juan Carlos Zabala (ARGENTINA) 2h 31m 36.0s*	Sam Ferris (G.B.) 2h 31m 55.0s	Armas Toivonen (FINLAND) 2h 32m 12.0s
1936	Kitei Son (JAPAN) 2h 29m 19.2s*	Ernest Harper (G.B.) 2h 31m 23.2s	Shoryu Nan (JAPAN) 2h 31m 42.0s
1948	Delfo Cabrera (ARGENTINA) 2h 34m 51.6s	Thomas Richards (G.B.) 2h 35m 07.6s	Etienne Gailly (BELGIUM) 2h 35m 33.6s
1952	Emil Zatopek (CZECHO.) 2h 23m 03.2s*	Reinaldo Gorno (ARGENTINA) 2h 25m 35.0s	Gustaf Jansson (SWEDEN) 2h 26m 07.0s
1956	Alain Mimoun (FRANCE) 2h 26m 00.0s	Franjo Mihalic (YUGOSLAVIA) 2h 26m 32.0s	Veikko Karvonen (FINLAND) 2h 27m 47.0s
1960	Abebe Bikila (ETHIOPIA) 2h 15m 16.2s*	Rhadi Ben Abdesselem (MOROCCO) 2h 15m 41.6s	A. Barry Magee (N.Z.) 2h 17m 18.2s
1964	Abebe Bikila (ETHIOPIA) 2h 12m 11.2s*	Basil Heatley (G.B.) 2h 16m 19.2s	Kokichi Tsuburaya (JAPAN) 2h 16m 22.8s
1968	Mamo Wolde (ETHIOPIA) 2h 20m 26.4s	Kenji Kimihara (JAPAN) 2h 23m 31.0s	Michael Ryun (NEW ZEALAND) 2h 23m 45.0s
1972			

---

[1] Distance was 40,000 metres.
[2] Velokas (GREECE) was third in 3h 06m 40.0s but was disqualified.
[3] Distance was 40,260 metres.
[4] Distance was 40,000 metres.
[5] Dorando Pietri (ITALY) finished 1st but was disqualified for assistance by officials over the final few hundred yards.
[6] Distance was 40,200 metres.
[7] Distance was 42,750 metres.
[8] O.R. as distance was even further than standard course.

The 400 metre hurdles being won in 1968 in world record time (48.1 seconds) by David Hemery (G.B.) by the exceptional margin of nearly a second from Garhard Hennige (W. Germany) and John Sherwood (G.B.).

110 METRES (120 yds. 1 ft.) HURDLES

	GOLD	SILVER	BRONZE
1896[1]	Thomas Curtis (U.S.) 17.6s	Grantley Goulding (G.B.) 18.0s	[2]
1900	Alvin Kraenzlein (U.S.) 15.4s*	John McLean (U.S.) 1½ ft.	Fred Moloney d.n.a.
1904	Fred Schule (U.S.) 16.0s	Thaddeus Shideler (U.S.) 2 yds.	L. Ashburner (U.S.) d.n.a.
1908	Forrest Smithson[3] (U.S.) 15.0s*	John Garrels (U.S.) 5 yds.	Arthur Shaw (U.S.) ½ yd.
1912	Fred Kelly (U.S.) 15.1s	James Wendell (U.S.) 15.2s	Martin Hawkins (U.S.) 15.3s
1920	Earl Thomson[4] (CANADA) 14.8s*	Harold Barron[4] (U.S.) 2½ yds.	Fred Murray (U.S.) d.n.a.
1924	Daniel Kinsey (U.S.) 15.0s	Sydney Atkinson (S. AFRICA) inches	Sten Pettersson[5] (SWEDEN) d.n.a.
1928	Sydney Atkinson (S. AFRICA) 14.8s[6]	Stephen Anderson (U.S.) 14.8s	John Collier (U.S.) 15.0s
1932	George Saling[7] (U.S.) 14.6s	Percy Beard (U.S.) 14.7s	Donald Finlay (G.B.) 14.8s
1936	Forrest Towns[8] (U.S.) 14.2s	Donald Finlay (G.B.) 14.4s	Fred Pollard (U.S.) 14.4s
1948	William Porter[9] (U.S.) 13.9s*	Clyde Scott (U.S.) 14.1s	Craig Dixon (U.S.) 14.1s
1952	W. Harrison Dillard[10] (U.S.) 13.7s*	Jack Davis (U.S.) 13.7s*	Art Barnard (U.S.) 14.1s

[1] Distance only 100 metres.
[2] Two other finalists did not run.
[3] Equalled O.R. of 15.4s in preliminaries.
[4] Equalled O.R. of 15.0s in preliminaries.
[5] George Guthrie (U.S.) finished third but was disqualified for knocking down three hurdles.
[6] George Weightman-Smith (S. AFRICA) set O.R. of 14.6s in preliminaries after he, Leighton Dye (U.S.) and Stephen Anderson (U.S.) had equalled mark of 14.8s.
[7] Set O.R. of 14.4s in preliminaries, after Jack Keller (U.S.) had set mark of 14.5s.
[8] Set O.R. of 14.1s in preliminaries.
[9] Equalled O.R. of 14.1s in preliminaries.
[10] Equalled O.R. of 13.9s in preliminaries.

	GOLD	SILVER	BRONZE
1956	Lee Calhoun (U.S.) 13.5s*	Jack Davis (U.S.) 13.5s*	Joel Shankle (U.S.) 14.1s
1960	Lee Calhoun (U.S.) 13.8s	Willie May (U.S.) 13.8s	Hayes Jones (U.S.) 14.0s
1964	Hayes Jones (U.S.) 13.6s	Blaine Lindgren (U.S.) 13.7s	Anatol Mikhailov (U.S.S.R.) 13.7s
1968	Willie Davenport (U.S.) 13.3s*	Erun Hall (U.S.) 13.4s	Eddy Ottoz (ITALY) 13.4s
1972			

400 METRES (437 yds. 1 ft.) HURDLES

	GOLD	SILVER	BRONZE
1896	Event not held		
1900	J. Walter Tewksbury (U.S.) 57.6s*	Henri Tauzin (FRANCE) d.n.a.	George Orton (U.S.) d.n.a.
1904[1]	Harry Hillman (U.S.) 53.0s	Frank Waller (U.S.) 2 yds.	George Poage (U.S.) d.n.a.
1908	Charles Bacon[2] (U.S.) 55.05s*	Harry Hillman[3] (U.S.) 1½ yds.	Leonard Tremeer (G.B.) 10 yds.
1912	Event not held		
1920	Frank Loomis (U.S.) 54.0s*	John Norton (U.S.) d.n.a.	August Desch (U.S.) d.n.a.
1924	F. Morgan Taylor (U.S.) 52.6s[5]	Erik Vilen[4] (FINLAND) 53.8s*	Ivan Riley (U.S.) 54.2s
1928	Lord Burghley (G.B.) 53.4s*	Frank Cuhel (U.S.) 53.6s	F. Morgan Taylor[6] (U.S.) 53.6s
1932	Robert Tisdall[7] (EIRE) 51.8s[8]	Glenn Hardin[7] (U.S.) 52.0s*	F. Morgan Taylor (U.S.) 52.2s
1936	Glenn Hardin (U.S.) 52.4s	John Loaring (CANADA) 52.7s	Miguel White (PHILIPPINES) 52.8s
1948	Roy Cochran[9] (U.S.) 51.1s*	Duncan White (CEYLON) 51.8s	Rune Larsson[9] (SWEDEN) 52.2s
1952	Charles Moore[10] (U.S.) 50.8s*	Yuriy Lituyev (U.S.S.R.) 51.3s	John Holland (N.Z.) 52.2s
1956	Glenn Davis (U.S.) 50.1s*	S. Eddie Southern[11] (U.S.) 50.8s	Joshua Culbreath (U.S.) 51.6s
1960	Glenn Davis (U.S.) 49.3s*	Clifton Cushman (U.S.) 49.6s	Richard Howard (U.S.) 49.7s
1964	Warren Cawley (U.S.) 49.6s	John Cooper (G.B.) 50.1s	Salvador Morale (ITALY) 50.1s
1968	David Hemery (G.B.) 48.1s*	Gerhard Hennige (W. GERMANY) 49.0s	John Sherwood (G.B.) 49.0s
1972			

---

[1] Hurdles only 2 ft. 6 in. high instead of more usual 3 ft. 0 in.
[2] Set O.R. of 57.0s in preliminaries.
[3] Set O.R. of 56.4s in preliminaries.
[4] Charles Brookins (U.S.) finished second but was disqualified for leaving his lane.
[5] Record not allowed because a hurdle was knocked down.
[6] Set O.R. of 53.4s in preliminaries.
[7] Set O.R. of 52.8s in preliminaries.
[8] Record not allowed because a hurdle was knocked down. Actual times for medal winners (those shown above being the officially rounded figures) were 51.7s, 51.9s, 52.0s respectively.
[9] Set O.R. of 51.9s in preliminaries.
[10] Set O.R. of 50.8s in preliminaries.
[11] Set O.R. of 50.1s in preliminaries.

3000 METRES (1 mile 1,520 yds. 1 ft.) STEEPLECHASE

	GOLD	SILVER	BRONZE
1896	Event not held		
1900[1]	George Orton (U.S.)[2] 7m 34.4s	Sidney Robinson (G.B.) 5 yds.	Jacques Chastanié (FRANCE) d.n.a.
	John Rimmer (G.B.) 12m 58.4s	Charles Bennett (G.B.) d.n.a.	Sidney Robinson (G.B.) d.n.a.

Horace Ashenfelter (U.S.), wearing 998, won the gold medal in the 3,000 metres steeplechase in 1952 at Helsinki, beating Vladimir Kazantsev (U.S.S.R.) wearing 436 by about 6 seconds. The leader here is the Finn Olavi Rinteenpää.

	GOLD	SILVER	BRONZE
1904[3]	James Lightbody (U.S.) 7m 39.6s	John Daly (IRELAND) 100 yds.	Arthur Newton (U.S.) 30 yds.
1908[4]	Arthur Russell (G.B.) 10m 47.8s	A. J. Robertson (G.B.) 10m 48.8s	J. L. Eisele (U.S.) 11m 00.8s
1912	Event not held		
1920	Percy Hodge (G.B.) 10m 00.4s*	Patrick Flynn (U.S.) 100 yds.	Ernesto Ambrosini (ITALY) 40 yds.
1924	Ville Ritola (FINLAND) 9m 33.6s*	Elias Katz[8] (FINLAND) 9m 44.0s	Paul Bontemps (FRANCE) 9m 45.2s
1928	Toivo Loukola (FINL'AND) 9m 21.8s*	Paavo Nurmi (FINLAND) 9m 31.2s	Ove Andersen (FINLAND) 9m 35.6s
1932[5]	Volmari Iso-Hollo[6] (FINLAND) 10m 33.4s	Thomas Evenson[6] (G.B.) 10m 46.0s	Joseph McCluskey (U.S.) 10m 46.2s
1936	Volmari Iso-Hollo (FINLAND) 9m 03.8s*	Kaarlo Tuominen (FINLAND) 9m 06.8s	Alfred Dompert (GERMANY) 9m 07.2s
1948	Tore Sjöstrand (SWEDEN) 9m 04.6s	Erik Elmsäter (SWEDEN) 9m 08.2s	Göte Hagström (SWEDEN) 9m 11.8s
1952	Horace Ashenfelter[7] (U.S.) 8m 45.4s*	Vladimir Kazantsev[7] (U.S.S.R.) 8m 51.6s	John Disley (G.B.) 8m 51.8s

[1] Two steeplechase events held, over 2500 metres and 4000 metres.
[2] Was actually Canadian.
[3] Held over 2500 metres.
[4] Held over 3200 metres.
[5] Distance in final was 3460 metres due to error on part of lap-scoring official.
[6] In preliminaries O.R. set up first by Evenson with 9m 18.8s then by Iso-Hollo with 9m 14.6s.
[7] In preliminaries O.R. set up first by Kazantsev with 8m 58.0s then by Ashenfelter with 8m 51.0s.
[8] Set O.R. of 9m 43.8s in preliminaries.

GOLD	SILVER	BRONZE
1956 Christopher Brasher[9] (G.B.) 8m 41.2s*	Sandor Rozsnyoi (HUNGARY) 8m 43.6s	Ernst Larsen (NORWAY) 8m 44.0s
1960 Zdzislaw Krzyszkowiak (POLAND) 8m 34.2s*	Nikolay Sokolov (U.S.S.R.) 8m 36.4s	Semyon Rzhishchin (U.S.S.R.) 8m 42.2s
1964 Gaston Roelants (BELGIUM) 8m 30.8s*	Maurice Herriott (G.B.) 8m 32.4s	Ivan Belyayev (U.S.S.R.) 8m 33.8s
1968 Amos Biwott (KENYA) 8m 51.0s	Benjamin Kogo (KENYA) 8m 51.6s	George Young (U.S.) 8m 51.8s
1972		

4 × 100 METRES (109 yds. 1 ft.) RELAY

1896–1908 Event not held		
1912 G.B.[1] 42.4s[3]	SWEDEN[2] 42.6s	
David Jacobs	Ivan Möller	
Harold Macintosh	Charles Luther	
Victor d'Arcy	Ture Persson	
William Applegarth	Knut Lindberg	
1920 U.S. 42.2s*	FRANCE 42.6s	SWEDEN d.n.a.
Charles Paddock	René Tirard	Agne Helmström
Jackson Scholz	René Lorain	William Pettersson
Loren Murchison	René Mourlon	Sven Malm
Morris Kirksey	Ali Khan	Nils Sandstrom
1924 U.S.[4] 41.0s*	G.B. 41.2s	NETHS. 41.8s
Frank Hussey	Harold Abrahams	J. Boot
Louis Clark	Walter Rangeley	H. Broos
Loren Murchison	Lancelot Royle	J. de Vries
J. Alfred Le Coney	William Nicol	M. van den Berge
1928 U.S. 41.0s*	GERMANY 41.2s	G.B. 41.8s
Frank Wykoff	Georg Lammers	Cyril Gill
James Quinn	Richard Corts	Eric Smouha
Charles Borah	Hubert Houben	Walter Rangeley
Henry Russell	Helmut Kornig	Jack London
1932 U.S.[5] 40.0s*	GERMANY 40.9s	ITALY 41.2s
Robert Kiesel	Helmut Kornig	Giuseppe Castelli
Emmett Toppino	Walter Hendrix	Luigi Facelli
Hector Dyer	Erich Borchmeyer	Ruggero Maregatti
Frank Wykoff	Arthur Jonath	Edgardo Toetti
1936 U.S.[6] 39.8s*	ITALY 41.1s	GERMANY[7] 41.2s
Jesse Owens	Orazio Mariani	Wilhelm Leichum
Ralph Metcalfe	Gianni Caldana	Erich Borchmeyer
Foy Draper	Elio Ragni	Erwin Gillmeister
Frank Wykoff	Tullio Gonnelli	Gerd Hornberger
1948 U.S.[8] 40.6s	G.B. 41.3s	ITALY 41.5s
H. Norwood Ewell	John Archer	Enrico Perucconi
Lorenzo Wright	John Gregory	Antonio Siddi
W. Harrison Dillard	Alistair McCorquodale	Carlo Monti
Melvin Patton	Ken Jones	Michele Tito
1952 U.S. 40.1s	U.S.S.R. 40.3s	HUNGARY 40.5s
F. Dean Smith	Boris Tokaryev	Laszlo Zarandi
W. Harrison Dillard	Lev Kalyayev	Geza Varasdi
Lindy Remigino	Levan Sanadze	Gyorgy Csanyi
Andy Stanfield	Vladimir Sukharyev	Bela Goldovanyi

[1] U.S. were disqualified in preliminaries after setting time of 42.2s.
[2] GERMANY finished 2nd but were disqualified.
[3] GERMANY set O.R. of 42.3s in preliminaries.
[4] Set O.R. of 41.2s in preliminaries after G.B. and NETHS. had set O.R. of 42.0s earlier.
[5] Set O.R. of 40.6s in preliminaries.
[6] Equalled O.R. of 40.0s in preliminaries.
[7] NETHS. finished 3rd but were disqualified.
[8] U.S. were disqualified but later reinstated.

	GOLD	SILVER	BRONZE
1956	U.S. 39.5s*	U.S.S.R. 39.8s	GERMANY 40.3s
	Ira Murchison	Boris Tokaryev	Lothar Knorzer
	Leamon King	Vladimir Sukharyev	Leonhard Pohl
	W. Thane Baker	Leonid Bartenyev	Heinz Futterer
	Bobby-Joe Morrow	Yuriy Konovalov	Manfred Germar
1960	GERMANY[9], [10] 39.5s*	U.S.S.R. 40.1s	G.B. 40.2s
	Bernd Cullman	Gusman Kosanov	Peter Radford
	Armin Hary	Leonid Bartenyev	David Jones
	Walter Mahlendorf	Yuriy Konovalov	David Segal
	Martin Lauer	Edvin Ozolin	J. Neville Whitehead
1964	U.S. 39.0s*	POLAND 39.3s	FRANCE 39.3s
	Paul Drayton	Andrzej Zielinski	Paul Genevay
	Garry Ashworth	Wieslaw Maniak	Bernard Laidebeur
	Richard Stebbins	Marian Foik	Claude Piquemal
	Robert Hayes	Marian Dudziak	Jocelyn Delecour
1968	U.S. 38.2s*	CUBA 38.3s	FRANCE 38.4s
	Charles Greene	Hermes Ramirez	G. Fenouil
	Melvin Pender	J. Morales	J. Delecour
	Ronnie Ray Smith	Pablo Montes	Claude Piquemal
	James Hines	Enriques Figuerola	Roger Bambuck
1972			

---

[9] Set O.R. of 39.5s in preliminaries.
[10] U.S. finished 1st by about 1 yard but were disqualified.

4 × 400 METRES (437 yds. 1 ft.) RELAY

1896–1908	Event not held		
1912	U.S. 3m 16.6s*	FRANCE 3m 20.7s	G.B. 3m 23.2s
	Melvin Sheppard	Charles Poulenard	George Nicol
	Frank Lindberg	Pierre Faillot	Ernest Henley
	James Meredith	Charles Rollot	J. Soutter
	Charles Reidpath	M. Schurrer	C. Seedhouse
1920	G.B. 3m 22.2s	S. AFRICA d.n.a.	FRANCE d.n.a.
	Cecil Griffiths	Harry Davel	George André
	Robert Lindsay	Clarence Oldfield	Gaston Féry
	John Ainsworth-Davis	Jack Oosterlaak	Maurice Delvart
	Guy Butler	Bevil Rudd	Maurice Devaux
1924	U.S. 3m 16.0s*	SWEDEN 3m 17.0s	G.B. 3m 17.4s
	C. S. Cochran	Artur Svensson	Edward Toms
	William Stevenson	Erik Bylén	George Renwick
	James McDonald	Gustaf Wejnarth	Richard Ripley
	Allan Hellfrich	Nils Engdahl	Guy Butler
1928	U.S. 3m 14.2s*	GERMANY 3m 14.8s	CANADA 3m 15.4s
	George Baird	Otto Neumann	Alex Wilson
	Emerson Spencer	R. Krebs	Philip Edwards
	Frederick Alderman	Harry Storz	Stanley Glover
	Raymond Barbuti	Hermann Engelhard	James Ball
1932	U.S.[1] 3m 08.2s*	G.B. 3m 11.2s	CANADA 3m 12.8s
	Ivan Fuqua	Crew Stoneley	Raymond Lewis
	Edgar Ablowich	Thomas Hampson	James Ball
	Karl Warner	Lord Burghley	Philip Edwards
	William Carr	Godfrey Rampling	Alex Wilson
1936	G.B. 3m 09.0s	U.S. 3m 11.0s	GERMANY 3m 11.8s
	Frederick Wolff	Harold Cagle	Helmut Hamann
	Godfrey Rampling	Robert Young	Friedrich v. Stulpnagel
	William Roberts	Edward O'Brien	Harry Voigt
	A. Godfrey Brown	Alfred Fitch	Rudolf Harbig
1948	U.S. 3m 10.4s	FRANCE 3m 14.8s	SWEDEN 3m 16.3s
	Arthur Harnden	Jean Kerebel	Kurt Lundkvist
	Clifford Bourland	Francis Schewetta	Lars-Enk Wolfbrandt
	Roy Cochran	Robert Chef d'Hotel	Folke Alnevik
	Malvin Whitfield	Jacques Lunis	Rune Larsson

	GOLD	SILVER	BRONZE
1952	JAMAICA 3m 03.9s*	U.S. 3m 04.0s	GERMANY 3m 06.6s
	Arthur Wint	Ollie Matson	Gunther Steines
	Leslie Laing	Gene Cole	Hans Geister
	Herbert McKenley	Charles Moore	Heinz Ulzheimer
	George Rhoden	Malvin Whitfield	Karl-Friedrich Haas
1956	U.S. 3m 04.8s	AUSTRALIA 3m 06.2s	G.B. 3m 07.2s
	Lou Jones	Leslie Gregory	John Salisbury
	Jesse Mashburn	David Lean	Michael Wheeler
	Charles Jenkins	Graham Gipson	F. Peter Higgins
	Thomas Courtney	Kevin Gosper	Derek Johnson
1960	U.S. 3m 02.2s*	GERMANY 3m 02.7s	BRITISH W.I.[2] 3m 04.0s
	Jack Yerman	Manfred Kinder	George Kerr
	Earl Young	Joachim Reske	James Wedderburn
	Glenn Davis	Johannes Kaiser	Keith Gardner
	Otis Davis	Carl Kaufmann	Malcolm Spence
1964	U.S. 3m 00.7s	G.B. 3m 01.6s	TRINIDAD
	Ollan Cassell	Timothy Graham	Edwin Skinner
	Michael Larrabee	Adrian Metcalfe	Kent Bernard
	Ulis Williams	John Cooper	Edwin Roberts
	Henry Carr	Robbie Brightwell	Wendell Mottley
1968	U.S. 2m 56.1s*	KENYA 2m 59.6s	GERMANY 3m 00.5s
	Vincent Matthews	Daniel Rudisha	Helmar Muller
	Ronald Freeman	Hezekiah Nyamau	Manfred Kinder
	Larry James	Naftali Bon	Gerhard Hennige
	Lee Evans	Charles Asah	Marhn Jellinghaus
1972			

---

[1] Set O.R. of 3m 11.8s in preliminaries.
[2] Wedderburn is from Barbados, the others from Jamaica.

20,000 METRES (12 miles 752 yds.) WALK

1896–1952	Event not held		
1956	Leonid Spirin (U.S.S.R.) 1h 31m 27.4s*	Antonas Mikenas (U.S.S.R.) 1h 32m 03.0s	Bruno Junk (U.S.S.R.) 1h 32m 12.0s
1960	Vladimir Golubnichiy (U.S.S.R.) 1h 34m 07.2s	Noel Freeman (AUSTRALIA) 1h 34m 16.4s	Stan Vickers (G.B.) 1h 34m 56.4s
1964	Kenneth Matthews (G.B.) 1h 29m 34.0s*	Dieter Lindner (GERMANY) 1h 31m 13.2s	Vladimir Golubnichiy (U.S.S.R.) 1h 31m 59.4s
1968	Vladimir Golubnichiy (U.S.S.R. 1h 33m 58.4s	Jose Pedrazza (MEXICO) 1h 34m 0.0s	Nickolay Smaga (U.S.S.R.) 1h 34m 03.4s
1972			

50,000 METRES (31 miles 120 yds.) WALK

1896–1928	Event not held		
1932	Thomas Green (G.B.) 4h 50m 10.0s*	Janis Dalinsh (LATVIA) 4h 47m 20.0s	Ugo Frigerio (ITALY) 4h 59m 06.0s
1936	Harold Whitlock (G.B.) 4h 30m 41.1s*	Arthur Schwab (SWITZ.) 4h 32m 09.2s	Adalberts Bubenko (LATVIA) 4h 32m 42.2s
1948	John Ljunggren (SWEDEN) 4h 41m 52.0s	Gaston Godel (SWITZ.) 4h 48m 17.0s	Tebbs Lloyd (G.B.) 4h 48m 31.0s
1952	Guiseppe Dordoni (ITALY) 4h 28m 07.8s*	Josef Dolezal (Czecho.) 4h 30m 17.8s	Antal Roka (HUNGARY) 4h 31m 27.2s
1956	Norman Read (N.Z.) 4h 30m 42.8s	Yevgeniy Maskinskov (U.S.S.R. 4h 32m 57.0s	John Ljunggren (SWEDEN) 4h 35m 02.0s

GOLD	SILVER	BRONZE
1960 Don Thompson (G.B.) 4h 25 m 30.0s*	John Ljunggren (SWEDEN) 4h 25m 47.0s	Abdon Pamich (ITALY) 4h 27m 55.4s
1964 Abdon Pamich (ITALY) 4h 11m 12.4s*	Paul Nihill (G.B.) 4h 11m 31.2s	Ingvar Pettersson (SWEDEN) 4h 14m 17.4s
1968 Christopher Höhne (E. GERMANY) 4h 20m 13.6s	Antal Kiss (HUNGARY) 4h 30m 17.0s	Larry Young (U.S.) 4h 31m 55.4s
1972		

HIGH JUMP

1896 Ellery Clark (U.S.) 5' 11¼"*	James Connolly (U.S.) 5' 7¼"	Robert Garrett (U.S.) 5' 7⅜"
1900 Irving Baxter (U.S.) 6' 2¾"*	Patrick Leahy (G.B.) 5' 10⅛"	Lajor Gönczy (HUNGARY) 5' 8⅞"
1904 Samuel Jones (U.S.) 5' 11"	Garrett Serviss (U.S.) 5' 10"	Paul Weinstein (GERMANY) 5' 10"

Harold Osborn (U.S.) won the high jump in Paris in 1924 with a leap of 6' 6" (1.98 metres). When he tried for 2.02 metres (above) the right end of the bar teetered off. He also won the decathlon in 1924.

Dick Fosbury (U.S.) whose back flip style in winning the high jump in 1968 at 7 feet 4¼ inches, caught the imagination of the stadium and television viewers all over the world.

	GOLD	SILVER	BRONZE
1908	Harry Porter (U.S.) 6′ 3″*	[1]	[1]
1912	Alma Richards (U.S.) 6′ 4″*	Hans Liesche (GERMANY) 6′ 3¼″	George Horine (U.S.) 6′ 2⅜″
1920	Richmond Landon (U.S.) 6′ 4⅜″*	Harold Muller (U.S.) 6′ 2¾″	Bo Ekelund (SWEDEN) 6′ 2¾″
1924	Harold Osborn (U.S.) 6′ 6″*	Leroy Brown (U.S.) 6′ 4¾″	Pierre Lewden (FRANCE) 6′ 3⅝″
1928[2]	Robert King (U.S.) 6′ 4⅜″	Ben Hedges (U.S.) 6′ 3¼″	Claude Ménard (FRANCE) 6′ 3¼″
1932[3]	Duncan McNaughton (CANADA) 6′ 5½″	Robert Van Osdel (U.S.) 6′ 5½″	Simeon Toribio (PHILIPPINES) 6′ 5½″
1936[4]	Cornelius Johnson (U.S.) 6′ 7⅞″*	David Albritton (U.S.) 6′ 6¾″	Delos Thurber (U.S.) 6′ 6¾″
1948	John Winter (AUSTRALIA) 6′ 6″	Björn Paulsen (NORWAY) 6′ 4¾″	George Stanich (U.S.) 6′ 4¾″
1952	Walter Davis (U.S.) 6′ 8⅜″*	Kenneth Wiesner (U.S.) 6′ 7⅛″	Jose Tellesda Conceicao (BRAZIL) 6′ 6″
1956	Charles Dumas (U.S.) 6′ 11½″*	Charles Porter (AUSTRALIA) 6′ 10⅝″	Igor Kashkarov (U.S.) 6′ 9⅞″
1960	Robert Shavlakadze (U.S.S.R.) 7′ 1⅛″*	Valeriy Brumel (U.S.S.R.) 7′ 1⅛″*	John Thomas (U.S.) 7′ 0¼″
1964	Valeriy Brumel (U.S.S.R.) 7′ 1¾″*	John Thomas (U.S.) 7′ 1¾″	John Rambo (U.S.) 7′ 1″
1968	Richard Fosbury (U.S.) 7′ 4¼″*	Edward Caruthers (U.S.) 7′ 3½″	Valentin Gavrilov (U.S.S.R.) 7′ 2⅝″
1972			

[1] Con Leahy (G.B.), István Somodi (HUNGARY) and Géo Andre (FRANCE) tied with 6′ 2″ and were all given silver medals.
[2] Places from second to fifth were decided by a jump-off.
[3] Places from first to fourth were decided by a jump-off.
[4] Places from second to fourth were decided by a jump-off.

Bob Seagren retained the U.S. unbeaten gold medal run in the pole vault, but only on the "count back" from two Germans who also cleared 17 feet 8½ inches in 1968.

POLE VAULT

	GOLD	SILVER	BRONZE
1896	William Hoyt (U.S.) 10′ 10″*	Albert Tyler (U.S.) 10′ 8″	Joannis Theodoropoulos (GREECE) 9′ 4¼″
1900[1]	Irving Baxter (U.S.) 10′ 10″*	M. B. Colkett (U.S.) 10′ 8″	Carl-Albert Andersen (NORWAY) 10′ 6″
1904	Charles Dvorak (U.S.) 11′ 6″*	Leroy Samse (U.S.) 11′ 3″	L. Wilkins (U.S.) 11′ 3″
1908	[2] 12′ 2″*		Ernest Archibald (CANADA) 11′ 9″
1912	Henry Babcock (U.S.) 12′ 11½″*	[3] 12′ 7½″	
1920	Frank Foss (U.S.) 13′ 5″*	Henry Petersen (DENMARK) 12′ 1¾″	Edwin Meyers[4] (U.S.) 11′ 9¾″
1924	Lee Barnes[5] (U.S.) 12′ 11½″	Glenn Graham (U.S.) 12′ 11½″	James Brooker (U.S.) 12′ 9½″
1928	Sabin Carr (U.S.) 13′ 9¼″*	William Droegemuller (U.S.) 13′ 5½″	Charles McGinnis[6] (U.S.) 12′ 11½″
1932	William Miller (U.S.) 14′ 1⅞″*	Shuhei Nishida (JAPAN) 14′ 1¼″	George Jefferson (U.S.) 13′ 9½″
1936	Earle Meadows (U.S.) 14′ 3¼″*	Shuhei Nishida (JAPAN) 13′ 11¼″	Sueo Oe (JAPAN) 13′ 11¼″
1948	O. Guinn Smith (U.S.) 14′ 1¼″	Erkki Kataja (FINLAND) 13′ 9½″	Robert Richards (U.S.) 13′9½″
1952	Robert Richards (U.S.) 14′ 11¼″*	Donald Laz (U.S.) 14′ 9¼″	Ragnar Lundberg (SWEDEN) 14′ 5¼″
1956	Robert Richards (U.S.) 14′ 11½″*	Robert Gutowski (U.S.) 14′ 10¼″	Georgios Roubanis (GREECE) 14′ 9¼″

[1] The best Americans did not compete as the event was held on a Sunday. A special contest held later for them resulted in a win for D. Horton (U.S.) with 11′ 3¾″.
[2] Alfred Gilbert (U.S.) and Edward Cook (U.S.) tied for first place.
[3] Frank Nelson (U.S.) and Marc Wright (U.S.) tied for second place.
[4] Places from third to sixth decided by a jump-off.
[5] First place decided by a jump-off.
[6] Places from third to fifth decided by a jump-off.

	GOLD	SILVER	BRONZE
1960	Donald Bragg (U.S.) 15′ 5″*	Ron Morris (U.S.) 15′ 1¼″	Eeles Landstrom (FINLAND) 14′ 11¼″
1964	Fred Hansen (U.S.) 16′ 8¾″*	Wolfgang Reinhardt (GERMANY) 16′ 6¾″	Klaus Lehnertz (GERMANY) 16′ 5″
1968	Bob Seagren (U.S.) 17′ 8½″*	Claus Schiprowski (GERMANY) 17′ 8½″*	Wolfgang Nordwig (E. GERMANY) 17′ 8½*
1972			

BROAD JUMP (LONG JUMP)

1896	Ellery Clark (U.S.) 20′ 10″*	Robert Garrett (U.S.) 20′ 3¼″	James Connolly (U.S.) 20′ 0½″
1900	Alvin Kraenzlein (U.S.) 23′ 6⅞″*	Myer Prinstein (U.S.) 23′ 6½″	Con Leahy (G.B.) 22′ 9½″
1904[1]	Myer Prinstein (U.S.) 24′ 1″*	Daniel Frank (U.S.) 22′ 7¼″	Robert Stangland (U.S.) 22′ 7″
1908	Frank Irons (U.S.) 24′ 6½″*	Daniel Kelly (U.S.) 23′ 3¼″	Calvin Bricker (CANADA) 23′ 3″
1912	Albert Gutterson (U.S.) 24′ 11¼″*	Calvin Bricker (CANADA) 23′ 7¾″	Georg Aberg (SWEDEN) 23′ 6¾″
1920	William Pettersson (SWEDEN) 23′ 5½″	Carl Johnson (U.S.) 23′ 3¼″	Eric Abrahamsson (SWEDEN) 23′ 2¾″
1924	William De Hart Hubbard (U.S.) 24′ 5″	Edward Gourdin (U.S.) 23′ 10½″	Sverre Hansen (NORWAY) 23′ 9¾″
1928	Edward Hamm (U.S.) 25′ 4¼″*[2]	Silvio Cator (HAITI) 24′ 10½″	Alfred Bates (U.S.) 24′ 3¼″
1932	Edward Gordon (U.S.) 25′ 0¾″	C. Lambert Redd (U.S.) 24′ 11¼″	Chuhei Nambu (JAPAN) 24′ 5¼″
1936	Jesse Owens (U.S.) 26′ 5¼″*	Luz Long (U.S.) 25′ 9¾″	Naoto Tajima (JAPAN) 25′ 4¾″
1948	Willie Steele (U.S.) 25′ 8″	Thomas Bruce (AUSTRALIA) 24′ 9¼″	Herbert Douglas (U.S.) 24′ 9″
1952	Jerome Biffle (U.S.) 24′ 10″	Meredith Gourdine (U.S.) 24′ 8½″	Odön Foldessy[3] (HUNGARY) 23′ 11½″

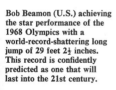

Bob Beamon (U.S.) achieving the star performance of the 1968 Olympics with a world-record-shattering long jump of 29 feet 2½ inches. This record is confidently predicted as one that will last into the 21st century.

	GOLD	SILVER	BRONZE
1956	Gregory Bell (U.S.) 25′ 8¼″	John Bennett (U.S.) 25′ 2¼″	Jorma Valkama[4] (FINLAND) 24′ 6½″
1960	Ralph Boston (U.S.) 26′ 7¾″*	Irvin Roberson (U.S.) 26′ 7¼″	Igor Ter-Ovanesyan (U.S.S.R.) 26′ 4¼″
1964	Lynn Davies (G.B.) 26′ 5¾″	Ralph Boston (U.S.) 26′ 4″	Igor Ter-Ovanesyan (U.S.S.R.) 26′ 2½″
1968	Robert Beaman (U.S.) 29′ 2½″*	Klaus Beer (E.GERMANY) 26′ 10½″	Ralph Boston (U.S.) 26′ 9¼″
1972			

[1] All seven competitors were from the U.S.
[2] In the 1924 Pentathlon Robert LeGendre (U.S.) had iumped 25′ 5¾″ but this was not classed as the Olympic broad jump record.
[3] Neville Price (S. AFRICA) jumped 24′ 1¾″ in the qualifying round but from 1936 such marks do not count in the final.
[4] Henryk Grabowski (POLAND) jumped 24′ 8″ in the qualifying round.

TRIPLE JUMP[1]

1896	James Connolly (U.S.) 44′ 11¾″*	Alexandre Tuffere (FRANCE) 41′ 8″	Joannis Persakis (GREECE) 41′ 1″
1900	Myer Prinstein (U.S.) 47′ 5¾″*	James Connolly (U.S.) 45′ 10″	L. P. Sheldon (U.S.) 44′ 9″
1904	Myer Prinstein (U.S.) 47′ 1″	Fred Englehardt (U.S.) 45′ 7¼″	Robert Stangland (U.S.) 43′ 10¼″
1908	Timothy Ahearne (G.B.) 48′ 11¼″*	J. Garfield MacDonald (CANADA) 48′ 5¼″	Edvard Larsen (NORWAY) 47′ 2¾″
1912	Gustaf Lindblom (SWEDEN) 48′ 5″	Georg Aberg (SWEDEN) 47′ 7¼″	Erik Almlöf (SWEDEN) 46′ 5¾″
1920	Vilho Tuulos (FINLAND) 47′ 7″	Folke Jansson (SWEDEN) 47′ 6″	Erik Almlöf (SWEDEN) 46′ 10″
1924	Anthony Winter (AUSTRALIA) 50′ 11¼″*	Luis Brunetto (ARGENTINA) 50′ 7¼″	Vilho Tuulos (FINLAND) 50′ 5″

[1] Formerly known as the Hop, Step and Jump.

George G. Avery (Australia) the silver medal winner in the 1948 hop, step and jump triple jump).

	GOLD	SILVER	BRONZE
1928	Mikio Oda (JAPAN) 49′ 10¾″	Levi Casey (U.S.) 49′ 9¼″	Vilho Tuulos (FINLAND) 49′ 7″
1932	Chuhei Nambu (JAPAN) 51′ 7″*	Erik Svensson (SWEDEN) 50′ 3¼″	Kenkichi Oshima (JAPAN) 49′ 7¼″
1936	Naoto Tajima (JAPAN) 52′ 6″*	Masao Harada (JAPAN) 51′ 4½″	Jack Metcalfe (AUSTRALIA) 50′ 10¼″
1948	Arne Ahman (SWEDEN) 50′ 6¼″	George Avery (AUSTRALIA) 50′ 5″	Ruhi Sarialp (TURKEY) 49′ 3½″
1952	Adhemar Ferreira da Silva (BRAZIL) 53′ 2½″*	Leonid Shcherbakov (U.S.S.R.) 52′ 5¼″	Arnoldo Devonish (VENEZUELA) 50′ 11″
1956	Adhemar Ferreira da Silva (BRAZIL) 53′ 7¾″*	Vilhjalmur Einarsson (ICELAND) 53′ 4¼″	Vitold Kreyer (U.S.S.R.) 52′ 6¾″
1960	Jozef Schmidt (POLAND) 55′ 1¾″*	Vladimir Goryayev (U.S.S.R.) 54′ 6½″	Vitold Kreyer (U.S.S.R.) 53′ 10¾″
1964	Jozef Schmidt (POLAND) 55′ 3½″*	Olyeg Fyedoseyev (U.S.S.R.) 54′ 4¾″	Victor Kravchenko (U.S.S.R.) 54′ 4¼″
1968	Viktor Saneyev (U.S.S.R.) 57′ 0¾″	Nelson Prudencio (BRAZIL) 56′ 8″	Giuseppe Gentile (ITALY) 56′ 6″
1972			

Queen Alexandra presenting world recordholder Ralph Rose (U.S.) with his gold medal for winning the shot put in London in 1908 with a best effort of 46 ft. 7½ ins. Rose had also won this event in 1904, and was second in 1912.

SHOT PUT[1]

1896[2]	Robert Garrett (U.S.) 36′ 9¾″*	Miltiades Gouscos (GREECE) 36′ 9″	Georgios Papasideris (GREECE) 34′ 0″
1900[2]	Richard Sheldon (U.S.) 46′ 3″*	Josiah McCracken (U.S.) 42′ 2″	Robert Garrett (U.S.) 40′ 7″
1904	Ralph Rose (U.S.) 48′ 7″*	Wesley Coe (U.S.) 47′ 3″	L. E. J. Feuerbach (U.S.) 43′ 10½″
1908	Ralph Rose (U.S.) 46′ 7½″	Dennis Horgan (G.B.) 44′ 8¼″	John Garrels (U.S.) 43′ 3″

[1] Weight 7.257 kilograms (16 lb.) from 7-foot circle.
[2] From a 7-foot square.

Randy Matson (U.S.) won the shot put in the 1968 Olympics with 67 feet 4¾ inches, far short of his world record of 71 feet 5½ inches, set in 1967.

	GOLD	SILVER	BRONZE
1912	Patrick McDonald (U.S.) 50′ 4″*	Ralph Rose (U.S.) 50′ 0½″	Lawrence Whitney (U.S.) 45′ 8½″
1920	Ville Pörhölä (FINLAND) 48′ 7″	Elmer Niklander (FINLAND) 46′ 5¼″	Harry Liversedge (U.S.) 46′ 5″
1924	L. Clarence Houser (U.S.) 49′ 2¼″	Glenn Hartranft (U.S.) 49′ 2″	Ralph Hills (U.S.) 48′ 0½″
1928	John Kuck (U.S.) 52′ 0¾″*	Herman Brix[3] (U.S.) 51′ 8″	Emil Hirschfield (GERMANY) 51′ 7″
1932	Leo Sexton (U.S.) 52′ 6⅛″*	Harlow Rothert (U.S.) 51′ 5⅛″	Frantisek Douda (CZECHO.) 51′ 2½″
1936	Hans Wöllke (GERMANY) 53′ 1¾″*	Sulo Barlund (FINLAND) 52′ 10¾″	Gerhard Stöck (GERMANY) 51′ 4½″
1948	Wilbur Thompson (U.S.) 56′ 2″*	James Delaney (U.S.) 54′ 8¾″	James Fuchs (U.S.) 53′ 10½″
1952	W. Parry O'Brien (U.S.) 57′ 1½″*	Darrow Hooper (U.S.) 57′ 0¾″	James Fuchs (U.S.) 55′ 11¾″
1956	W. Parry O'Brien (U.S.) 60′ 11¼″*	William Nieder (U.S.) 59′ 7¾″	Jiri Skobla (CZECHO.) 57′ 11″
1960	William Nieder (U.S.) 65′ 6¾″*	W. Parry O'Brien (U.S.) 62′ 8¼″	Dallas Long (U.S.) 62′ 4¼″
1964	Dallas Long (U.S.) 66′ 8½″*	Randy Matson (U.S.) 66′ 3¼″	Vilmos Varju (HUNGARY) 63′ 7½″
1968	Randy Matson[4] (U.S.) 67′ 4¾″	George Woods (U.S.) 66′ 0¼″	Eduard Gushchin (U.S.S.R.) 65′ 11″
1972			

[3] Later became movie star under name of Bruce Bennett.
[4] Set O.R. 67′ 10¼″ in qualifying.

DISCUS THROW[1]

	GOLD	SILVER	BRONZE
1896	Robert Garrett (U.S.) 95' 7¾"*	Panagiotis Paraskevopoulos (GREECE) 95' 0"	Sotirios Versis (GREECE) 91' 1¾"
1900	Rudolf Bauer (HUNGARY) 118' 3"*	Frantisek Janda (BOHEMIA) 115' 7¾"	Richard Sheldon (U.S.) 113' 2¼"
1904	Martin Sheridan[2] (U.S.) 128' 10½"*	Ralph Rose (U.S.) 128' 10½"*	Nicolas Georgantos (GREECE) 123' 7½"
1908	Martin Sheridan (U.S.) 134' 2"*	M. H. Giffin (U.S.) 133' 6½"	Marquis Horr (U.S.) 129' 5¼"
1912	Armas Taipale (FINLAND) 148' 4"*	Richard Byrd (U.S.) 138' 10"	James Duncan (U.S.) 138' 8½"
1920	Elmer Niklander (FINLAND) 146' 7½"	Armas Taipale (FINLAND) 144' 11½"	Augustus Pope (U.S.) 138' 2¼"
1924	L. Clarence Houser (U.S.) 151' 5"*	Vilho Niittymaa (FINLAND) 147' 5½"	Thomas Lieb (U.S.) 147' 1"
1928	L. Clarence Houser (U.S.) 155' 3"*	Antero Kivi (FINLAND) 154' 11½"	James Corson (U.S.) 154' 6½"
1932	John Anderson (U.S.) 162' 4½"*	Henri Laborde (FRANCE) 159' 0½"	Paul Winter (FRANCE) 157' 0"

[1] Weight 2 kilograms (4 lbs. 6 oz.) from 7-foot circle.
[2] First place decided by a throw-off.

(Left) Al Oerter (U.S.), winner of the discus throw in four successive Olympics—1956, 1960, 1964 and 1968—wears the Winged Foot emblem of the New York Athletic Club.

Matthew McGrath (U.S.) gold medal winner in the 16-lb. hammer throw at the 1912 Olympics in Stockholm, also placed second in 1908 and 1924.

Jim Thorpe (U.S.), winner of the decathlon and pentathlon (the latter no longer contested) in 1912, and an American Indian, was the greatest all-round athlete seen up to that time. Because of a previous minor infraction of the rules (see page 16) his two gold medals had to be returned and re-awarded to the runners-up. Thorpe's name was struck from the Roll of Champions, but he went on to become a professional baseball player and record-holding star in American football.

Bob Mathias (U.S.), winner of the 1948 decathlon, ready to put the shot in 1952 at Helsinki in the gruelling decathlon, in which he retained his title.

	GOLD	SILVER	BRONZE
1936	Kenneth Carpenter (U.S.) 165′ 7½″*	Gordon Dunn (U.S.) 161′ 11″	Giorgio Oberweger (ITALY) 161′ 6″
1948	Adolfo Consolini (ITALY) 172′ 2″*	Giuseppe Tosi (ITALY) 169′ 10½″	Fortune Gordien (U.S.) 166′ 7″
1952	Sim Iness (U.S.) 180′ 6½″*	Adolfo Consolini (ITALY) 176′ 5″	James Dillion (U.S.) 174′ 9½″
1956	Alfred Oerter (U.S.) 184′ 11″*	Fortune Gordien (U.S.) 179′ 10″	Desmond Koch (U.S.) 178′ 5½″
1960	Alfred Oerter (U.S.) 194′ 1¾″*	Richard Babka (U.S.) 190′ 4¼″	Richard Cochran (U.S.) 187′ 6¼″
1964	Alfred Oerter (U.S.) 200′ 1½″*	Ludvik Danek (CZECHO.) 198′ 6½″	David Weill (U.S.) 195′ 2″
1968	Alfred Oerter (U.S.) 212′ 6½″*	Lothar Milde (E. GERMANY) 206′ 11½″	Ludvik Danek (CZECHO.) 206′ 5″
1972			

HAMMER THROW[1]

1896	Event not held		
1900[2]	John Flanagan (U.S.) 163′ 2″*	Truxton Hare (U.S.) 161′ 2″	Josiah McCracken (U.S.) 139′ 3½″
1904	John Flanagan (U.S.) 168′ 1″*	John DeWitt (U.S.) 164′ 11″	Ralph Rose (U.S.) 150′ 0½″
1908	John Flanagan (U.S.) 170′ 4¼″*	Matthew McGrath (U.S.) 167′ 11″	Cornelius Walsh (CANADA) 159′ 1½″
1912	Matthew McGrath (U.S.) 179′ 7″*	Duncan Gillis (CANADA) 158′ 9″	Clarence Childs (U.S.) 158′ 0½″
1920	Patrick Ryan (U.S.) 173′ 5½″	Carl Johan Lind (SWEDEN) 160′ 2¼″	Basil Bennett (U.S.) 158′ 3½″
1924	Fred Tootell (U.S.) 174′ 10″	Matthew McGrath (U.S.) 166′ 9½″	Malcolm Nokes (G.B.) 160′ 4″
1928	Patrick O'Callaghan (IRELAND) 168′ 7″	Ossian Skiöld (SWEDEN) 168′ 3″	Edmund Black (U.S.) 160′ 10″
1932	Patrick O'Callaghan (IRELAND) 176′ 11″	Ville Pörhölä (FINLAND) 171′ 6″	Peter Zaremba (U.S.) 165′ 1½″
1936	Karl Hein (GERMANY) 185′ 4″*	Erwin Blask (GERMANY) 180′ 7″	Fred Warngard (SWEDEN) 179′ 10½″
1948	Imre Nemeth (HUNGARY) 183′ 11½″	Ivan Gubijan (YUGOSLAVIA) 178′ 0½″	Robert Bennett (U.S.) 176′ 3½″
1952	József Csermak (HUNGARY) 197′ 11½″*	Karl Storch (GERMANY) 193′ 1″	Imre Nemeth (HUNGARY) 189′ 5″
1956	Harold Connolly (U.S.) 207′ 3½″*	Mikhail Krivonosov (U.S.S.R.) 206′ 9½″	Anatoliy Samotsvetov (U.S.S.R.) 205′ 3″
1960	Vasiliy Rudenkov (U.S.S.R.) 220′ 1¾″*	Gyula Zsivotzky (HUNGARY) 215′ 10″	Tadeusz Rut (POLAND) 215′ 4½″
1964	Romuald Klim (U.S.S.R.) 228′ 10½″*	Gyula Zsivozky (HUNGARY) 226′ 8″	Uwe Beyer (GERMANY) 223′ 4½″
1968	Gyula Zsivotzky (HUNGARY) 240′ 8″*	Romuald Klim (U.S.S.R.) 240′ 5″	Lazar Lovasz (HUNGARY) 228′ 11″
1972			

[1] Weight 7.257 kilograms (16 lbs.) from 8-foot 2½ inch circle.
[2] From 9-foot circle.

JAVELIN THROW[1]

1896–1904	Event not held		
1908	Erik Lemming (SWEDEN) 179′ 10½″*	Arne Halse (NORWAY) 165′ 11″	Otto Nilsson (SWEDEN) 154′ 6¼″
1912	Erik Lemming (SWEDEN) 198′ 11½″*	Juho Saaristo[2] (FINLAND) 192′ 5½″	Mor Koczan (HUNGARY) 182′ 1″
1920	Jonni Myyra (FINLAND) 215′ 9½″*	Urko Peltonen (FINLAND) 208′ 8″	Pekka Johansson (FINLAND) 207′ 0″

[1] Weight 800 grams (1 lb. 12.218 oz.).
[2] Later in the "two-handed" event he threw 200′ 1½″.

GOLD	SILVER	BRONZE
1924 Jonni Myyra (FINLAND) 206' 6½"	Gunnar Lindstrom (SWEDEN) 199' 10½"	Eugene Oberst (U.S.) 191' 5"
1928 Erik Lundkvist (SWEDEN) 218' 6"*	Bela Szepes (HUNGARY) 214' 1"	Olav Sunde (NORWAY) 209' 10½"
1932 Matti Jaervinen (FINLAND) 238' 6½"*	Martti Sippala (FINLAND) 229' 0"	Eino Penttila (FINLAND) 225' 4½"
1936 Gerhard Stöck (GERMANY) 235' 8½"	Yrjo Nikkanen (FINLAND) 232' 2"	Kalervo Toivonen (FINLAND) 232' 0"
1948 Tapio Rautavaara (FINLAND) 228' 11"	Steve Seymour[3] (U.S.) 221' 8"	Jozsef Varszegi (HUNGARY) 219' 11".
1952 Cyrus Young (U.S.) 242' 0½"*	William Miller (U.S.) 237' 8½"	Toivo Hyytiainen (FINLAND) 235' 10½"
1956 Egil Danielsen (NORWAY) 281' 2½"*	Janusz Sidlo (POLAND) 262' 4½"	Viktor Tsibulenko (U.S.S.R.) 260' 10"
1960 Viktor Tsibulenko (U.S.S.R.) 277' 8½"	Walter Kruger (GERMANY) 260' 4½"	Gergely Kulscar (HUNGARY) 257' 9¼"
1964 Pauli Nevala (FINLAND) 271' 2"	Gergely Kulscar (HUNGARY) 270' 0½"	Janis Lusis (U.S.S.R.) 264' 2"
1968 Janis Lusis (U.S.S.R.) 295' 7"*	Jorma Kinnunen (FINLAND) 290' 0"	Gergely Kulcsar (HUNGARY) 285' 7½"
1972		

---

[3] Martin Biles (U.S.) threw 222' 0½" in qualifying round.

DECATHLON[1]

1896–1908 Event not held		
1912 Hugo Wieslander[3] (SWEDEN) 6,162 pts.	Charles Lomberg (SWEDEN) 5,943 pts.	Gösta Holmer[3] (SWEDEN) 5,956 pts.
1920 Helge Lövland (NORWAY) 5,970 pts.	Brutus Hamilton (U.S.) 5,912 pts.	Bertil Ohlson (SWEDEN) 5,825 pts.
1924 Harold Osborn (U.S.) 6,668 pts.	Emerson Norton (U.S.) 6,360 pts.	Aleksander Kolmpere (ESTONIA) 6,260 pts.
1928 Paavo Yrjola (FINLAND) 6,770 pts.	Akilles Jaervinen (FINLAND) 6,815 pts.	Kenneth Doherty (U.S.) 6,593 pts.
1932 James Bausch (U.S.) 6,896 pts.	Akilles Jaervinen (FINLAND) 7,038 pts.	Wolrad Eberle (GERMANY) 6,830 pts.
1936 Glenn Morris (U.S.) 7,421 pts.	Robert Clark (U.S.) 7,226 pts.	Jack Parker (U.S.) 6,918 pts.
1948 Robert Mathias (U.S.) 6,326 pts.	Ignace Heinrich (FRANCE) 6,740 pts.	Floyd Simmons (U.S.) 6,711 pts.
1952 Robert Mathias (U.S.) 7,731 pts.	Milton Campbell (U.S.) 7,132 pts.	Floyd Simmons (U.S.) 7,069 pts.
1956 Milton Campbell (U.S.) 7,708 pts.	Rafer Johnson (U.S.) 7,568 pts.	Vasiliy Kuznetsov (U.S.S.R.) 7,461 pts.
1960 Rafer Johnson (U.S.) 8,001 pts.	Yang Chuan-Kwang (FORMOSA) 7,921 pts.	Vasiliy Kuznetsov (U.S.S.R.) 7,624 pts.
1964 Willi Holdorf (GERMANY) 7,887 pts.	Rein Aun (U.S.S.R.) 7,842 pts.	Hans-Joachim Walde (GERMANY) 7,809 pts.
1968 William Toomey (U.S.) 8,193 pts.*	Hans-Joachim Walde (W. GER.) 8,111 pts.	Kurt Bendlin (W. GER.) 8,064 pts.
1972		

---

[1] Consisting of 10 events within two consecutive days—100m, broad jump, shot put, high jump, 400m on the first day; 110m hurdles, discus throw, pole vault, javelin throw, 1500m on the second day.
All scores shown are based on the present day point-scoring system.
[2] Jim Thorpe (U.S.) finished first with 6,754 pts. but was later disqualified.
[3] Old scoring system made him third.

Wyomia Tyus (U.S.) successfully defends her 100 metres title in 1968 in the world record time of 11.0 seconds.

17b. Track and Field Athletics (Women)

100 METRES (109 yds. 1 ft.)

	GOLD	SILVER	BRONZE
1928	Elizabeth Robinson (U.S.) 12.2s*	Bobby Rosenfeld (CANADA) 12.2s	Ethel Smith (CANADA) 12.2s
1932	Stanislawa Walasiewicz[1] (POLAND) 11.9s*	Hilda Strike[1] (CANADA) 11.9s	Wilhelmina von Bremen (U.S.) 12.0s
1936	Helen Stephens (U.S.) 11.5s[2]	Stanislawa Walasiewicz (POLAND) 11.7s	Kathe Krauss (GERMANY) 11.9s
1948	Francina Blankers-Koen (NETHS.) 11.9s*	Dorothy Manley (G.B.) 12.2s	Shirley Strickland (AUSTRALIA) 12.2s
1952	Marjorie Jackson[3] (AUSTRALIA) 11.5s*	Daphne Hasenjager (S. AFRICA) 11.8s	Shirley Strickland (AUSTRALIA) 11.9s
1956	Betty Cuthbert[4]* (AUSTRALIA) 11.5s	Christa Stubnick (GERMANY) 11.7s	Marlene Mathews (AUSTRALIA) 11.7s
1960	Wilma Rudolph[5] (U.S.) 11.0s[6]*	Dorothy Hyman (G.B.) 11.3s	Giuseppina Leone (ITALY) 11.3s
1964	Wyomia Tyus (U.S.) 11.4s[7]	Edith Maguire (U.S.) 11.6s	Ewa Kobukowska (POLAND) 11.6s

[1] Set O.R. of 11.9s in preliminaries, after Marie Dollinger (GERMANY) had equalled record of 12.2s.
[2] Final was wind-assisted as were heat of 11.4s and semi-final of 11.5s.
[3] Set O.R. of 11.5s in preliminaries.
[4] Set O.R. of 11.4s in preliminaries.
[5] Set O.R. of 11.3s in preliminaries.
[6] Final was wind-assisted.
[7] Set O.R. of 11.2s in preliminaries.

	GOLD	SILVER	BRONZE
1968	Wyomia Tyus (U.S.) 11.0s*	Barbara Ferrel (U.S.) 11.1s	Irena Szewinska (POLAND) 11.1s
1972			

The 200 metres final in 1960 with Wilma Rudolph (U.S.), the gold medal winner of the 100 metres dash as well, wearing No. 117; Jutta Heine (Germany), the silver medal winner wearing No. 77; and Dorothy Hyman (G.B.), the bronze medal winner wearing No. 100. Also in the photo is Giuseppina Leone (Italy) No. 181, bronze medal winner in the 100 metres dash.

200 METRES (218 yds. 2 ft.)

1928–1936	Event not held		
1948	Francina Blankers-Koen[1] (NETHS.) 24.4s	Audrey Williamson (G.B.) 25.1s	Audrey Patterson (U.S.) 25.2s
1952	Marjorie Jackson[2] (AUSTRALIA) 23.7s	Bertha Brouwer (HOLLAND) 24.2s	Nadyezhda Khnykina (U.S.S.R.) 24.2s
1956	Betty Cuthbert (AUSTRALIA) 23.4s*	Christa Stubnick (GERMANY) 23.7s	Marlene Mathews (AUSTRALIA) 23.8s
1960	Wilma Rudolph[3] (U.S.) 24.0s	Jutta Heine (GERMANY) 24.4s	Dorothy Hyman (G.B.) 24.7s
1964	Edith Maguire (U.S.) 23.0s*	Irena Kirszenstein (POLAND) 23.1s	Marilyn Black (AUSTRALIA) 23.1s
1968	Irena Szewinska (POLAND) 22.5s*	Raelene Boyle (AUSTRALIA) 22.7s	Jennifer Lamy (AUSTRALIA) 22.8s
1972			

[1] Set O.R. of 24.3s in preliminaries.
[2] Set O.R. of 23.4s in preliminaries, bettering her previous O.R. of 23.6s set earlier after Khnykina (U.S.S.R.) had equalled old record of 24.3s.
[3] Set O.R. of 23.2s in preliminaries.

400 METRES (437 yds. 1 ft.)

1928–1960	Event not held		
1964	Betty Cuthbert (AUSTRALIA) 52.0s*	Ann Packer (G.B.) 52.2s[1]	Judith Amoore (AUSTRALIA) 53.4s
1968	Colette Besson (FRANCE) 52.0s	Lilian Board (G.B.) 52.1s	Natalya Pyechenkina (U.S.S.R.) 52.2s
1972			

[1] Set O.R. of 53.1 in preliminaries, and 52.7 in semi-final.

One of the closest finishes in the 1968 Games—Colette Besson (France) beats the late Lilian Board (G.B.) by one-tenth of a second in 52.0 seconds in the 400 metres.

800 METRES (874 yds. 2 ft.)

	GOLD	SILVER	BRONZE
1928	Lina Radke (GERMANY) 2m 16.8s*	Kinuye Hitomi (JAPAN) 2m 17.6s	Inga Gentzel (SWEDEN) 2m 17.6s
1932–1956	Event not held		
1960	Ludmila Shevtsova (U.S.S.R.) 2m 04.3s*[1]	Brenda Jones (AUSTRALIA) 2m 04.4s	Ursula Donath (GERMANY) 2m 05.6s
1964	Ann Packer (G.B.) 2m 01.1s*	Maryvonne Dupureur (FRANCE) 2m 01.9s[2]	Marise Chamberlain (N.Z.) 2m 02.8s
1968	Madeline Manning (U.S.) 2m 00.9s*	Ilona Silai (RUMANIA) 2m 02.5s	Maria Gommers (NETHS.) 2m 02.6s
1972			

[1] In preliminaries O.R. progressively beaten by Antje Gleichfeld (GERMANY) 2m 10.9s, Ursula Donath (GERMANY) 2m 07.8s and Dixie Willis (AUSTRALIA) 2m 05.2s.
[2] Set O.R. of 2m 04.1s in semi-final.

1500 METRES (1640 yds. 1 ft.)

1928–68 Event not held.

1972

100 METRES (109 yds. 1 ft.) HURDLES

1928–68 Event not held.

1972

Gisela Kohler (Germany), silver medal winner, leading over the last hurdle in a heat of the now superseded 80 metres event in 1956 at Melbourne.

The previous event (100 metres hurdles) supersedes the 80 metres hurdles which was held 8 times from 1932 to 1968 and for which Gold, Silver and Bronze medals were won as follows: Australia 3–1–3; Germany 1–2–2; U.S. 1–1–0; U.S.S.R. 1–1–0; Italy 1–0–0; Netherlands 1–0–0–; G.B. 0–2–0; Poland 0–1–0; Canada 0–0–1; Formosa 0–0–1; South Africa 0–0–1.

4 × 100 METRES (109 yds. 1 ft.) RELAY

	GOLD	SILVER	BRONZE
1928	CANADA 48.4s*	U.S. 48.8s	GERMANY 49.0s
	Myrtle Cook	Mary Washburn	E. Kellner
	Ethel Smith	Jessie Gross	Leni Schmidt
	Bobby Rosenfeld	Loretta McNeil	A. Holdmann
	Florence Bell	Elizabeth Robinson	Leni Junker
1932	U.S. 47.0s*	CANADA 47.0s*	G.B. 47.6s
	Mary Carew	Mildred Frizell	Ethel Johnson
	Evelyn Furtsch	Lilian Palmer	Gwendoline Porter
	Annette Rogers	Mary Frizell	Violet Webb
	Wilhelmina von Bremen	Hilda Strike	Nellie Halstead
1936	U.S. 46.9s[1]	G.B. 47.6s	CANADA 47.8s
	Harriett Bland	Eileen Hiscock	Dorothy Brookshaw
	Annette Rogers	Violet Olney	Hilda Cameron
	Elizabeth Robinson	Audrey Brown	Aileen Meagher
	Helen Stephens	Barbara Burke	Mildred Dolson
1948	NETHS. 47.5s	AUSTRALIA 47.6s	CANADA 48.0s
	Xenia de Jongh	Shirley Strickland	Viola Myers
	Nettie Timmers	Joy Maston	Nancy Mackay
	Gerda Koudijs	Betty McKinnon	Doris Foster
	Francina Blankers-Koen	Joyce King	Patricia Jones
1952	U.S. 45.9s*[2]	GERMANY 45.9s*	G.B. 46.2s
	Mae Faggs	Ursula Knab	Sylvia Cheeseman
	Barbara Jones	Maria Sander	June Foulds
	Janet Moreau	Helga Klein	Jean Desforges
	Catherine Hardy	Marga Petersen	Heather Armitage
1956	AUSTRALIA[3] 44.5s*	G.B. 44.7s	U.S. 44.9s
	Shirley Strickland	Anne Pashley	Mae Faggs
	Norma Crocker	Jean Scrivens	Margaret Matthews
	Fleur Mellor	June Paul[4]	Wilma Rudolph
	Betty Cuthbert	Heather Armitage	Isabelle Daniels

[1] GERMANY set O.R. of 46.4s in preliminaries but dropped baton in final.
[2] AUSTRALIA set O.R. of 46.1s in preliminaries but dropped baton in final.
[3] Set O.R. of 44.9s in preliminaries, later equalled by GERMANY.
[4] Formerly Foulds.

The most talked-about woman athlete in 1948 was the winner of 4 gold medals: Fanny Blankers-Koen (Netherlands), known as "The Flying Dutchwoman." Her medals came in the 100 m, 200 m, 80 m hurdles and as a member of the 4 × 100 m relay team.

	GOLD	SILVER	BRONZE
1960	U.S.[1] 44.5s	GERMANY 44.8s	POLAND 45.0s
	Martha Hudson	Martha Langbein	Tereza Wieczorek
	Lucinda Williams	Anni Biechl	Barbara Janiszewska
	Barbara Jones	Brunhilde Hendrix	Celina Jesionowska
	Wilma Rudolph	Jutta Heine	Halina Richter

[1] Set O.R. of 44.4s in preliminaries.

Close finish in the 4 × 100 metres relay in 1956, which produced a world record and gold medals for Australia with Betty Cuthbert (middle) the winner over Great Britain's anchor girl Heather Armitage.

	GOLD	SILVER	BRONZE
1964	POLAND 43.6s*	U.S. 43.9s	G.B. 44.0s
	Teresa Ciepla	Willye White	Janet Simpson
	Irena Kirzsenstein	Wyomia Tyus	Mary Rand
	Halina Gorecka	Marilyn White	Daphne Arden
	Ewa Klobukowska	Edith Maguire	Dorothy Hyman
1968	U.S. 42.8s*	CUBA 43.3s	U.S.S.R. 43.4s
	Barbara Ferrell	Marlene Elejarde	Lyudmila Zharkova
	Margaret Bailes	Fulgencia Romay	Galina Bukharina
	Mildrette Netter	Violeta Quesada	Vyera Popkova
	Wyomia Tyus	Miguellina Cobian	Ludmila Samotyesova
1972			

4 × 400 METRES (437 yds. 1 ft.) RELAY

1928–68 Event not held
1972

HIGH JUMP

1928	Ethel Catherwood (CANADA) 5′ 2⅝″*	[1]	[1]
1932	Jean Shiley (U.S.) 5′ 5″*	Mildred Didrikson (U.S.) 5′ 5″*	Eva Dawes (CANADA) 5′ 3″
1936	Ibolya Csak (HUNGARY) 5′ 3″	Dorothy Odam (G.B.) 5′ 3″	Elfriede Kaun (GERMANY) 5′ 3″
1948	Alice Coachman (U.S.) 5′ 6⅛″*	Dorothy Tyler[2] (G.B.) 5′ 6⅛″*	Micheline Ostermeyer (FRANCE) 5′ 3⅜″
1952	Esther Brand (S. AFRICA) 5′ 5¾″	Sheila Lerwill (G.B.) 5′ 5″	Alexandra Chudina (U.S.S.R.) 5′ 4⅛″
1956	Mildred McDaniel (U.S.) 5′ 9¼″*	[3]	[3]
1960	Iolanda Balas (RUMANIA) 6′ 0⅞″*	[4]	[4]
1964	Iolanda Balas (RUMANIA) 6′ 2¾″*	Michele Brown (AUSTRALIA) 5′ 11″	Taisia Chenchik (U.S.S.R.) 5′ 10″
1968	Miloslava Rezkova (CZECHO.) 5′ 11⅝″	Antonina Okorokova (U.S.S.R.) 5′ 10⅞″	Valentina Kozyr (U.S.S.R.) 5′ 10⅞″
1972			

[1] Tie for second place by Carolina Gisolf (HOLLAND) and Mildred Wiley (U.S.) at 5′ 1½″.
[2] Formerly Odam.
[3] Tie for second place by Thelma Hopkins (G.B.) and Maria Pisaryeva (U.S.S.R.) at 5′ 5¾″.
[4] Tie for second place by Jaroslawa Jozwiakowska (POLAND) and Dorothy Shirley (G.B.) at 5′ 7¼″.

LONG JUMP

1928–1936 Event not held

1948	Olga Gyarmati (HUNGARY) 18′ 8¼″*	Noemi Simonetto (ARGENTINA) 18′ 4½″	Anne Leyman (SWEDEN) 18′ 3⅜″
1952	Yvette Williams (N.Z.) 20′ 5⅝″*	Alexandra Chudina (U.S.S.R.) 20′ 1¾″	Shirley Cawley (G.B.) 19′ 5″
1956	Elzbieta Krzesinska (POLAND) 20′ 10″*	Willye White (U.S.) 19′ 11¾″	Nadyezhda Dvalishvili[1] (U.S.S.R.) 19′ 11″
1960	Vyera Krepkina (U.S.S.R.) 20′ 10¾″*	Elzbieta Krzesinska (POLAND) 20′ 6¾″	Hildrun Claus (GERMANY) 20′ 4½″

[1] Formerly Khnykina.

Mary Rand (Great Britain) in the act of breaking the world long jump record with 22 feet 2¼ inches during the 1964 Olympics.

	GOLD	SILVER	BRONZE
1964	Mary Rand (G.B.) 22′ 2¼″*	Irena Kirszenstein (POLAND) 21′ 7¾″	Tatyana Schelkanova (U.S.S.R.) 21′ 0¾″
1968	Viorica Viscopoleanu (RUMANIA) 22′ 4½″*	Sheila Sherwood (G.B.) 21′ 11″	Tatynana Talysheva (U.S.S.R.) 21′ 10¼″
1972			

SHOT PUT[1]

1928–1936	Event not held		
1948	Micheline Ostermeyer (FRANCE) 45′ 1½″*	Amelia Piccinini (ITALY) 42′ 11¼″	Ina Schäffer (AUSTRIA) 42′ 10⅞″
1952	Galina Zybina (U.S.S.R.) 50′ 1½″*	Marianne Werner (GERMANY) 47′ 9⅝″	Klavdia Tochenova (U.S.S.R.) 47′ 6⅞″
1956	Tamara Tyshkyevich (U.S.S.R.) 54′ 5″*	Galina Zybina (U.S.S.R.) 54′ 2¾″	Marianne Werner (GERMANY) 51′ 2½″
1960	Tamara Press (U.S.S.R.) 56′ 10″*	Johanna Lüttge (GERMANY) 54′ 6″	Earlene Brown (U.S.) 53′ 10½″
1964	Tamara Press (U.S.S.R.) 59′ 6″*	Renate Garisch (GERMANY) 57′ 9¼″	Galina Zybina (U.S.S.R.) 57′ 3″
1968	Margarita Gummel (E. GERMANY) 64′ 4″*	Marita Lange (E. GERMANY) 61′ 7½″	Nadezhda Chizhova (U.S.S.R.) 59′ 8¼″
1972			

[1] Weight 4 kilograms (8 lbs. 13 oz.) from 7-foot circle.

DISCUS THROW[1]

1928	Helena Konopacka (POLAND) 129′ 11¾″*	Lilian Copeland (U.S.) 121′ 7⅞″	Ruth Svedberg (SWEDEN) 117′ 10¼″
1932	Lilian Copeland (U.S.) 133′ 1⅝″*	Ruth Osburn (U.S.) 131′ 7½″	Jadwiga Wajsowna (POLAND) 127′ 1¼″

[1] Weight 1 kilogram (2 lbs. 3 oz.) from 7-foot circle.

Tamara Andreyevna Tyshkyevich, the Russian's 244 lb. gold medal winner in the shot put in 1956.

	GOLD	SILVER	BRONZE
1936	Gisela Mauermayer (GERMANY) 156′ 3¼″*	Jadwiga Wajsowna (POLAND) 151′ 7¾″	Paula Mollenhauer (GERMANY) 130′ 6⅞″
1948	Micheline Ostermeyer (FRANCE) 137′ 6⅛″	Edera Gentile (ITALY) 135′ 0⅞″	Janine Mazeas (FRANCE) 132′ 7⅜″
1952	Nina Romashkova (U.S.S.R.) 168′ 8½″*	Yelizaveta Bagryantseva (U.S.S.R.) 154′ 5⅝″	Nina Dumbadze (U.S.S.R.) 151′ 10½″
1956	Olga Fikotova (CZECHO.) 176′ 1½″*	Irina Beglyakova (U.S.S.R.) 172′ 4½″	Nina Ponomaryeva[2] (U.S.S.R.) 170′ 8″
1960	Nina Ponomaryeva[2] (U.S.S.R.) 180′ 9¼″*	Tamara Press (U.S.S.R.) 172′ 6½″	Lia Manoliu (RUMANIA) 171′ 9½″
1964	Tamara Press (U.S.S.R.) 187′ 10½″*	Ingrid Lotz (GERMANY) 187′ 8½″	Lia Manoliu (RUMANIA) 187′ 5″

[2] Formerly Romashkova.

	GOLD	SILVER	BRONZE
1968	Lia Manoliu (RUMANIA) 191′ 2½″*	Laesel Westermann (W. GER.) 189′ 6″	Jolan Kleiber (HUNGARY) 180′ 1½″
1972			

JAVELIN THROW[1]

1928	Event not held		
1932	Mildred Didrikson (U.S.) 143′ 4″*	Ellen Braumüller (GERMANY) 142′ 8⅝″	Tilly Fleischer (GERMANY) 141′ 6⅞″
1936	Tilly Fleischer (GERMANY) 148′ 2¾*	Liesl Kruger (GERMANY) 142′ 0⅜″	Marja Kwasniewska (POLAND) 137′ 1¼″
1948	Hermine Bauma (AUSTRIA) 149′ 6″*	Kaisa Parviäinen (FINLAND) 143′ 8⅛″	Lily Carlstedt (DENMARK) 140′ 5⅛″
1952	Dana Zatopkova (CZECHO.) 165′ 7″*	Alexandra Chudina (U.S.S.R.) 164′ 0⅞″	Yelena Gorchakova (U.S.S.R.) 163′ 3⅛″
1956	Inese Jaunzeme (U.S.S.R.) 176′ 8½″*	Marlene Ahrens (CHILE) 165′ 3½″	Nadyezhda Konyayeva (U.S.S.R.) 164′ 11½″
1960	Elvira Ozolina (U.S.S.R.) 183′ 8″*	Dana Zatopkova (CZECHO.) 176′ 5¼″	Birute Kalediene (U.S.S.R.) 175′ 4½″
1964	Mihaela Penes (RUMANIA) 198′ 7½″	Marta Rudasne (HUNGARY) 191′ 2″	Yelena Gorchakova (U.S.S.R.) 187′ 2½″[2]
1968	Angela Nemeth (HUNGARY) 198′ 0½″	Mihaela Penes (RUMANIA) 196′ 7″	Eva Janko (AUSTRIA) 190′ 5″
1972			

[1] Weight 600 grams (1 lb. 5 oz.).
[2] Set O.R. of 204′ 8½″ in qualifying round.

Dana Zatopkova (Czechoslovakia), whose husband won 4 gold medals, won a gold medal in the javelin throw herself in the 1952 Olympics, for a unique married-couple record.

Irina Press (shown here) is half of Russia's star sister combination. Irina won the 80 metres hurdles in 1968 and the pentathlon in 1964. Tamara Press won the shot put in 1960 and 1964 and the discus throw in 1964.

PENTATHLON[1]

1928–1960 Event not held

1964 Irina Press (U.S.S.R.) 5,246 pts.	Mary Rand (G.B.) 5,035 pts.	Galina Bystrova (U.S.S.R.) 4,956 pts.
1968 Ingrid Becker (W. GER.) 5,098 pts.	Liesel Prokop (AUSTRIA) 4,966 pts.	Anna-Maria Toth (HUNGARY) 4,959pts.
1972		

---

[1] Consisting of five events within two consecutive days—80 metres hurdles, shot put, high jump on the first day; long jump and 200 metres on the second.

18. Volleyball

This sport was introduced for the 1964 Games.

MEN

	GOLD	SILVER	BRONZE
1964	U.S.S.R. 17 pts.	CZECHO. 17 pts.	JAPAN 16 pts.
	Yury Chesnokov	Vaclav Smidl	Yataka Demachi
	Yury Vengerovsky	Josef Humhal	Tsutomu Koyama
	Eduard Sibiryakov	Josef Labuda	Sadatoshi Sugahara
	Dmitry Voskobornikov	Josef Musil	Naohiro Ikeda
	Vazha Kacharava	Petr Kop	Yasutaka Sato
	Stanislaw Ljugailo	Milan Cuda	Toshiaki Kosedo
	Vitaly Kovalenko	Karel Paulus	Tokihiko Higuchi
	Yury Poyarkov	Bohumil Golian	Masayuki Minami
	Ivan Bugaenkov	Boris Perusic	Takeshi Tokutomi
	Nikolay Burobin	Pavel Schenk	Teruhisa Moriyama
	Valery Kalachikhin	Ladislav Toman	Yuzo Nakamura
	Georgy Mondzolevsky		Katsutoshi Nekoda
1968	U.S.S.R. 16 pts.	JAPAN 14 pts.	CZECHO. 14 pts.
	Eduard Sibiryakov	Naohiro Ikeda	Antonin Prochazka
	Valery Kravchenko	Masayuki Minami	Jiri Svoboda
	Vladimir Belyaev	Katsutoshi Nekoda	Lubomir Zajicek
	Evgeny Lapinsky	Mamoru Shiragami	Josef Musil
	Oleg Antropov	Isao Koizumi	Josef Smolka
	Vasilijus Matushevas	Kenji Kimura	Vladimir Petlak
	Victor Mikhalchuk	Yasuaki Mitsumori	Petr Kop
	Yuri Poyarkov	Jungo Morita	Frantisek Sokol
	Boris Tereshuk	Tadayoshi Yokota	Bohumil Golian
	Vladimir Ivanov	Seiji Ohko	Zdenek Groessl
	Ivan Bugaenkov	Tetsuo Sato	Pavel Schenk
	Georgy Mondzolevsky	Kenji Shimaoka	Drahomir Koudelka
1972			

WOMEN

1964	JAPAN 10 pts.	U.S.S.R. 9 pts.	POLAND 8 pts.
	Masai Kasai	Antonina Ryzhova	Krystyna Czajkowska
	Emiko Miyamoto	Astra Bittauer	Jozefa Ledwig
	Kinuko Tanida	Ninel Lukanina	Maria Goliniowska
	Yuriko Handa	Ludmila Buldakova	Jadwiga Rutkowska
	Yoshiko Matsumara	Nelly Abramova	Danuta Kordaczuk
	Sada Isobe	Tamara Tikhonina	Krystyna Jakubowska
	Masaku Kondo	Valentina Kamenek	Jadwiga Marko
	Ayano Shibuki	Inna Ryksal	Maria Sliwka
	Katsumi Matsumari	Marita Katusheva	Zofia Szczesniewska
	Yoko Shinozaki	Tatyana Roschina	Krystyna Krupa
	Yuko Fujimoto	Valentina Mishak	Hanna Krystyna Busz
		Ludmila Gureeva	Barbara Hermel
1968	U.S.S.R. 14 pts.	JAPAN 12 pts.	POLAND 10 pts.
	Ljudmila Buldakova	Setsuko Yoshida	Krystyna Czajkowska
	Ljudmila Mikhailovskaya	Suzue Takayama	Jozefa Ledwig
	Tatyana Veinberg	Toyoko Iwahara	Elzbieta Porzec
	Vera Lantratova	Youko Kasahara	Wanda Wiecha
	Vera Galushka	Aiko Onozawa	Zofia Szczesniewska
	Tatyana Sarycheva	Yukiyo Kojima	Krystyna Jakubowska
	Tatyana Ponyaeva	Sachiko Fukunaka	Lidia Chmielnicka
	Nina Smoleeva	Kunie Shishikura	Barbara Niemczyk
	Inna Ryksal	Setsuko Inoue	Halina Aszkielowicz
	Galina Leontieva	Sumie Oinuma	Krystyna Krupa
	Roza Salikhova	Makiko Furukawa	Jad-wiga Ksiazek
	Valentina Vinogradova	Keiko Hama	Krystyna Ostromecka
1972			

19. Water Polo

	GOLD	SILVER	BRONZE
1896	Event not held		
1900	G.B.[1]	BELGIUM	FRANCE[2]
1904	U.S.[3]	U.S.	U.S.
	D. Bratton		
	Louis Handley		
	D. Hesser		
	L. B. Goodwin		
	Joseph Ruddy		
	J. Steen		
	G. van Cleef		
1908	G.B.[4]	BELGIUM	SWEDEN
	Charles Smith	A. Michant	Thorsten Kumfeldt
	G. Nevinson	Herman Meyboom	Axel Runström
	George Cornet	Victor Boin	Harald Julin
	T. Thould	Joseph Pletinex	Pontus Hansson
	George Wilkinson	S. Feyaerts	Gunnar Wennerström
	Paul Radmilovic[5]	Oscar Grégoire	Robert Andersson
	C. G. E. Forsyth	Herman Donners	Erik Bergvall
1912	G.B. 3 pts.	SWEDEN 2	BELGIUM 1
	Charles Smith	Thorsten Kumfeldt	Albert Durant
	George Cornet	Harald Julin	Herman Donners
	Charles Bugbee	Max Gumpel	Victor Boin
	Arthur Hill	Pontus Andersson	Joseph Pletinex
	George Wilkinson	Wilhelm Andersson	Oscar Grégoire
	Paul Radmilovic	Robert Andersson	Herman Meyboom
	Isaac Bentham	Eric Bergqvist	Félicien Courbet
1920	G.B.[6]	BELGIUM	SWEDEN
	Charles Smith	Gerald Blitz	Harald Julin
	Paul Radmilovic	Maurice Blitz	Robert Andersson
	Charles Bugbee	Albert Durant	Wilhelm Andersson
	N. M. Purcell	Joseph Pletinex	Eric Bergqvist
	C. Jones	Pierre Vermetten	Max Gumpel
	W. Peacock	Joseph Claudts	Pontus Hansson
	W. H. Dean	Félicien Courbet	Erik Andersson
			Nils Backlund
			Ake Naumann
1924	FRANCE[7]	BELGIUM	U.S.
	Paul Dujardin	Gerald Blitz	Arthur Austin
	Henri Padou	Maurice Blitz	Oliver Horn
	Rigal	Albert Durant	Frederick Lauer
	Deborgie	Joseph Pletinex	Edward Mitchell
	Delberghe	Joseph Claudts	John Norton
	Desmettre	Joseph de Combe	Wallace O'Connor
	Mayraud	Pierre Dewin	George Schroth
		Georges Fleurix	Harold Vollmer
		Paul Gailly	Johnny Weismuller
		Jules Thiry	James Handy
		Pierre Vermetten	Harold Kruger
			Elmer Collett
			John Curren
1928	GERMANY[8]	HUNGARY	FRANCE
	Erich Rademacher	István Barta	Paul Dujardin
	Fritz Gunst	Sándor Ivády	Henri Padou
	Otto Cordes	Márton Hommonay	Keignaert
	Emil Benecke	Alajos Keserü	Bulteel
	Joachim Rademacher	Olivér Halassy	A. Triboullet
	Karl Bähre	József Vértesy	Henri Cuvelier
	Max Amann	Ferenc Keserü	Roget
			van de Plancke
			A. Thévenon

---

[1] G.B. bt BELGIUM in final 7–2.
[2] Tie for third place between Libellule, Paris, and Enfants de Neptun, Tourcoing.
[3] New York A.C. bt Chicago A.C. in final 6–0; Missouri A.C. placed third.
[4] G.B. bt BELGIUM 9–2; BELGIUM bt SWEDEN 8–4.
[5] Also won a gold medal in 4 × 200 metres free-style relay.
[6] G.B. bt BELGIUM in final 3–2.

	GOLD	SILVER	BRONZE
1932	HUNGARY 8 pts.[9]	GERMANY 5	U.S. 5
	György Bródy	Erich Rademacher	Herbert Wildman
	Sándor Ivády	Fritz Gunst	Wallace O'Connor
	Márton Hommonay	Otto Cordes	Calvert Strong
	Olivér Halassy	Emil Benecke	Philip Daubenspeck
	József Vértesi	Joachim Rademacher	Harold McAllister
	János Németh	Hans Schwartz	Charles Finn
	Alajos Keserü	Hans Schulze	Austin Clapp
	Béla Komjádi		
	István Barta		
	Miklós Sárkány		
1936	HUNGARY 5 pts.[10]	GERMANY 5	BELGIUM 2
	György Bródy	Paul Klingenburg	Albert Castelyns
	Kálmán Hazai	Bernhard Baier	Gérard Blitz
	Márton Hommonay	Gustav Schürger	Pierre Coppieters
	Olivér Halassy	Fritz Gunst	Fernand Isselé
	Jenö Brandi	Josef Hauser	Joseph de Combe
	János Németh	Hans Schneider	Henry Stoelen
	György Kutasi	Hans Schulze	Henry d'Isy
	Mihály Bozsi	Alfred Kienzle	
	István Molnár	Heinrich Krug	
	Sandor Tarics	Helmuth Schwenn	
		Fritz Stolze	
1948	ITALY 6 pts.[11]	HUNGARY 3	NETHS. 2
	Pasquale Buonocore	László Jenei	J. Rohner
	Emilio Bulgarelli	Miklós Holop	Cornelius Korevaar
	Cesare Rubini	Dezsö Gyarmati	Cor Braasem
	Geminio Ognio	Károly Szittya	H. Stam
	Ermenegildo Arena	Oszkár Csuvik	A. Ruimschotel
	Aldo Ghira	István Szivós	Rudolph van Feggelen
	Tullio Pandolfini	Dezsö Lemhényi	Frits Smol
	Mario Majoni	Jenö Brandi	H. Z. Kestelaar
	Gianfranco Pandolfini	Dezsö Fábián	J. Cabout
		Pál Pók	P. Salomons
		Endre Györfi	M. Smael
1952	HUNGARY 5 pts.[12]	YUGOSLAVIA 5	ITALY 2
	László Jenei	Zdravko Kovacic	Raffaello Gambino
	György Vizvári	Veljko Bakasun	Cesare Rubini
	Dezsö Gyarmati	Ivo Stakula	Maurizio Mannelli
	Kálmán Markovits	Ivo Kurtini	Geminio Ognio
	Antal Bolvári	Bosko Vuksanovic	Ermenegildo Arena
	István Szivós	Zdravko Jezic	Renato de Sanzuane
	György Kárpáti	Lovro Radonic	Carlo Peretti
	Róbert Antal	Vladimir Ivkovic	Renato Traiola
	Dezsö Fábián	Marko Brainovic	Vincenzo Polito
	Károly Szittya	Dragoslav Siljak	Salvatore Gionta
	Dezsö Lemhényi		Lucio Ceccarini
	István Hasznos		
	Miklós Martin		
1956	HUNGARY 10 pts.[13]	YUGOSLAVIA 7	U.S.S.R. 6
	Otto Boras	Zdravko Kovacic	Boris Goikhman
	Dezsö Gyarmati	Hrvoje Kacic	Vyacheslav Kurrenoy
	Kálmán Markovits	Marijan Zuzej	Yuriy Chaliapin
	István Hevesi	Ivo Cipci	Valentin Prokopov
	György Kárpáti	Tomislav Franjkovic	Boris Markarov
	Mihály Mayer	Lovro Radonic	Petr Mchvenieradze
	Antal Bolvári	Zdravko Jezic	Petr Breus
	László Jenei	Vladimir Ivkovic	Mikhail Ryzhak
	Tivadar Kanisza		Viktor Ageyev
	István Szivós		Nodar Gvakharia
	Ervin Zador		Georgiy Lezin

[7] FRANCE bt BELGIUM in final 3–0.
[8] GERMANY bt HUNGARY in final 5–2.
[9] HUNGARY bt GERMANY 6–2, and U.S. 7–0; GERMANY drew with U.S. 4–4.
[10] HUNGARY drew with GERMANY 2–2, and bt BELGIUM 3–0; GERMANY bt BELGIUM 4–1.
[11] ITALY bt HUNGARY 4–3, and bt NETHS. 4–2; HUNGARY drew with NETHS. 4–4.

GOLD	SILVER	BRONZE
1960 ITALY 5 pts.[14]	U.S.S.R. 3	HUNGARY 2
Danio Bardi	Vladimir Semyenov	Otto Boras
Giuseppe d'Altrui	Anatoliy Kartashyev	István Hevesi
Franco Lavoratori	Vladimir Novikov	Mihály Mayer
Gianni Lonzi	Petr Mchvenieradze	Kálmán Markovits
Rosario Parmeggiani	Yuriy Grigorovskiy	Tivadar Kanizsa
Eraldo Pizzo	Viktor Ageyev	Zoltán Domotor
Dante Rossi	Givi Chikvanaya	György Kárpáti
Amedeo Ambron	Leri Gogoladze	László Jenei
Salvatore Gionta	Vyacheslav Kurrenoy	Peter Rusoran
Luigi Mannelli	Boris Goikhman	Andras Katona
Brunello Spinelli[15]	Evgeniy Saltsyn	Dezsö Gyarmati
1964 HUNGARY 5 pts.[16]	YUGOSLAVIA 5 pts.	U.S.S.R. 2 pts.
Miklós Ambius	Milan Muskatirovic	Igor Grabovsky
László Felkai	Ivo Trumbic	Vladimir Kuznetsov
János Konrad	Vinco Rosio	Boris Grishin
Zoltan Domotov	Slatco Simenc	Boris Popov
Tivador Kanizsa	Bozidor Stanisic	Nikolay Kalashnikov
Peter Rusoran	Ante Nardeli	Zenon Bortevich
György Karpati	Zoran Jankovic	Nicolay Kuznetsov
Dezsö Gyarmati	Frane Nonkovic	Vladimir Semionov
Denes Pocsik	Karlo Stipanic	Victor Ageev
Mihály Mayer		Leonid Osipov
Andras Bodnar		Eduar Yegorov
Otto Boras[15]		
1968 YUGOSLAVIA[17]	U.S.S.R.	HUNGARY
Karlo Stipanic	Vadim Guljaev	Endre Molnar
Ivo Trumbic	Givi Chikvanaya	Mihály Mayer
Ozren Bonacic	Boris Grishin	István Szivos
Uros Marovic	Alexander Dolgushin	János Konrad II
Ronald Lopanty	Aleksey Barkalov	László Sarosi
Zoran Jankovic	Yuriy Grigorovskiy	László Felkai
Miroslav Poljak	Vladimir Semenov	Ferenc Konrad III
Dejan Dabovic	Alexander Shidlovsky	Denes Pocsik
Djordje Perisic	Vjacheslav Skok	Andras Bodnar
Mirko Sandic	Leonid Osipov	Zoltan Domotor
Zdravko Hebel	Oleg Bovin	Janos Steinmetz
1972		

---

[12] HUNGARY drew with YUGOSLAVIA 2–2 and bt ITALY 7–2; YUGO-
SLAVIA bt ITALY 3–1.

[13] HUNGARY bt YUGOSLAVIA 2–1, and U.S.S.R. 4–0: YUGOSLAVIA
bt U.S.S.R. 3–2.

[14] ITALY bt U.S.S.R. 2–0, drew with HUNGARY 3–3; U.S.S.R. drew with
HUNGARY 3–3.

[15] Lists of team-members include, where known, names of all who played in
preliminaries as well as finals.

[16] HUNGARY drew with YUGOSLAVIA 4–4 and bt U.S.S.R. 5–2. YUGO-
SLAVIA drew with U.S.S.R. 2–0.

[17] YUGOSLAVIA bt HUNGARY 8–6 and bt U.S.S.R. 13–11. U.S.S.R. bt
ITALY 8–5.

20. Weight-Lifting

BANTAMWEIGHT

	GOLD	SILVER	BRONZE
1896–1936	Event not held		
1948[1]	Joseph de Pietro (U.S.) 678 lb.*	Julian Creus (G.B.) 655¾ lb.	Richard Tom (U.S.) 650¼ lb.
1952[1]	Ivan Udodov (U.S.S.R.) 694½ lb.*	Mahmoud Namdjou (IRAN) 678 lb.	Ali Mirzai (IRAN) 661¼ lb.
1956[1]	Charles Vinci (U.S.) 754½ lb.*	Vladimir Stogov (U.S.S.R.) 743½ lb.	Mahmoud Namdjou (IRAN) 732½ lb.
1960[1]	Charles Vinci (U.S.) 759 lb.*	Yoshinobu Miyake (JAPAN) 742½ lb.	Esmail Khan (IRAN) 726 lb.
1964[1]	Alexey Vakhonin (U.S.S.R.) 787¾ lb.*	Imre Földi (HUNGARY) 782¼ lb.	Shiro Ichinoseki (JAPAN) 765¾ lb.
1968	Mohammad Nasiri Seresht (IRAN) 809¾ lb.*	Imre Földi (HUNGARY) 809¾ lb.*	Henryk Trebicki (POLAND) 787¾ lb.
1972			

[1] Weight up to 56 kilograms (123½ lb.).

FEATHERWEIGHT

	GOLD	SILVER	BRONZE
896–1912	Event not held		
920[1]	F. de Haes (BELGIUM) 485 lb.	Alfred Schmidt (ESTONIA) 468½ lb.	E. Ritter (SWITZ.) 463 lb.
924[1]	Pierino Gabetti (ITALY) 887¼ lb.[2]	Andreas Stadler (AUSTRIA) 848¾ lb.	A. Reinmann (SWITZ.) 843¼ lb.
928[1]	Franz Andrysek (AUSTRIA) 633¾ lb.	Pierino Gabetti (ITALY) 622¾ lb.	Hans Wölpert (GERMANY) 622¾ lb.
932[1]	Raymond Suvigny (FRANCE) 633¾ lb.	Hans Wölpert (GERMANY) 622¾ lb.	Anthony Terlazzo (U.S.) 617¼ lb.
936[1]	Anthony Terlazzo (U.S.) 689 lb.	Saleh Moh Soliman (EGYPT) 672½ lb.	Ibrahim Shams (EGYPT) 661¼ lb.
48[1]	Mahmoud Fayad (EGYPT) 733 lb.*	Rodney Wilkes (TRINIDAD) 700 lb.	Jaffar Salmassi (IRAN) 689 lb.
52[1]	Rafael Chimishkyan (U.S.S.R.) 774 lb.*	Nikolay Saksonov (U.S.S.R.) 733 lb.	Rodney Wilkes (TRINIDAD) 711 lb.
56[1]	Isaac Berger (U.S.) 776½ lb.*	Evgeniy Minayev (U.S.S.R.) 754¾ lb.	Marian Zielinski (POLAND) 738 lb.
60[1]	Evgeniy Minayev (U.S.S.R.) 819½ lb.*	Isaac Berger (U.S.) 797½ lb.	Sebastiano Manníroni (ITALY) 775½ lb.
64[1]	Yoshinobu Miyake (JAPAN) 876 lb.*	Isaac Berger (U.S.) 842¾ lb.	Mieczyslaw Nowak (POLAND) 832 lb.
68	Yoshinobu Miyake (JAPAN) 865 lb.	Dito Shanidze (U.S.S.R.) 854 lb.	Yoshiyuki Miyake (JAPAN) 848½ lb.
72			

Weight up to 60 kilograms (132 lb.).
Total of 5 lifts.

LIGHTWEIGHT

	GOLD	SILVER	BRONZE
6–1912	Event not held		
20[1]	Alfred Neyland (ESTONIA) 567¾ lb.	R. Williquet (BELGIUM) 529 lb.	J. Rooms (BELGIUM) 507 lb.
4[1]	Edmond Décottignies (FRANCE) 970 lb.[2]	Anton Zwerzina (AUSTRIA) 942½ lb.	Bohumil Durdys (CZECHO.) 937 lb.
8[1]	Kurt Helbig (GERMANY) 711 lb.[3] Hans Haas (AUSTRIA) 711 lb.	—	F. Arnout (FRANCE) 667 lb.

(Left) Yuriy Vlasov (U.S.S.R.), who set an Olympic record in the heavyweight contest in 1960. (Above) Isaac Berger (U.S.), who won the gold medal in the featherweight division in 1956 and the silver medal in 1960.

	GOLD	SILVER	BRONZE
1932[1]	René Duverger (FRANCE) 716½ lb.*	Hans Haas (AUSTRIA) 678 lb.	Gastone Pierini (ITALY) 667 lb.
1936[1]	Mohammed Mesbah (EGYPT) 755 lb.*[3] Robert Fein (AUSTRIA) 755 lb.*	—	Karl Jansen (GERMANY) 722 lb.
1948[1]	Ibrahim Shams (EGYPT) 793½ lb.*	Appia Hammouda (EGYPT) 793½ lb.*	James Halliday (G.B.) 749½ lb.
1952[1]	Thomas Kono (U.S.) 799 lb.*	Yevgeniy Lopatin (U.S.S.R.) 771½ lb.	Verdi Barberis (AUSTRALIA) 771½ lb.
1956[1]	Igor Rybak (U.S.S.R.) 837½ lb.*	Ravil Khabutdinov (U.S.S.R.) 821 lb.	Chang Hee Kim (KOREA) 815½ lb.
1960[1]	Viktor Bushuyev (U.S.S.R.) 876 lb.*	Tan Howe Liang (KOREA) 837½ lb.	Abdul Wahid Aziz (IRAQ) 837½ lb.
1964[1]	Waldemar Baszanowski (POLAND) 953½ lb.*	Vladimir Kaplunov (U.S.S.R.) 953½ lb.	Marian Zielinski (POLAND) 925½ lb.
1968	Waldemar Baszanowski (POLAND) 964½ lb.*	Parviz Jalayer (IRAN) 931½ lb.	Marian Zielinski (POLAND) 925½ lb.
1972			

[1] Weight up to 67.5 kilograms (149 lb.).
[2] Total of 5 lifts.
[3] Results and bodyweights being equal both were declared champions.

MIDDLEWEIGHT

	GOLD	SILVER	BRONZE
1896–1912	Event not held		
1920[1]	Henri Gance (FRANCE) 540 lb.	Ubaldo Bianchi (ITALY) 523½ lb.	Albert Pettersson (SWEDEN) 523½ lb.
1924[1]	Carlo Galimberti (ITALY) 1,085¾ lb.[2]	Alfred Neyland (ESTONIA) 1,003 lb.	J. Kikkas (ESTONIA) 992 lb.
1928[1]	Roger Francois (FRANCE) 738½ lb.	Carlo Galimberti (ITALY) 733 lb.	A. Scheffer (NETHS.) 722 lb.
1932[1]	Rudolf Ismayr (GERMANY) 760½ lb.*	Carlo Galimberti (ITALY) 749½ lb.	Karl Hipfinger (AUSTRIA) 744 lb.
1936[1]	Khadr El Thouni (EGYPT) 854¾ lb.*	Rudolf Ismayr (GERMANY) 777 lb.	Adolf Wagner (GERMANY) 777 lb.
1948[1]	Frank Spellman (U.S.) 860 lb.*	Peter George (U.S.) 843¼ lb.	Sung Kim (KOREA) 837¾ lb.
1952[1]	[3] Peter George (U.S.) 882 lb.*	Gerald Gratton (CANADA) 860 lb.	Sung Kim (S. KOREA) 843¾ lb.
1956[1]	Fyeodor Bagdanovskiy (U.S.S.R.) 925¾ lb.*	Peter George (U.S.) 909 lb.	Ermanno Pignatti (ITALY) 843 lb.
1960[1]	Aleksandr Kurynov (U.S.S.R.) 964¼ lb.*	Thomas Kono (U.S.) 942 lb.	Győző Veres (HUNGARY) 895 lb.
1964[1]	Hans Zdrazila (CZECHO.) 980¾ lb.*	Victor Kurentsov (U.S.S.R.) 969¾ lb.	Masashi Ohuchi (JAPAN) 964 lb.
1968	Viktor Kurentsov (U.S.S.R.) 1,046¾ lb.*	Masashi Ohuchi (JAPAN) 1,002¾ lb.*	Karoly Bakos (HUNGARY) 969¾ lb.
1972			

[1] Weight up to 75 kilograms (165¼ lb.).
[2] Total of 5 lifts.
[3] Class was described as Welterweight.

LIGHT-HEAVYWEIGHT

896–1912	Event not held		
920[1]	Ernest Cadine (FRANCE) 639 lb.	Fritz Hünenberger (SWITZ.) 606 lb.	Erik Pettersson (SWEDEN) 600½ lb.
924[1]	Charles Rigoulot (FRANCE) 1,107¾ lb.[2]	Fritz Hünenberger (SWITZ.) 1,080¼ lb.	Leopold Friedrich (AUSTRIA) 1,080¼ lb.
928[1]	Said Nosseir (EGYPT) 782½ lb.	Louis Hostin (FRANCE) 777 lb.	J. Verheyen (NETHS.) 744 lb.
932[1]	Louis Hostin (FRANCE) 804¾ lb.*	Svend Olsen (DENMARK) 793½ lb.	Henry Duey (U.S.) 727½ lb.
936[1]	Louis Hostin (FRANCE) 820 lb.*	Eugen Deutsch (GERMANY) 804¾ lb.	Ibrahim Wasif (EGYPT) 793½ lb.
948[1]	Stanley Stanczyk (U.S.) 920½ lb.*	Harold Sakata (U.S.) 837¾ lb.	Gösta Magnusson (SWEDEN) 826¾ lb.
952[1]	[3] Trofim Lomakin (U.S.S.R.) 920½ lb.*	Stanley Stanczyk (U.S.) 915 lb.	Arkhadiy Vorobyev (U.S.S.R.) 898¼ lb.
956[1]	Thomas Kono (U.S.) 986¼ lb.*	Vasiliy Styepanov (U.S.S.R.) 942 lb.	James George (U.S.) 920¼ lb.
960[1]	Ireneusz Palinski (POLAND) 975¼ lb.	James George (U.S.) 947¾ lb.	Jan Bochenek (POLAND) 925¾ lb.
964[1]	Rudolf Plyukeider (U.S.S.R.) 1,046 lb.*	Geza Toth (HUNGARY) 1,030¼ lb.	Gyozo Veres (HUNGARY) 1,030 lb.
968	Boris Selitsky (U.S.S.R.) 1,068¾ lb.*	Vladimir Belyaev (U.S.S.R.) 1,068¾ lb.*	Norbert Ozimek (POLAND) 1,041¼ lb.
972			

Weight up to 82.5 kilograms (182 lb.).
Total of 5 lifts (total of 709½ lb. for three Olympic lifts).
Class was described as Middleweight.

Paul Anderson (U.S.) set an Olympic record in winning the heavyweight class gold medal in 1956. A year later he raised 6,270 lb. on his back.

MIDDLE-HEAVYWEIGHT

	GOLD	SILVER	BRONZE
1896–1948	Event not held		
1952[1]	[2] Norbert Schemansky (U.S.) 981 lb.*	Grigoriy Novak (U.S.S.R.) 903¾ lb.	Lennox Kilgour (TRINIDAD) 887¼ lb.
1956[1]	Arkhadiy Vorobyev (U.S.S.R.) 1,019¼ lb.*	David Sheppard (U.S.) 975¼ lb.	Jean Debuf (FRANCE) 936¾ lb.
1960[1]	Arkhadiy Vorobyev (U.S.S.R.) 1,041¼ lb.*	Trofim Lomakin (U.S.S.R.) 1,008 lb.	Louis Martin (G.B.) 980½ lb.
1964[1]	Vladimir Golovanov (U.S.S.R.) 1,074 lb.*	Louis Martin (G.B.) 1,046½ lb.	Ireneusz Palinski (POLAND) 1,030 lb.
1968	Kaarlo Kangasniemi (FINLAND) 1,140½ lb.*	Yan Talts (U.S.S.R.) 1,118¼ lb.	Marek Golab (POLAND), 1,091 lb.
1972			

[1] Weight up to 90 kilograms (198¼ lb.).
[2] Class was described as Light-Heavyweight.

HEAVYWEIGHT

1896[1]	Viggo Jensen (DENMARK) 245¾ lb.	Launceston Elliott (G.B.) 245¾ lb.	Sotirios Versis (GREECE) 242½ lb.
1900	Event not held		
1904[1]	Perikles Kakousis (GREECE) 246 lb.*	Otto Osthoff (U.S.) 186 lb.	Frank Kungler (U.S.) 150 lb.
1908–1912	Event not held		
1920[2]	Filippo Bottino (ITALY) 595 lb.	Joseph Alzin (LUXEM.) 562 lb.	L. Bernot (FRANCE) 551 lb.
1924[2]	Giuseppe Tonani (ITALY) 1,140¾ lb.[3]	Franz Aigner (AUSTRIA) 1,135¼ lb.	H. Tammer (ESTONIA) 1,096¾ lb.
1928[2]	Josef Strassberger (GERMANY) 810 lb.	Arnold Luhaär (ESTONIA) 793½ lb.	Jaroslav Skobla (CZECHO.) 788 lb.

	GOLD	SILVER	BRONZE
1932[2]	Jaroslav Skobla (CZECHO.) 837¾ lb.*	Vaclav Psenicka (CZECHO.) 832¼ lb.	Josef Strassberger (GERMANY) 832¼ lb.
1936[2]	Josef Manger (AUSTRIA) 903¾ lb.*	Vaclav Psenicka (CZECHO.) 887¼ lb.	Arnold Luhaär (ESTONIA) 882 lb.
1948[2]	John Davis (U.S.) 996½ lb.*	Norbert Schemansky (U.S.) 937 lb.	A. Charite (NETHS.) 909¼ lb.
1952[4]	John Davis (U.S.) 1,014 lb.*	James Bradford (U.S.) 964½ lb.	Humberto Selvetti (ARGENTINA)953½lb.
1956[4]	Paul Anderson (U.S.) 1,102 lb.*	Humberto Selvetti (ARGENTINA) 1,102 lb.*	Alberto Pigaiani (ITALY) 997¼ lb.
1960[4]	Yuriy Vlasov (U.S.S.R.) 1,184½ lb.*	James Bradford (U.S.) 1,129½ lb.	Norbert Schemansky (U.S.) 1,102 lb.
1964[4]	Leonid Zhabotinsky (U.S.S.R.) 1,262 lb.*	Yury Vlasov (U.S.S.R.) 1,256 lb.	Norbert Schemansky (U.S.) 1,184¾ lb.
1968	Leonid Zhabotinsky (U.S.S.R.) 1,261¾ lb.	Serge Reding (BELGIUM) 1,223 lb.	Joseph Dube (U.S.) 1,223 lb.
1972			

[1] There was only one class irrespective of weight.
[2] Weight over 82.5 kilograms (182 lb.).
[3] Total of 5 lifts.
[4] Weight over 90 kilograms (198¼ lb.).

21. Wrestling

FREE-STYLE—FLYWEIGHT

	GOLD	SILVER	BRONZE
1896–1900	Event not held		
1904[1]	Robert Curry (U.S.)	John Heim (U.S.)	Gustav Thiefenthaler (U.S.)
1908–1936	Event not held		
1948[2]	Lennart Viitala (FINLAND)	Halit Balamir (TURKEY)	Thure Johansson (SWEDEN)
1952[2]	Hasan Gemici (TURKEY)	Yushu Kitano (JAPAN)	Mahmoud Mollaghassemi (IRAN)
1956[2]	Mirian Tsalkalamanidze (U.S.S.R.)	Mohamad Khojastehpour (IRAN)	Huseyin Akbas (TURKEY)
1960[2]	Ahmet Bilek (TURKEY)	Masayuki Matsubara (JAPAN)	Moha Saidabadi Safepour (IRAN)
1964[2]	Yoshikatsu Yoshida (JAPAN)	Chang-sun Chang (KOREA)	Said Alikbar Haydari (IRAN)
1968	Shigeo Nakata (JAPAN)	Richard Sanders (U.S.)	Surenjav Sukhbaatar (MONGOLIA)
1972			

[1] Weight up to 47.6 kilograms (105 lb.).
[2] Weight up to 52 kilograms (114½ lb.).

A free-style bout between bantamweights at Empress Hall, Earls Court, London in the 1948 Olympics. Nasuk Akkar (Turkey), the eventual gold medal winner, is on top of Charles Kouyos (France), who won the bronze medal.

FREE-STYLE—BANTAMWEIGHT

	GOLD	SILVER	BRONZE
1896–1900	Event not held		
1904[1]	I. Niflot (U.S.)	August Wester (U.S.)	Z. Strebler (U.S.)
1908[2]	George Mehnert (U.S.)	W. Press (G.B.)	A. Cote (CANADA)
1912–1920	Event not held		
1924[3]	Kustaa Pihlajamäki (FINLAND)	Kalle Makinen (FINLAND)	Bryant Hines (U.S.)
1928[3]	Kalle Makinen (FINLAND)	Edmond Spapen (BELGIUM)	James Trifonou (CANADA)
1932[3]	Robert Pearce (U.S.)	Odön Zombori (HUNGARY)	Aatos Jaskari (FINLAND)
1936[3]	Odön Zombori (HUNGARY)	Ross Flood (U.S.)	Johannes Herbert (GERMANY)
1948[4]	Nasuk Akkar (TURKEY)	Gerald Leeman (U.S.)	Charles Kouyos (FRANCE)
1952[4]	Shohachi Ishii (JAPAN)	Rashid Mamedbekov (U.S.S.R.)	Jadar Khan (INDIA)
1956[4]	Mustafa Dagistanli (TURKEY)	Mohamad Yaghoubi (IRAN)	Mikhail Chakhov (U.S.S.R.)
1960[4]	Terrence McCann (U.S.)	Nejdet Zalev (BULGARIA)	Tadeusz Trojanowski (POLAND)
1964[4]	Yojiro Uetake (JAPAN)	Huseyin Akbas (TURKEY)	Aidyn Ali Ogly (U.S.S.R.)
1968	Yojiro Uetake (JAPAN)	Donald Behm (U.S.)	Abutaleb Gorgori (IRAN)
1972			

---

[1] Weight up to 56.7 kilograms (125 lb.).
[2] Weight up to 54 kilograms (119 lb.).
[3] Weight up to 56 kilograms (123½ lb.).
[4] Weight up to 57 kilograms (125¼ lb.).

FREE-STYLE—FEATHERWEIGHT

GOLD	SILVER	BRONZE
1896–1900 Event not held		
1904[1] B. Bradshaw (U.S.)	T. McLeer (U.S.)	C. Clapper (U.S.)
1908[2] George Dole (U.S.)	J. P. Slim (G.B.)	W. McKie (G.B.)
1912 Event not held		
1920[3] Charles Ackerley (U.S.)	Samuel Gerson (U.S.)	P. Bernard (G.B.)
1924[4] Robin Reed (U.S.)	Chester Newton (U.S.)	Katsutoshi Naitoh (JAPAN)
1928[4] Allie Morrison (U.S.)	Kustaa Pihlajamäki (FINLAND)	Hans Minder (SWITZ.)
1932[4] Hermanni Pihlajamäki (FINLAND)	Edgar Nemir (U.S.)	Einar Karlsson (SWEDEN)
1936[4] Kustaa Pihlajamäki (FINLAND)	Francis Millard (U.S.)	Gösta Jönsson (SWEDEN)
1948[5] Gazanfer Bilge (TURKEY)	Ivar Sjölin (SWEDEN)	Adolf Müller (SWITZ.)
1952[5] Bayram Sit (TURKEY)	Nasser Guivethci (IRAN)	Josiah Henson (U.S.)
1956[5] Shozo Sasahara (JAPAN)	Joseph Mewis (BELGIUM)	Erkki Penttilä (FINLAND)
1960[5] Mustafa Dagistanli (TURKEY)	Stantcho Ivanov (BULGARIA)	Vladimir Rubashvili (U.S.S.R.)
1964[6] Osamu Watanabe (JAPAN)	Stantcho Ivanov (BULGARIA)	Nodar Khokhashvili (U.S.S.R.)
1968 Masaaki Kaneko (JAPAN)	Enio Todorov (BULGARIA)	Shamseddin Seyed-Abbassi (IRAN)
1972		

[1] Weight up to 61.2 kilograms (135 lb.).
[2] Weight up to 60.3 kilograms (133 lb.).
[3] Weight up to 62.5 kilograms (138 lb.).
[4] Weight up to 61 kilograms (134½ lb.).
[5] Weight up to 62 kilograms (136¾ lb.).
[6] Weight up to 63 kilograms (138¾ lb.).

FREE-STYLE—LIGHTWEIGHT

GOLD	SILVER	BRONZE
1896–1900 Event not held		
1904[1] O. Roehm (U.S.)	R. Tesing (U.S.)	G. Zukel (U.S.)
1908[2] G. de Relwyskow (G.B.)	W. Wood (G.B.)	A. Gingell (G.B.)
1912 Event not held		
1920[3] Kalle Antilla (FINLAND)	Gottfrid Svensson (SWEDEN)	P. Wright (G.B.)
1924[4] Russel Vis (U.S.)	Volmar Wickström (FINLAND)	Arve Haavisto (FINLAND)
1928[4] Osvald Käpp (ESTONIA)	Charles Pacome (FRANCE)	Eino Leino (FINLAND)
1932[5] Charles Pacome (FRANCE)	Károly Kárpáti (HUNGARY)	Gustaf Klarén (SWEDEN)
1936[4] Károly Kárpáti (HUNGARY)	Wolfgang Ehrl (FINLAND)	Hermanni Pihlajamäki (FINLAND)
1948[5] Celal Atik (TURKEY)	Gösta Frändfors (SWEDEN)	Hermann Baumann (SWITZ.)

[1] Weight up to 65.7 kilograms (144 lb.).
[2] Weight up to 66.6 kilograms (147 lb.).
[3] Weight up to 67.5 kilograms (149 lb.).
[4] Weight up to 66 kilograms (145½ lb.).
[5] Weight up to 65 kilograms (143¼ lb.).

GOLD	SILVER	BRONZE
1952[6] Olle Anderberg (SWEDEN)	Thomas Evans (U.S.)	Djahanbakte Torfighe (IRAN)
1956[6] Emmali Habibi (IRAN)	Shigeru Kasahara (JAPAN)	Alimbeg Bestayev (U.S.S.R.)
1960[6] Shelby Wilson (U.S.)	Viktor Sinyavskiy (U.S.S.R.)	Enio Dimov (BULGARIA)
1964[7] Enio Dimor (BULGARIA)	Klaus Rost (GERMANY)	Iwao Horiuchi (JAPAN)
1968 Abdollah Mohaved (IRAN)	Enio Valtchev (BULGARIA)	Sereeter Danzandarjaa (MONGOLIA)
1972		

[6] Weight up to 67 kilograms (147¾ lb.).
[7] Weight up to 70 kilograms (154¼ lb.).

FREE-STYLE—WELTERWEIGHT

1896–1900 Event not held		
1904[1] Charles Erickson (U.S.)	William Beckmann (U.S.)	J. Winholtz (U.S.)
1908–1920 Event not held		
1924[2] [3] Hermann Gehri (SWITZ.)	Eino Leino (FINLAND)	Adolf Müller (SWITZ.)
1928[2] [3] Arve Haavisto (FINLAND)	Lloyd Appleton (U.S.)	Morris Letchford (CANADA)
1932[2] [3] Jack van Bebber (U.S.)	Daniel MacDonald (CANADA)	Eino Leino (FINLAND)
1936[2] [3] Frank Lewis (U.S.)	Ture Andersson (SWEDEN)	Joseph Schleimer (CANADA)
1948[4] Yasar Dogu (TURKEY)	Richard Garrard (AUSTRALIA)	Leland Mervill (U.S.)
1952[4] William Smith (U.S.)	Per Berlin (SWEDEN)	Abdullah Modjtavabi (IRAN)
1956[4] Mitsuo Ikeda (JAPAN)	Ibrahim Zengin (TURKEY)	Vakhtang Balavadze (U.S.S.R.)
1960[4] Douglas Blubaugh (U.S.)	Ismail Ogan (TURKEY)	Muhammad Bashir (PAKISTAN)
1964[5] Ismail Ogan (TURKEY)	Guliko Sagaradze (U.S.S.R.)	Mohamad-Ali (IRAN) Sanatkaran
1968 Mahmut Atalay (TURKEY)	Daniel Robin (FRANCE)	Dagvasuren Purev (MONGOLIA)
1972		

[1] Weight up to 71.6 kilograms (158 lb.).
[2] Weight up to 72 kilograms (158¾ lb.).
[3] Class called Light middleweight.
[4] Weight up to 73 kilograms (161 lb.).
[5] Weight up to 78 kilograms (171¾ lb.).

FREE-STYLE—MIDDLEWEIGHT

1896–1904 Event not held		
GOLD	SILVER	BRONZE
1908[1] Stanley Bacon (G.B.)	G. de Relwyskow (G.B.)	F. Beck (G.B.)
1912 Event not held		
1920[2] Eino Leino (FINLAND)	Väino Penttala (FINLAND)	Charles Johnson (U.S.)
1924[3] Fritz Haggmann (SWITZ.)	Pierre Olivier (BELGIUM)	Vilho Pekkala (FINLAND)
1928[3] Ernst Kyburz (SWITZ.)	D. Stockton (CANADA)	S. Rabin (G.B.)
1932[3] Ivar Johansson (SWEDEN)	Kyösti Luukko (FINLAND)	Jozsef Tunyogi (HUNGARY)
1936[3] Emile Poilvé (FRANCE)	Richard Voliva (U.S.)	Ahmet Kirecci (TURKEY)

	GOLD	SILVER	BRONZE
1948[3]	Glen Brand (U.S.)	Adil Candemir (TURKEY)	Erik Linden (SWEDEN)
1952[3]	David Tsimakuridze (U.S.S.R.)	Gholamreza Takhti (IRAN)	György Gurics (HUNGARY)
1956[3]	Nikola Nikolov (BULGARIA)	Daniel Hodge (U.S.)	Georgiy Skhirtladze (U.S.S.R.)
1960[3]	Hassan Gungor (TURKEY)	Georgiy Skhirtladze (U.S.S.R.)	Hans Antonsson (SWEDEN)
1964[4]	Prodan Gardjer (BULGARIA)	Hasan Gungor (TURKEY)	Daniel Brand (U.S.)
1968	Boris Gurevitch (U.S.S.R.)	Munkhbat Jigjid (MONGOLIA)	Prodane Gardjev (BULGARIA)
1972			

---

[1] Weight up to 73 kilograms (161 lb.).
[2] Weight up to 75 kilograms (165¼ lb.).
[3] Weight up to 79 kilograms (174 lb.).
[4] Weight up to 87 kilograms (191¾ lb.).

FREE-STYLE—LIGHT-HEAVYWEIGHT

	GOLD	SILVER	BRONZE
1896–1912	Event not held		
1920[1]	Anders Larsson (SWEDEN)	Charles Courant (SWITZ.)	Walter Maurer (U.S.)
1924[2]	John Spellman (U.S.)	Rudolf Svensson (SWEDEN)	Charles Courant (SWITZ.)
1928[2]	Thure Sjöstedt (SWEDEN)	Anton Bögli (SWITZ.)	Henri Lefebre (FRANCE)
1932[2]	Peter Mehringer (U.S.)	Thure Sjöstedt (SWEDEN)	Eddie Scarf (AUSTRALIA)
1936[2]	Knut Fridell (SWEDEN)	August Néo (ESTONIA)	Erich Siebert (GERMANY)
1948[2]	Henry Wittenberg (U.S.)	Fritz Stöckli (SWITZ.)	Bengt Fahlkvist (SWEDEN)
1952[2]	Wiking Palm (SWEDEN)	Henry Wittenberg (U.S.)	Adil Atan (TURKEY)
1956[2]	Gholamreza Tahkti (IRAN)	Boris Koulayev (U.S.S.R.)	Peter Blair (U.S.)
1960[2]	Ismet Atli (TURKEY)	Gholamreza Tahkti (IRAN)	Anatoliy Albul (U.S.S.R.)
1964[3]	Alexandr Medred (U.S.S.R.)	Ahmet Ayik (TURKEY)	Said Sherifov (BULGARIA)
1968	Ahmet Ayik (TURKEY)	Shota Lomidze (U.S.S.R.)	Jozsef Csatari (HUNGARY)
1972			

---

[1] Weight up to 82.5 kilograms (182 lb.).
[2] Weight up to 87 kilograms (191¾ lb.).
[3] Weight up to 97 kilograms (213¾ lb.).

FREE-STYLE—HEAVYWEIGHT

	GOLD	SILVER	BRONZE
1896[1]	Karl Schumann (GERMANY)	Georges Tsitas (GREECE)	Stephanos Christopulos (GREECE)
1900	Event not held		
1904[2]	B. Hansen (U.S.)	Frank Kungler (U.S.)	F. Warmbold (U.S.)
1908[3]	G. C. O'Kelly (G.B.)	Jacob Gundersen (NORWAY)	Edward Barrett (G.B.)

---

[1] Only one class, regardless of weight.
[2] Weight over 71.6 kilograms (158 lb.).
[3] Weight over 73 kilograms (161 lb.).

	GOLD	SILVER	BRONZE
1912	Event not held		
1920[4]	Robert Rothe (SWITZ.)	Nathan Pendleton (U.S.)	Ernst Nilsson (SWEDEN) Frederick Meyer[5] (U.S.)
1924[6]	Harry Steele (U.S.)	Henry Wernli (SWITZ.)	A. McDonald (G.B.)
1928[6]	Johan Richthoff (SWEDEN)	Aukusti Sihvola (FINLAND)	E. Dame (FRANCE)
1932[6]	Johan Richthoff (SWEDEN)	John Riley (U.S.)	Nikolaus Hirschl (AUSTRIA)
1936[6]	Kristjan Palusalu (ESTONIA)	Josef Klapuch (CZECHO.)	Hjalmar Nyström (FINLAND)
1948[6]	Gyula Bóbis (HUNGARY)	Bertil Antonsson (SWEDEN)	Joseph Armstrong (AUSTRALIA)
1952[6]	Arsen Mekokishvili (U.S.S.R.)	Hans Antonsson (SWEDEN)	Kenneth Richmond (G.B.)
1956[6]	Hamit Kaplan (TURKEY)	Ussein Alichev (BULGARIA)	Taisto Kangasniemi (FINLAND)
1960[6]	Wilfried Dietrich (GERMANY)	Hamit Kaplan (TURKEY)	Sergey Sarasov (U.S.S.R.)
1964[7]	Alexandr Wanitsky (U.S.S.R.)	Liutvi Djiber (BULGARIA)	Hamit Kaplan (TURKEY)
1968	Alexander Medved (U.S.S.R.)	Osman Douraliev (BULGARIA)	Wilfried Dietrich (GERMANY)
1972			

[4] Weight over 82.5 kilograms (182 lb.).
[5] Tie for third place.
[6] Weight over 87 kilograms (191¾ lb.).
[7] Weight over 97 kilograms (213¾ lb.).

GRECO-ROMAN—FLYWEIGHT

1896–1936	Event not held		
1948[1]	Pietro Lombardi (ITALY)	Kenan Olcay (TURKEY)	Reino Kangasmäki (FINLAND)
1952[1]	Boris Gurevich (U.S.S.R.)	Ignazio Fabra (ITALY)	Leo Honkala (FINLAND)
1956[1]	Nikolay Solovyev (U.S.S.R.)	Ignazio Fabra (ITALY)	Dursan Egribas (TURKEY)
1960[1]	Dumitru Pirvulescu (RUMANIA)	Ossman Sayed (U.A.R.)	Mohamad Paziraye (IRAN)
1964[1]	Tsutomu Hanahara (JAPAN)	Angel Kerezov (BULGARIA)	Dumitru Pirvulescu (RUMANIA)
1968	Petar Kirov (BULGARIA)	Vladimir Bakulin (U.S.S.R.)	Miroslav Zeman (CZECHO.)
1972			

[1] Weight up to 52 kilograms (114¼ lb.).

GRECO-ROMAN—BANTAMWEIGHT

1896–1920	Event not held		
1924[1]	Edvard Pütsep (ESTONIA)	Anselm Ahlfors (FINLAND)	Väinö Ikonen (FINLAND)
1928[1]	Kurt Leucht (GERMANY)	Josef Maudr (CZECHO.)	Giovanni Gozzi (ITALY)
1932[1]	Jakob Brendel (GERMANY)	Marcello Nizzola (ITALY)	Louis Francois (FRANCE)

[1] Weight up to 58 kilograms (127¾ lb.).

	GOLD	SILVER	BRONZE
1936[2]	Marton Lorinc (HUNGARY)	Egon Svensson (SWEDEN)	Jakob Brendel (GERMANY)
1948[3]	Kurt Pettersson (SWEDEN)	Mahmoud Hassan Aly (EGYPT)	Hamit Kaya (TURKEY)
1952[3]	Imre Hódos (HUNGARY)	Zakaria Khihab (LEBANON)	Artem Teryan (U.S.S.R.)
1956[3]	Konstantin Vyrupayev (U.S.S.R.)	Edvin Vesterby (SWEDEN)	Francisc Horvat (RUMANIA)
1960[3]	Olyeg Karavayev (U.S.S.R.)	Ion Cernea (RUMANIA)	Dinko Stoikov (BULGARIA)
1964[3]	Masamitsu Ichiguchi (JAPAN)	Vladlen Trostiansky (U.S.S.R.)	Ion Cernea (RUMANIA)
1968	Janos Varga (HUNGARY)	Ion Baciu (RUMANIA)	I. Kochergin (U.S.S.R.)
1972			

[2] Weight up to 56 kilograms (123¼ lb.).
[3] Weight up to 57 kilograms (125¾ lb.).

GRECO-ROMAN—FEATHERWEIGHT

	GOLD	SILVER	BRONZE
1896–1908	Event not held		
1912[1]	Kalle Koskelo (FINLAND)	Georg Gerstacker (GERMANY)	Otto Lasanen (FINLAND)
1920[2]	Oskari Friman (FINLAND)	Heikki Kähkönen (FINLAND)	Fridtjof Svensson (SWEDEN)
1924[2]	Kalle Anttila (FINLAND)	Aleksanteri Toivola (FINLAND)	Erik Malmberg (SWEDEN)
1928[2]	Voldemar Väli (ESTONIA)	Erik Malmberg (SWEDEN)	Girolamo Quaglia (ITALY)
1932[2]	Giovanni Gozzi (ITALY)	Wolfgang Ehrl (GERMANY)	Lauri Koskela (FINLAND)
1936[3]	Yasar Erkan (TURKEY)	Aarne Reini (FINLAND)	Einar Karlsson (SWEDEN)
1948[2]	Mohammed Oktav (TURKEY)	Olle Anderberg (SWEDEN)	Ferenc Tóth (HUNGARY)
1952[2]	Yakov Punkin (U.S.S.R.)	Imre Polyák (HUNGARY)	Abdel Rashed (EGYPT)
1956[2]	Rauno Mäkinen (FINLAND)	Imre Polyák (HUNGARY)	Roman Dzneladze (U.S.S.R.)
1960[2]	Müzahir Sille (TURKEY)	Imre Polyák (HUNGARY)	Konstantin Vyrupayev (U.S.S.R.)
1964[4]	Imre Polyak (HUNGARY)	Roman Rurua (U.S.S.R.)	Branko Martinovic (YUGOSLAVIA)
1968	Roman Rurua (U.S.S.R.)	Hideo Fujimoto (JAPAN)	Simion Popescu (RUMANIA)
1972			

[1] Weight up to 60 kilograms (132 lb.).
[2] Weight up to 62 kilograms (136¼ lb.).
[3] Weight up to 61 kilograms (134¼ lb.).
[4] Weight up to 63 kilograms (138¾ lb.).

GRECO-ROMAN—LIGHTWEIGHT

	GOLD	SILVER	BRONZE
1896–1904	Event not held		
1908[1]	Enrico Porro (ITALY)	Nikolay Orlov (RUSSIA)	Arvo Linden-Linko (FINLAND)
1912[2]	Eemil Wäre (FINLAND)	Gustaf Malmström (SWEDEN)	Edvin Matiasson (SWEDEN)
1920[2]	Eemil Wäre (FINLAND)	Taavi Tamminen (FINLAND)	Fritjof Andersen (NORWAY)
1924[3]	Oskari Friman (FINLAND)	Lajos Keresztes (HUNGARY)	Kalle Westerlund (FINLAND)

	GOLD	SILVER	BRONZE
1928[3]	Lajos Keresztes (HUNGARY)	Edvard Sperling (GERMANY)	Edvard Westerlund (FINLAND)
1932[3]	Erik Malmberg (SWEDEN)	Abraham Kurland (DENMARK)	Edvard Sperling (GERMANY)
1936[4]	Lauri Koskela (FINLAND)	Josef Herda (CZECHO.)	Voldemar Väli (ESTONIA)
1948[2]	Karl Freij (SWEDEN)	Aage Eriksen (NORWAY)	Károly Ferencz (HUNGARY)
1952[3]	Shazam Safin (U.S.S.R.)	Karl Freij (SWEDEN)	Mikulas Athanasov (CZECHO.)
1956[2]	Kyösti Lehtonen (FINLAND)	Riza Dogan (TURKEY)	Gyula Tóth (HUNGARY)
1960[3]	Avtandil Koridze (U.S.S.R.)	Bozidar Martinovic (YUGOSLAVIA)	Roland Freij (SWEDEN)
1964[5]	Kazim Ayvaz (TURKEY)	Valerin Bularca (RUMANIA)	David Gvantseladze (U.S.S.R.)
1968	Muneji Munemura (JAPAN)	Stevan Horvat (YUGOSLAVIA)	Petros Galaktopoulos (GREECE)
1972			

---

[1] Weight up to 66.6 kilograms (147 lb.).
[2] Weight up to 67.5 kilograms (149 lb.).
[3] Weight up to 67 kilograms (147¾ lb.).
[4] Weight up to 66 kilograms (145¼ lb.).
[5] Weight up to 70 kilograms (154¼ lb.).

GRECO-ROMAN—WELTERWEIGHT

1896–1928 Event not held

	GOLD	SILVER	BRONZE
1932[1] [2]	Ivar Johansson (SWEDEN)	Väinö Kajander-Kajukorpi (FINLAND)	Ercole Gallegatti (ITALY)
1936[2] [3]	Rudolf Svedberg (SWEDEN)	Fritz Schäfer (GERMANY)	Eino Virtanen (FINLAND)
1948[4]	Gösta Andersson (SWEDEN)	Miklós Szilvási (HUNGARY)	Carl Hansen (DENMARK)
1952[4]	Miklós Szilvási (HUNGARY)	Gösta Andersson (SWEDEN)	Khalil Taha (LEBANON)
1956[4]	Mithat Bayrak (TURKEY)	Vladimir Maneyev (U.S.S.R.)	Per Berlin (SWEDEN)
1960[4]	Mithat Bayrak (TURKEY)	Günther Maritschnigg (GERMANY)	René Schiermeyer (FRANCE)
1964[5]	Anatoly Koleslav (U.S.S.R.)	Cyril Todorov (BULGARIA)	Bertil Nystrom (SWEDEN)
1968	Rudolf Vesper (E. GERMANY)	Daniel Robin (FRANCE)	Karoly Bajko (HUNGARY)
1972			

---

[1] Weight up to 75 kilograms (165¼ lb.).
[2] Class called Light middleweight.
[3] Weight up to 72 kilograms (158¾ lb.).
[4] Weight up to 73 kilograms (161 lb.).
[5] Weight up to 78 kilograms (171¾ lb.).

GRECO-ROMAN—MIDDLEWEIGHT

1896–1904 Event not held

	GOLD	SILVER	BRONZE
1908[1]	Fritjof Martensson (SWEDEN)	Mauritz Andersson (SWEDEN)	Anders Andersen (DENMARK)
1912[2]	Claes Johansson (SWEDEN)	Max Klein (RUSSIA)	Alfred Asikainen (FINLAND)
1920[2]	Carl Westergren (SWEDEN)	Artur Lindfors (FINLAND)	Masa Perttila (FINLAND)

	GOLD	SILVER	BRONZE
1924[2][3]	Edvard Westerlund (FINLAND)	Artur Lindfors (FINLAND)	Roman Steinberg (ESTONIA)
1928[2][3]	Väinö Kokkinen (FINLAND)	László Papp (HUNGARY)	Albert Kusnetz (SWEDEN)
1932[4]	Väinö Kokkinen (FINLAND)	Johann Földeák (GERMANY)	Axel Cadier (SWEDEN)
1936[4]	Ivar Johansson (SWEDEN)	Ludwig Schweikert (GERMANY)	József Palotás (HUNGARY)
1948[4]	Axel Grönberg (SWEDEN)	Mohamed Tayfur (TURKEY)	Ercole Gallegatti (ITALY)
1952[4]	Axel Grönberg (SWEDEN)	Kalervo Rauhala (FINLAND)	Nikolay Belov (U.S.S.R.)
1956[4]	Guivi Kartozia (U.S.S.R.)	Dimitar Dobrev (BULGARIA)	Karl-Axel Jansson (SWEDEN)
1960[4]	Dimitar Dobrev (BULGARIA)	Lothar Metz (GERMANY)	Ion Taranu (RUMANIA)
1964[5]	Branislav Simic (YUGOSLAVIA)	Jiri Kormanik (CZECHO.)	Lothar Metz (GERMANY)
1968	Lothar Metz (E. GERMANY)	Valentin Olenik (U.S.S.R.)	Branislav Simic (YUGOSLAVIA)
1972			

---

[1] Weight up to 73 kilograms (161 lb.).
[2] Weight up to 75 kilograms (165¼ lb.).
[3] Class called Light middleweight.
[4] Weight up to 79 kilograms (174 lb.).
[5] Weight up to 87 kilograms (191¾ lb.).

GRECO-ROMAN—LIGHT-HEAVYWEIGHT

	GOLD	SILVER	BRONZE
1896–1904	Event not held		
1908[1]	Verner Weckman (FINLAND)	Yrjö Saarela (FINLAND)	Carl Jensen (DENMARK)
1912[2][3]	Anders Ahlgren[4] (SWEDEN) Ivar Bohling (FINLAND)	—	Béla Vargya (HUNGARY)
1920[2]	Claes Johansson (SWEDEN)	Edil Rosenquist (FINLAND)	Johnsen Eriksen (DENMARK)
1924[2]	Carl Westergren (SWEDEN)	Rudolf Svensson (SWEDEN)	Onni Pellinen (FINLAND)
1928[5][6]	Ibrahim Moustafa (EGYPT)	Adolf Rieger (GERMANY)	Onni Pellinen (FINLAND)
1932[7]	Rudolf Svensson (SWEDEN)	Onni Pellinen (FINLAND)	Mario Gruppioni (ITALY)
1936[7]	Axel Cadier (SWEDEN)	Edwins Bietags (LITHUANIA)	August Néo (ESTONIA)
1948[7]	Karl Nilsson (SWEDEN)	Kaelpo Gröndahl (FINLAND)	Ibrahim Orabi (EGYPT)
1952[7]	Kaelpo Gröndahl (FINLAND)	Shalva Shikhladze (U.S.S.R.)	Karl Nilsson (SWEDEN)
1956[7]	Valentin Nikolayev (U.S.S.R.)	Petko Sirakov (BULGARIA)	Karl Nilsson (SWEDEN)
1960[7]	Terfik Kis (TURKEY)	Kraliu Bimbalov (BULGARIA)	Guivi Kartozia (U.S.S.R.)
1964[8]	Boyan Alexandrov (BULGARIA)	Pev Svensson (SWEDEN)	Heinz Kiehl (GERMANY)

---

[1] Weight up to 93 kilograms (205 lb.)
[2] Weight up to 82.5 kilograms (182 lb.).   [3] Class called Middleweight B.
[4] Declared a draw after wrestling for over six hours without a decision.
[5] Weight up to 82 kilograms (180¾ lb.).   [6] Class called Middleweight.
[7] Weight up to 87 kilograms (191¼ lb.).
[8] Weight up to 97 kilograms (213¾ lb.).

	GOLD	SILVER	BRONZE
1968	Boian Radev (BULGARIA)	Nikolai Yakovenko (U.S.S.R.)	Nicolae Martinescu (RUMANIA)

GRECO-ROMAN—HEAVYWEIGHT

	GOLD	SILVER	BRONZE
1896–1904	Event not held		
1908[1]	Richard Weisz (HUNGARY)	A. Petrov (RUSSIA)	Sören Jensen (DENMARK)
1912[2]	Yrjö Saarela (FINLAND)	Johan Olin (FINLAND)	Sören Jensen (DENMARK)
1920[2]	Adolf Lindfors (FINLAND)	Paul Hansen (DENMARK)	Martti Nieminen (FINLAND)
1924[2]	Henry Deglane (FRANCE)	Edil Rosenquist (FINLAND)	Raymund Badó (HUNGARY)
1928[3]	Rudolf Svensson (SWEDEN)	Hjalmar Nyström (FINLAND)	Georg Gehring (GERMANY)
1932[4]	Carl Westergren (SWEDEN)	Josef Urban (CZECHO.)	Nikolaus Hirschl (AUSTRIA)
1936[4]	Kristjan Palusalu (ESTONIA)	John Nyman (SWEDEN)	Kurt Hornfischer (GERMANY)
1948[4]	Ahmed Kirecci (TURKEY)	Tor Nilsson (SWEDEN)	Guido Fantoni (ITALY)
1952[4]	Johannes Kotkas (U.S.S.R.)	Josef Ruzicka (CZECHO.)	Tauro Kovanen (FINLAND)
1956[4]	Anatoliy Parfenyov (U.S.S.R.)	Wilfried Dietrich (GERMANY)	Adelmo Bulgarelli (ITALY)
1960[4]	Ivan Bogdan (U.S.S.R.)	Wilfried Dietrich (GERMANY)	Karoly Kubat (CZECHO.)
1964[5]	István Kozma (HUNGARY)	Anatoly Roshin (U.S.S.R.)	Wilfried Dietrich (GERMANY)
1968	István Kozma (HUNGARY)	Anatoly Roshin (U.S.S.R.)	Petr Kment (CZECHO.)
1972			

---

[1] Weight over 93 kilograms (205 lb.).
[2] Weight over 82.5 kilograms (182 lb.).
[3] Weight over 82 kilograms (180¾ lb.).

[4] Weight over 87 kilograms (191¾ lb.).
[5] Weight over 97 kilograms (213¾ lb.).

22. Yachting

The 5.5 metres class which was contested from 1952 to 1968 has been discontinued. Gold, Silver, and Bronze medals for that event were won as follows: Sweden 2–1–1; U.S. 2–0–1; Australia 1–0–1; Great Britain 0–1–1; Switzerland 0–1–1; Denmark 0–1–0; Finland 0–1–0.

SOLING

1896–1968	Event not held	
1972		

TEMPEST

1896–1968	Event not held	
1972		

DRAGON

1896–1936	Event not held		
1948	"Pan" Thor Thorvaldsen Sigve Lie Hakon Barfod (NORWAY) 4,746 pts.	"Slaghoken" Folke Bohlin V. Johnson F. Brodin (SWEDEN) 4,621	"Snap" William Berntsen Ole Berntsen K. Baess (DENMARK) 4,223
1952	"Pan" Thor Thorvaldsen Sigve Lie Hakon Barfod (NORWAY) 6,130 pts.	"Tornado" Per Gedda Leif Boldt-Christmas Erland Almkvist (SWEDEN) 5,556	"Gustel X" Theodor Thomsen Erich Natusch Georg Nowka (GERMANY) 5,352
1956	"Slaghoken II" Folke Bohlin Bengt Palmquist Leif Wikström (SWEDEN) 5,723 pts.	"Tip" Ole Berntsen Cyril Andresen Christian von Bülow (DENMARK) 5,723[1]	"Bluebottle" Graham Mann Ronald Backus Jonathan Janson (G.B.) 4,547
1960	"Nirefs" Prince Constantine Odysseus Eskidjoglou Georges Zaimis (GREECE) 6,733 pts.	"Tango" Jorge Chavez Salas Hector Calegaris Jorge del Rio (ARGENTINA) 5,715	"Venilia" Antonio Cosentino Antonio Ciciliano Giulio de Stefano (ITALY) 5,704
1964	"White Lady" Ole Berntsen Chris Van Bulow Ole Poulsen (DENMARK) 5,854 pts.	"Mutafo" P. Ahrendt U. Mens W. Lorenz (GERMANY) 5,826	"Aphrodite" Lowell North C. Rogers R. Deaver (U.S.) 5,523
1968	"Willi Waw" George Friedrichs (U.S.) 6.0 pts.	"Chock" Aage Birch (DENMARK) 26.4	"Mutafo" Paul Borowski (E. GERMANY) 32.7
1972			

---

[1] Order decided on number of first places.

STAR

GOLD	SILVER	BRONZE
1896–1928 Event not held		
1932 "Jupiter" Gilbert Gray Andrew Libano jr. (U.S.) 46 pts.	"Joy" Colin Ratsey Peter Jaffe (G.B.) 35	"Swedish Star" Gunnar Asther Daniel Sundén-Cullberg (SWEDEN) 28
1936 "Wannesee" Peter Bischoff Hans-Joachim Wiese (GERMANY) 80 pts.	"Sunshine" Arved Laurin Uno Wallentin (SWEDEN) 64	"Bemm II" Adriaan Maas Willem de Vries Lentsch (NETHS.) 63
1948 "Hilarius" Hilary Smart Paul Smart (U.S.) 5,828 pts.	"Kurush II" Carlos de Cardenas Carlos de Cardenas jr. (CUBA) 4,849	"Starita" Adriaan Maas Edward Stutterheim (NETHS.) 4,731
1952 "Merope" Agostino Straulino Nicoló Rode (ITALY) 7,635 pts.	"Comanche" John Reid John Price (U.S.) 7,216	"Espadarte" Francisco de Andrade Joaquim Fiuza (PORTUGAL) 4,903
1956 "Kathleen" Herbert Williams Lawrence Low (U.S.) 5,876 pts.	"Merope III" Agostino Straulino Nicoló Rode (ITALY) 5,649	"Gem IV" Durward Knowles Sloan Farrington (BAHAMAS) 5,223
1960 "Tornado" Timir Pinegin Fyedor Shutkov (U.S.S.R.) 7,619 pts.	"Ma' Lindo" Mario Quina José Quina (PORTUGAL) 6,665	"Shrew II" William Parks Robert Halperin (U.S.) 6,269
1964 "Gem" D. Knowles C. Cook (BAHAMAS) 5,664 pts.	"Glider" R. Stearns L. Williams (U.S.) 5,585	"Humbug V" P. Pettersson H. Sundstrom (SWEDEN) 5,527
1968 "North Star" Lowell North (U.S.) 14.4 pts.	"Sirene" Peder Lunde (NORWAY) 43.7	"Romance" Franco Cavallo (ITALY) 44.7
1972		

Paul Elvström (Denmark), who has won the gold medal in the Finn class each of the two times the event was held—in 1956 and 1960. He is the only one ever to have won gold medals in four successive Olympic Games.

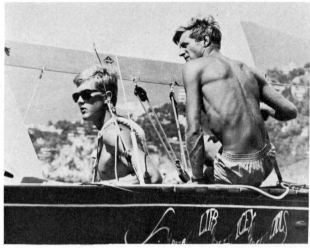

"Superdocious" (G.B.), the Flying Dutchman gold medal winner, with Rodney Pattisson (helmsman) and Iain McDonald-Smith (crew) who came first in five races out of six—a record for an Olympic Regatta.

FLYING DUTCHMAN

	GOLD	SILVER	BRONZE
1896–1956	Event not held		
1960	"Sirene"	"Skum"	"Macky VI"
	Peder Lunde	Hans Fogh	Rolf Mulka
	Bjorn Bergvall	Ole Erik Petersen	Ingo von Bredow
	(NORWAY) 6,774 pts.	(DENMARK) 5,991	(GERMANY) 5,882
1964	"Pandora"	"Lady C"	"Widgeon"
	Helman Pederson	Keith Musto	H. Melges
	E. Wells	Anthony Morgan	W. Benson
	(N.Z.) 6,255 pts.	(G.B.) 5,556	(U.S.) 5,158
1968	"Superdocious"	"Leda"	"Mach"
	Rodney Pattisson	Ullrich Libor	Ralph Conrad
	Iain Macdonald-Smith	(W. GERMANY) 43.7	(BRAZIL) 48.4
	(G.B.) 3 pts.		
1972			

FINN

1896–1952	Event not held		
1956	Paul Elvström	Andre Nelis	John Marvin
	(DENMARK) 7,509 pts.	(BELGIUM) 6,254	(U.S.) 5.953
1960	Paul Elvström	Aleksandr Tyukelov	Andre Nelis
	(DENMARK) 8,171 pts.	(U.S.S.R.) 6,250	(BELGIUM) 5,934
1964	Willi Kuhweide	Peter Barrett	Henning Wind
	(GERMANY) 7,638 pts.	(U.S.) 6,373	(DENMARK) 6,190
1968	Valentin Mankin	Hubert Raudaschl	Fabio Albarelli
	(U.S.S.R.) 11.7 pts.	(AUSTRIA) 53.4	(ITALY) 55.1
1972			

ROLL OF OLYMPIC MEDAL WINNERS
IN THE WINTER EVENTS SINCE 1908

Nordic Skiing—Men

15 KM. (9.3 miles) CROSS-COUNTRY[1]

	GOLD	SILVER	BRONZE
1908–1920	Sport not held		
1924	Thorleif Haug (NORWAY) 1h 14m 31.0s	Johan Gröttumsbraaten (NORWAY) 1h 15m 51.0s	Tipani Niku (FINLAND) 1h 26m 26.0s
1928	Johan Gröttumsbraaten (NORWAY) 1h 37m 01.0s	Ole Hegge (NORWAY) 1h 39m 01.0s	Reidar Ödegaard (NORWAY) 1h 40m 11.0s
1932	Sven Utterström (SWEDEN) 1h 23m 07.0s	Axel Wikström (SWEDEN) 1h 25m 07.0s	Veli Saarinen (FINLAND) 1h 25m 24.0s
1936	Erik-August Larsson (SWEDEN) 1h 14m 38.0s	Oddbjörn Hagen (NORWAY) 1h 15m 33.0s	Pekki Niemi (FINLAND) 1h 16m 59.0s
1948	Martin Lundström (SWEDEN) 1h 13m 50.0s	Nils Östensson (SWEDEN) 1h 14m 22.0s	Gunnar Eriksson (SWEDEN) 1h 16m 06.0s
1952	Hallgeir Brenden (NORWAY) 1h 1m 34.0s	Tapio Mákelá (FINLAND) 1h 2m 09.0s	Paavo Lonkila (FINLAND) 1h 2m 20.0s
1956	Hallgeir Brenden (NORWAY) 49m 39s	Sixten Jernberg (SWEDEN) 50m 14.0s	Pavel Koltschin (U.S.S.R.) 50m 17.0s
1960	Haakon Brusveen (NORWAY) 51m 55.5s	Sixten Jernberg (SWEDEN) 51m 58.6s	Veikko Hakulinen (FINLAND) 52m 03.0s
1964	Eero Maentyranta (FINLAND) 50m 54.1s	H. Grönningen (NORWAY) 51m 34.8s	Sixten Jernberg (SWEDEN) 51m 42.2s
1968	H. Grönningen (NORWAY) 47m 54.2s	Eero Maentyranta (FINLAND) 47m 56.1s	Gunnar Larsson (SWEDEN) 48m 33.7s
1972	Sven-Ake Lundback (SWEDEN) 45m 28.24s	Fedor Simaschov (U.S.S.R.) 46m 00.84s	Ivar Formo (NORWAY) 46m 02.86s

[1]Decided over 18 km. (11.1 miles) 1924–1948.

30 KM. (18.6 miles) CROSS-COUNTRY

	GOLD	SILVER	BRONZE
1908–1952	Event not held		
1956	Veikko Hakulinen (FINLAND) 1h 44m 06.0s	Sixten Jernberg (SWEDEN) 1h 44m 30.0s	Pavel Koltschin (U.S.S.R.) 1h 45m 45.0s
1960	Sixten Jernberg (SWEDEN) 1h 51m 03.9s	Rolf Rämgård (SWEDEN) 1h 51m 16.9s	Nikolay Anikin (U.S.S.R.) 1h 52m 28.2s
1964	Eero Maentyranta (FINLAND) 1h 30m 50.7s	H. Grönningen (NORWAY) 1h 32m 02.3s	I. Voronchikin (U.S.S.R.) 1h 32m 15.8s
1968	Franco Nones (ITALY) 1h 35m 39.2s	Odd Martinsen (NORWAY) 1h 36m 28.9s	Eero Maentyranta (FINLAND) 1h 36m 55.3s
1972	Viaceslav Vedenin (U.S.S.R.) 1h 36m 31.2s	Paal Tyldum (NORWAY) 1h 37m 25.3s	Johs Harviken (NORWAY) 1h 37m 32.4s

50 KM. (31 miles) CROSS-COUNTRY

	GOLD	SILVER	BRONZE
1924	Thorleif Haug (NORWAY) 3h 44m 32.0s	Thoralf Strömstad (NORWAY) 3h 46m 23.0s	Johan Gröttumsbraaten (NORWAY) 3h 47m 46.0s
1928	Per Erik Hedlund (SWEDEN) 4h 52m 03.3s	Gustaf Jonsson (SWEDEN) 5h 05m 30.0s	Volger Andersson (SWEDEN) 5h 05m 46.0s
1932	Veli Saarinen (FINLAND) 4h 28m 00.0s	Väinö Liikkanen (FINLAND) 4h 28m 20.0s	Arne Rustadstuen (NORWAY) 4h 31m 20.0s

GOLD	SILVER	BRONZE
1936 Elis Wiklund (SWEDEN) 3h 30m 11.0s	Axel Wikström (SWEDEN) 3h 33m 20.0s	Nils-Joel Englund (SWEDEN) 3h 34m 10.0s
1948 Nils Karlsson (SWEDEN) 3h 47m 48.0s	Harald Eriksson (SWEDEN) 3h 52m 20.0s	Benjamin Vanninen (FINLAND) 3h 57m 28.0s
1952 Veikko Hakulinen (FINLAND) 3h 33m 33.0s	Eero Kolehmainen (FINLAND) 3h 38m 11.0s	Magnar Estenstad (NORWAY) 3h 38m 28.0s
1956 Sixten Jernberg (SWEDEN) 2h 50m 27.0s	Veikko Hakulinen (FINLAND) 2h 51m 45.0s	Fyedor Terentyev (U.S.S.R.) 2h 53m 32.0s
1960 Kalevi Hämäläinen (FINLAND) 2h 59m 06.3s	Veikko Hakulinen (FINLAND) 2h 59m 26.7s	Rolf Rämgård (SWEDEN) 3h 02m 46.7s
1964 Sixten Jernberg (SWEDEN) 2h 43m 52.6s	A. Roennlund (SWEDEN) 2h 44m 58.2s	A. Tiainen (FINLAND) 2h 45m 30.4s
1968 Olle Ellefsaeter (NORWAY) 2h 28m 45.8s	Viaceslav Vedenin (U.S.S.R.) 2h 29m 02.5s	Josef Haas (SWITZERLAND) 2h 29m 14.8s
1972 Paal Tyldrum (NORWAY) 2h 43m 14.75s	Magne Myrmo (NORWAY) 2h 43m 29.45s	Viaceslav Vedenin (U.S.S.R.) 2h 44m 00.19s

RELAY RACE 4 × 10 KM. (6 miles 376 yds.)

Event not held 1908–1932

Year	Gold	Silver	Bronze
1936	FINLAND 2h 41m 33.0s Nurmela Karppinen Lähde Jalkanen	NORWAY 2h 41m 39.0s Hagen Hoffsbakken Brodahl Iversen	SWEDEN 2h 43m 03.0s Berger Larsson Häggblad Matsbo
1948	SWEDEN 2h 32m 08.0s Östensson Täpp Eriksson Lundström	FINLAND 2h 41m 06.0s Silvennoinen Laukkanen Rytky Kiuru	NORWAY 2h 44m 33.0s Evensen Ökern Nyborg Hagen
1952	FINLAND 2h 20m 16.0s Hasu Lonkila Korhonen Mäkelä	NORWAY 2h 23m 13.0s Estenstad Kirkholt Stokken Brenden	SWEDEN 2h 24m 13.0s Täpp Andersson Josefsson Lundström
1956	U.S.S.R. 2h 15m 30.0s Terentyev Koltschin Anikin Kusin	FINLAND 2h 21m 31.0s Kiuru Kortelainen Viitanen Hakulinen	SWEDEN 2h 17m 42.0s Larsson Samuelsson Larsson Jernberg
1960	FINLAND 2h 18m 45.6s Alatalo Mäntyranta Huhtala Hakulinen	NORWAY 2h 18m 46.4s Grönningen Brenden Östby Brusveen	U.S.S.R. 2h 21m 21.6s Schelyuchin Vaganov Kusnetsov Anikin
1964	SWEDEN 2h 18m 34.6s Asph Jernberg Stefansson Roennlund	FINLAND 2h 18m 42.4s Huhtala Tiainen Launla Mähtyranta	U.S.S.R. 2h 18m 46.9s Uhobin Vaganov Voronchikin Kolchin
1968	NORWAY 2h 08m 33.5s Martinsen Tyldum Grönningen Ellefsaeter	SWEDEN 2h 10m13.2s Halvarsson Andersson G. Larsson Roennlund	FINLAND 2h 10m 56.7s Oikarainen Taipale Laurila Maentyranta
1972	U.S.S.R. 2h 04m 47.94s Voroakov Skobov Fimachov Vedenin	NORWAY 2h 04m 57.06s Braa Tyldrum Formo Harviken	SWITZER. 2h 07m 00.06s Kaflin Giger Koelin Hauser

Nordic Skiing—Women

5 KM. CROSS-COUNTRY (3 miles 188 yds.)

GOLD	SILVER	BRONZE
1924–60 Event not held		
1964 Klaudia Boyerskikh (U.S.S.R.) 17m 50.5s	M. Lehtonen (FINLAND) 17m 52.9s	A. Kolchina (U.S.S.R.) 18m 08.4s
1968 Toini Gustafsson (SWEDEN) 16m 45.2s	Galina Koulakova (U.S.S.R.) 16m 48.4s	Alevtina Koltchina (U.S.S.R.) 16m 51.6s
1972 Galina Koulakova (U.S.S.R.) 17m 00.50s	Marjatta Kajosmaa (FINLAND) 17m 05.50s	Helena Sikolova (CZECHO.) 17m 07.32s

10 KM. CROSS-COUNTRY (6.2 miles)

1952 Lydia Widemen (FINLAND) 41m 40.0s	Mirja Hietamies (FINLAND) 42m 39.0s	Siiri Rantanen (FINLAND) 42m 50.0s
1956 Lyubov Kosyryeva (U.S.S.R.) 38m 11.0s	Radya Yeroschina (U.S.S.R.) 38m 16.0s	Sonja Edström (SWEDEN) 38m 23.0s
1960 Maria Gusakova (U.S.S.R.) 39m 46.6s	Lyubov Baranova-Kosyryeva (U.S.S.R.) 40m 04.2s	Radya Yeroschina (U.S.S.R.) 40m 06.0s
1964 Klaudia Boyarskikh (U.S.S.R.) 40m 24.3s	E. Mekshilo (U.S.S.R.) 40m 26.6s	Maria Gusakova (U.S.S.R.) 40m 46.6s
1968 Toini Gustafsson (SWEDEN) 36m 46.5s	Berit Moerdre (NORWAY) 37m 54.6s	Inger Aufles (NORWAY) 37m 59.9s
1972 Galina Koulakova (U.S.S.R.) 34m 17.8s	Alevitina Olunina (U.S.S.R.) 34m 54.1s	Marjatta Kajosmaa (FINLAND) 34m 56.5s

3 × 5 KM. RELAY

1924–1952 Event not held

1956 FINLAND 1h 9m 01.0s Polkunen Hietamies Rantanen	U.S.S.R. 1h 9m 28.0s Kosyryeva Koltschina Yeroschina	SWEDEN 1h 9m 48.0s Johansson Eriksson Edström
1960 SWEDEN 1h 4m 21.4s Johansson Strandberg Ruthström-Edström	U.S.S.R. 1h 5m 2.6s Yeroschina Gusakova Baranova-Kosyryeva	FINLAND 1h 6m 27.5s Rantanen Ruoppa Pöysti
1964 U.S.S.R. 59m 20.2s Koltschina Mekshilo Boyarskikh	SWEDEN 1h 1m 27.0s Martinsson Strandberg Gustafsson	FINLAND 1h 2m 45.1s Pusula Pöysti Lehstonen
1968 NORWAY 57m 30.0s Aufles Enger Damon Moerdre	SWEDEN 57m 51.0s Strandberg Gustafsson Martinsson	U.S.S.R. 58m 13.6s Koltschina Achkina Koulacova
1972 U.S.S.R. 48m 46.15s Moukhateva Olunina Koulakova	FINLAND 49m 19.57s Takolo Kuntola Kajosmaa	NORWAY 49m 51.49s Aufles Dahl Moerdrelammedal

Ski Jumping

1924–1960 held on one hill only

BIG HILL (80 metres)

1964 Toralf Engan (NORWAY) 230.70 pts.	Veikko Kankkonen (FINLAND) 228.90 pts.	T. Brandtzaeg (NORWAY) 227.20 pts.

Toralf Engan (Norway) shows how he won the ski jump title in the 1964 Olympics. Besides winning the gold medal on the Big Hill, he captured the silver medal on the Small Hill.

(90 metres)

	GOLD	SILVER	BRONZE
1968	Vladimir Beloussov (U.S.S.R.) 231.3 pts.	Jiri Raska (CZECHOSLOVAKIA) 229.4 pts.	Lars Grini (NORWAY) 214.3 pts.
1972	Wojciech Fortuna (POLAND) 219.8 pts.	Walter Steiner (SWITZ.) 219.8 pts.	Rainer Schmidt (EAST GERMANY 219.3 pts

SMALL HILL (70 metres)

1964	Veikko Kankkonen (FINLAND) 229.90 pts.	Toralf Engan (NORWAY) 226.30 pts.	T. Brandtzaeg (NORWAY) 222.90 pts.
1968	Jiri Raska (CZECHOSLOVAKIA) 216.5 pts.	Reinhold Bachler (AUSTRIA) 214.2 pts.	Baldur Preiml (AUSTRIA) 212.6 pts.
1972	Yukio Kasaya (JAPAN) 244.2 pts.	Akitsugo Konno (JAPAN) 234.8 pts.	Seiji Aochi (JAPAN) 229.5 pts.

NORDIC COMBINED (15 km. and jumping)

1908–1920	Event not held		
1924[1]	Thorleif Haug (NORWAY)	Thoralf Strömstad (NORWAY)	Johan Gröttumsbraaten (NORWAY)
1928[1]	Johan Gröttumsbraaten (NORWAY)	Hans Vinjarengen (NORWAY)	John Snersrud (NORWAY)
1932	Johan Gröttumsbraaten (NORWAY) 446.0 pts.	Ole Stenen (NORWAY) 436.05 pts.	Hans Vinjarengen (NORWAY) 434.60 pts.
1936	Oddbjorn Hagen (NORWAY) 430.30 pts.	Olaf Hoffsbakken (NORWAY) 419.80 pts.	Sverre Brodahl (NORWAY) 408.10 pts.
1948	Heikki Hasu (FINLAND) 448.80 pts.	Martti Huhtala (FINLAND) 433.65 pts.	Sfen Israelsson (SWEDEN) 433.40 pts.

[1] In 1924 and 1928, the scoring was decided upon a different basis from that used from 1932 onwards.

	GOLD	SILVER	BRONZE
1952	Simon Slattvik (NORWAY) 451.952 pts.	Heikki Hasu (FINLAND) 447.5 pts.	Sverre Stenersen (NORWAY) 436.335 pts.
1956	Sverre Stenersen (NORWAY) 455.0 pts.	Bengt Eriksson (SWEDEN) 473.4 pts.	Franciszek Gron-Gasienica (POLAND) 436.8 pts.
1960	Georg Thoma (GERMANY) 457.952 pts.	Tormod Knutsen (NORWAY) 453.0 pts.	Nikolay Gusakow (U.S.S.R.) 452.0 pts.
1964	Tormod Knutsen (NORWAY) 469.28 pts.	N. Kiselev (U.S.S.R.) 453.04 pts.	Georg Thoma (GERMANY) 452.88 pts.
1968	Frantz Keller (WEST GERMANY) 449.04 pts.	Alois Kaelin (SWITZERLAND) 447.94 pts.	Andreas Kunz (EAST GERMANY) 444.10 pts.
1972	Ulrich Wehling (EAST GERMANY) 413.34 pts.	Rauno Miettinen (FINLAND) 405.50 pts.	Karl-Heinz Luck (EAST GERMANY) 398.80 pts.

Biathlon

1960	Klas Lestander (SWEDEN) 1h 33m 21.6s	Antti Tyrvainen (FINLAND) 1h 33m 57.7s	Aleksandr Privalov (U.S.S.R.) 1h 34m 54.2s
1964	Vladimir Melyanin (U.S.S.R.) 1h 20m 26.8s	Aleksandr Privalov (U.S.S.R.) 1h 23m 42.5s	O. Jordet (NORWAY) 1h 24m 38.8s
1968	Magnar Solberg (NORWAY) 1h 13m 45.9s	Alexander Tikhonov (U.S.S.R.) 1h 14m 40.4s	Vladimir Goundartsev (U.S.S.R.) 1h 18m 27.4s
1972	Magnar Solberg (NORWAY) 1h 15m 55.5s	Hans-Jürg Knauthe (EAST GERMANY) 1h 16m 07.6s	Lars Arwidson (SWEDEN) 1h 16m 27.0s

Biathlon Relay

1968	U.S.S.R. Tikhonov Pousanov Mamatov Goundartsev 2h 13m 2.4s	NORWAY Waerhuag Jordet Solberg Istad 2h 14m 50.2s	SWEDEN Arwidson Eriksson Petrusson Olsson 2h 17m 26.3s
1972	U.S.S.R. Safin Biakov Mamakov Tikhonov 1h 51m 44.9s	FINLAND Saira Suutarinen Ikola Röppänen 1h 54m 37.2s	EAST GERMANY Knauthe Mischner Speer Koschla 1h 54m 57.6s

Alpine Skiing—Men

GIANT SLALOM

1952	Stein Erikson (NORWAY) 2m 25.0s	Christian Pravda (AUSTRIA) 2m 26.9s	Toni Spiss (AUSTRIA) 2m 28.8s
1956	Anton Sailer (AUSTRIA) 3m 00.1s	Andreas Molterer (AUSTRIA) 3m 0.63s	Walter Schuster (AUSTRIA) 3m 07.2s
1960	Roger Staub (SWITZ.) 1m. 48.3s	Josef Stiegler (AUSTRIA) 1m 48.7s	Ernst Hinterseer (AUSTRIA) 1m 49.1s
1964	Francois Boulieu (FRANCE) 1m 46.71s	Karl Schranz (AUSTRIA) 1m 47.09s	Josef Stiegler (AUSTRIA) 1m 48.05s
1968	Jean-Claude Killy (FRANCE) 3m 29.28s	Willy Favre (SWITZ.) 3m 31.50s	Heinrich Messner (AUSTRIA) 3m 31.83s
1972	Gustavo Thoeni (ITALY) 3m 09.62s	Edmund Bruggmann (SWITZ.) 3m 10.75s	Werner Mattle (SWITZ.) 3m 10.99s

SLALOM

	GOLD	SILVER	BRONZE
1948	Edi Reinalter (SWITZ.) 2m 10.3s	James Couttet (FRANCE) 2m 10.8s	Henri Oreiller (FRANCE) 2m 12.8s
1952	Othmar Schneider (AUSTRIA) 2m 00.0s	Stein Eriksen (NORWAY) 2m 01.2s	Guttorm Berge (NORWAY) 2m 01.7s
1956	Anton Sailer (AUSTRIA) 3m 14.7s	Chiharu Igaya (JAPAN) 3m 18.7s	Stig Sollander (SWEDEN) 3m 20.2s
1960	Ernst Hinterseer (AUSTRIA) 2m 08.9s	Matthias Lietner (AUSTRIA) 2m 10.3s	Charles Bozon (FRANCE) 2m 10.4s
1964	Josef Stiegler (AUSTRIA) 2m 21.13s	William Kidd (U.S.) 2m 21.27s	James Heuga (U.S.) 2m 21.52s
1968	Jean-Claude Killy (FRANCE) 1m 39.73s	Herbert Huber (AUSTRIA) 1m 39.82s	Alfred Matt (AUSTRIA) 1m 40.09s
1972	Francisco Fernandez Ochoa (SPAIN) 1m 49.27s	Gustavo Thoeni (ITALY) 1m 50.28s	Rolando Thoeni (ITALY) 1m 50.30s

DOWNHILL

	GOLD	SILVER	BRONZE
1948	Henri Oreiller (FRANCE) 2m 55.0s	Franz Gabl (AUSTRIA) 2m 59.1s	Karl Molitor (SWITZ.) 3m 00.3s / Rolf Olinger (SWITZ.) 3m 00.3s
1952	Zeno Coló (ITALY) 2m 30.8s	Othmar Schneider (AUSTRIA) 2m 32.0s	Christian Pravda (AUSTRIA) 2m 32.4s
1956	Anton Sailer (AUSTRIA) 2m 52.2s	Raymond Fellay (SWITZ.) 2m 55.7s	Andreas Molterer (AUSTRIA) 2m 56.2s
1960	Jean Vuarnet (FRANCE) 2m 06.0s	Hans-Peter Lanig (GERMANY) 2m 06.5s	Guy Perillat (FRANCE) 2m 06.9s
1964	Egon Zimmermann (AUSTRIA) 2m 18.16s	L. Lacroix (FRANCE) 2m 18.90s	W. Bartels (GERMANY) 2m 19.48s
1968	Jean-Claude Killy (FRANCE) 1m 59.85s	Guy Périllat (FRANCE) 1m 59.93s	J. Daniel Daetwyler (SWITZ.) 2m 00.32s
1972	Bernhard Russi (SWITZ.) 1m 51.43s	Roland Collombin (SWITZ.) 1m 52.07s	Heinrich Messner (AUSTRIA) 1m 52.40s

Jean-Claude Killy (France) who achieved the great triple in Alpine skiing of Downhill, Slalom and Giant Slalom before a home crowd at Grenoble in 1968.

Alpine Skiing—Women

GIANT SLALOM

	GOLD	SILVER	BRONZE
1952	Andrea Lawrence-Mead (U.S.) 2m 06.8s	Dagmar Rom (AUSTRIA) 2m 09.0s	Annemarie Buchner (GERMANY) 2m 10s
1956	Ossi Reichert (GERMANY) 1m 56.5s	Josefine Franal (AUSTRIA) 1m 57.8s	Dorothea Hochleitner (AUSTRIA) 1m 58.2s
1960	Yvonne Rüegg (SWITZ.) 1m 39.9s	Penelope Piton (U.S.) 1m 40.0s	Giuliana Chenal-Minuzzo (ITALY) 1m 40.2s
1964	Marielle Goitschel (FRANCE) 1m 52.24s	Christine Goitschel (FRANCE) 1m 53.11s	Jean Saubert (U.S.) 1m 53.11s
1968	Nancy Greene (CANADA) 1m 51.97s	Annie Famose (FRANCE) 1m 54.61s	Fernande Bochatay (SWITZ.) 1m 54.74s
1972	Marie-Therese Nadig (SWITZ.) 1m 29.90s	Annemarie Pröll (AUSTRIA) 1m 30.75s	Wiltrud Drexel (AUSTRIA) 1m 32.35s

SLALOM

1948	Gretchen Frazer (U.S.) 1m 57.2s	Antoinette Meyer (SWITZ.) 1m 57.7s	Erika Mahringer (AUSTRIA) 1m 58.0s
1952	Andrea Lawrence-Mead (U.S.) 2m 10.6s	Ossi Reichert (GERMANY) 2m 11.4s	Annemarie Buchner (GERMANY) 2m 13.3s
1956	Renée Colliard (SWITZ.) 1m 52.3s	Regina Schöpf (AUSTRIA) 1m 55.4s	Jevginija Sidorova (U.S.S.R.) 1m 56.7s
1960	Anne Heggtveit (CANADA) 1m 49.6s	Betsy Snite (U.S.) 1m 52.9s	Barbi Henneberger (GERMANY) 1m 56.6s
1964	Christine Goitschel (FRANCE) 1m 29.86s	Marielle Goitschel (FRANCE) 1m 30.77s	Jean Saubert (U.S.) 1m 31.36s
1968	Marielle Goitschel (FRANCE) 1m 25.86s	Nancy Greene (CANADA) 1m 26.15s	Annie Famose (FRANCE) 1m 27.89s
1972	Barbara Cochran (U.S.A.) 1m 31.24s	Daniele Debernard (FRANCE) 1m 31.26s	Florence Steurer (FRANCE) 1m 32.69s

DOWNHILL

1948	Hedy Schlernegger (SWITZ.) 2m 28.2s	Trude Beiser (AUSTRIA) 2m 29.1s	Resi Hammerer (AUSTRIA) 2m 30.2s
1952	Trude Jochum-Beiser (AUSTRIA) 1m 47.1s	Annemarie Buchner (GERMANY) 1m 48.0s	Giuliana Minuzzo (ITALY) 1m 49.0s
1956	Madeleine Berthod (SWITZ.) 1m 40.7s	Frieda Danzer (SWITZ.) 1m 45.4s	Lucile Wheeler (CANADA) 1m 45.9s
1960	Heidi Biebl (GERMANY) 1m 37.6s	Penelope Piton (U.S.) 1m 38.6s	Traudl Hecher (AUSTRIA) 1m 38.9s
1964	Christl Haas (AUSTRIA) 1m 55.39s	Edith Zimmerman (AUSTRIA) 1m 56.42s	Traudl Hecher (AUSTRIA) 1m 56.66s
1968	Olga Pall (AUSTRIA) 1m 40.87s	Isabelle Mir (FRANCE) 1m 41.33s	Christl Haas (AUSTRIA) 1m 41.41s
1972	Marie-Therese Nadig (SWITZ.) 1m 36.68s	Annemarie Pröll (AUSTRIA) 1m 37.00s	Susan Corrock (U.S.A.) 1m 37.68s

Figure Skating—Men

1908	Ulrich Sachow (SWEDEN) 1,886.5 pts.	Richard Johansson (SWEDEN) 1,826.0 pts.	Per Thoren (SWEDEN) 1,787.0 pts.
1920	Gillis Grafström (SWEDEN) 2,575.25 pts.	Andreas Krogh (NORWAY) 2,634 pts.	Martin Stuxrud (NORWAY) 2,561 pts.
1924	Gillis Grafström (SWEDEN) 2,575.25 pts.	Willy Böckl (AUSTRIA) 2,518.75 pts.	Georges Gautschi (SWITZ.) 2,233.5 pts.
1928	Gillis Grafström (SWEDEN) 2,698.25 pts.	Willy Böckl (AUSTRIA) 2,682.50 pts.	Robert v. Zeebroeck (BELGIUM) 2,578.75 pts.

	GOLD	SILVER	BRONZE
1932	Karl Schafer (AUSTRIA) 2,602.0 pts.	Gillis Grafström (SWEDEN) 2,514.5 pts.	Montgomery Wilson (CANADA) 2,448.3 pts.
1936	Karl Schafer (AUSTRIA) 2,959.0 pts.	Ernst Baier (GERMANY) 2,805.3 pts.	Felix Kaspar (AUSTRIA) 2,801.0 pts.
1948	Richard Button (U.S.) 1,720.6 pts.	Hans Gerschwiler (SWITZ.) 1,630.1 pts.	Edi Rada (AUSTRIA) 1,603.2 pts.
1952	Richard Button (U.S.) 1,730.3 pts.	Helmut Seibt (AUSTRIA) 1,621.3 pts.	James Grogan (U.S.) 1,627.4 pts.
1956	Hayes Alan Jenkins (U.S.) 1,497.95 pts.	Ronald Robertson (U.S.) 1,492.15 pts.	David Jenkins (U.S.) 1,465.41 pts.
1960	David Jenkins (U.S.) 1,440.2 pts.	Karol Divin (CZECHO.) 1,414.3 pts.	Donald Jackson (CANADA) 1,401.0 pts.
1964	Manfred Schnelldorfer (GERMANY) 1,916.9 pts.	Alain Calmat (FRANCE) 1,876.5 pts.	Scott Allen (U.S.) 1,873.6 pts.
1968	Wolfgang Schwarz (AUSTRIA) 1,094.1 pts.	Timothy Wood (U.S.) 1,891.6 pts.	Patrick Péra (FRANCE) 1,864.5 pts.
1972	Ondrej Nepela (CZECHO.) 2,739.1 pts.	Sergei Chetverukhin (U.S.S.R.) 2,672.4 pts.	Patrick Pera (FRANCE) 2,653.1 pts.

Figure Skating—Women

	GOLD	SILVER	BRONZE
1908	Madge Syers (G.B.) 1,262.5 pts.	Elsa Rendschmidt (GERMANY) 1,055.0 pts.	Dorothy Greenhough-Smith (G.B.) 960.5 pts.
1920	Magda Julin-Mauroy (SWEDEN)	Svea Norén (SWEDEN) 887.75 pts.	Theresa Weld (U.S.) 890.0 pts.
1924	Heima Planck-Szabo (AUSTRIA) 2,094.25 pts.	Beatrix Loughran (U.S.) 1,959.0 pts.	Ethel Muckelt (G.B.) 1,750.50 pts.
1928	Sonja Henie (NORWAY) 2,452.25 pts.	Fritzi Burger (AUSTRIA) 2,248.50 pts.	Beatrix Loughran (U.S.) 2,254.50 pts.
1932	Sonja Henie (NORWAY) 2,302.5 pts.	Fritzi Burger (AUSTRIA) 2,167.1 pts.	Maribel Vinson (U.S.) 2,158.5 pts.
1936	Sonja Henie (NORWAY) 2,971.4 pts.	Cecilia Colledge (G.B.) 2,926.8 pts.	Vivi-Anne Hultén (SWEDEN) 2,763.2 pts.
1948	Barbara Scott (CANADA) 1,467.7 pts.	Eva Pawlik (AUSTRIA) 1,418.3 pts.	Jeanette Altwegg (G.B.) 1,405.5 pts.
1952	Jeanette Altwegg (G.B.) 1,455.8 pts.	Tenley Albright (U.S.) 1,432.2 pts.	Jacqueline du Bief (FRANCE) 1,422.0 pts.
1956	Tenley Albright (U.S.) 1,866.39 pts.	Carol Heiss (U.S.) 1,848.24 pts.	Ingrid Wendl (AUSTRIA) 1,753.91 pts.
1960	Carol Heiss (U.S.) 1,490.1 pts.	Sjoukje Dijkstra (HOLLAND) 1,424.8 pts.	Barbara Roles (U.S.) 1,414.8 pts.
1964	Sjoukje Dijkstra (HOLLAND) 2,018.5 pts.	Regine Heitzer (AUSTRIA) 1,945.5 pts.	Petra Burka (CANADA) 1,940.0 pts.
1968	Peggy Fleming (U.S.) 1,970.5 pts.	Gabrielle Seyfert (EAST GERMANY) 1,882.3 pts.	Hana Maskova (CZECHO.) 1,828.8 pts.
1972	Beatrix Schuba (AUSTRIA) 2,751.5 pts.	Karen Magnussen (CANADA) 2,672.2 pts.	Janet Lynn (U.S.) 2,663.1 pts.)

PAIRS

	GOLD	SILVER	BRONZE
908	Anna Hübler Heinrich Burger (GERMANY) 56.0 pts.	Phyllis W. Johnson James H. Johnson (G.B.) 51.5 pts.	Madge Syers Edgar Syers (G.B.) 48.0 pts.
920	Ludovika Jakobsson Walter Jakobsson (FINLAND) 80.75 pts.	Alexia Bryn Yngvar Bryn (NORWAY) 72.75 pts.	Phyllis W. Johnson Basi Williams (G.B.) 66.25 pts.

Soviet husband and wife skating team, Oleg Protopopov and Ludmilla Belousova, display the form in the pairs Figure Skating Championships that won them the first gold medal of the 1964 Winter Olympics.

	GOLD	SILVER	BRONZE
1924	Helene Engelmann Alfred Berger (AUSTRIA) 74.50 pts.	Ludovika Jakobsson Walter Jakobsson (FINLAND) 71.75 pts.	Andrée Joly Pierre Brunet (FRANCE) 69.25 pts.
1928	Andrée Joly Pierre Brunet (FRANCE) 100.50 pts.	Lilly Scholz Otto Kaiser (AUSTRIA) 99.25 pts.	Melitta Brunner Ludwig Wrede (AUSTRIA) 93.25 pts
1932	Andrée Brunet Pierre Brunet (FRANCE) 76.7 pts.	Beatrix Loughran Sherwin Badger (U.S.) 77.5 pts.	Emilia Rotter László Szollás (HUNGARY) 76.4 pts
1936	Maxi Herber Ernst Baier (GERMANY) 103.3 pts.	Ilse Pausin Erik Pausin (AUSTRIA) 102.7 pts.	Emilia Rotter László Szollás (HUNGARY) 97.6 pts
1948	Micheline Lannoy Pierre Baugniet (BELGIUM) 123.5 pts.	Andrea Kékessy Ede Király (HUNGARY) 122.2 pts.	Suzanne Morrow Wallace Diestelmeyer (CANADA) 121.0 pts.

	GOLD	SILVER	BRONZE
1952	Ria Falk Paul Falk (GERMANY) 102.6 pts.	Karol Estelle Kennedy Michael Kennedy (U.S.) 100.6 pts.	Marianna Nagy László Nagy (HUNGARY) 97.4 pts.
1956	Elisabeth Schwarz Kurt Oppelt (AUSTRIA) 101.8 pts.	Frances Dafoe Norris Bowden (CANADA) 101.9 pts.	Marianna Nagy László Nagy (HUNGARY) 99.3 pts.
1960	Barbara Wagner Robert Paul (CANADA) 80.2 pts.	Marika Kilius Hansjürgen Bäumler (GERMANY) 76.8 pts.	Nancy Ludington Ronald Ludington (U.S.) 76.2 pts.
1964	Ludmilla Belousova Oleg Protopopov (U.S.S.R.) 104.4 pts.	Marika Kilius Hansjürgen Bäumler (GERMANY) 103.6 pts.	D. Wilkes G. Revell (CANADA) 98.5 pts.
1968	Ludmilla Belousova Oleg Protopopov (U.S.S.R.) 315.2 pts.	Tatiana Chesternyava Alexander Gorelik (U.S.S.R.) 312.3 pts.	Margot Glockshuber Wolfgang Danne (WEST GERMANY) 304.4 pts.
1972	Irina Rodnina Alexei Ulanov (U.S.S.R.) 420.4 pts.	Ludmila Smirnova Andrei Suraikin (U.S.S.R.) 419.4 pts.	Manuela Gross Uwe Kagelmann (EAST GERMANY) 411.8 pts.

Speed Skating—Men

1908–1920 Event not held

500 METRES

	GOLD	SILVER	BRONZE
1924	Charles Jewtraw (U.S.) 44.0s	Oskar Olsen (NORWAY) 44.2s	Roald Larsen (NORWAY) 44.8s Clas Thunberg (FINLAND)
1928	Clas Thunberg (FINLAND) 43.4s* Bernt Evensen (NORWAY)		John O'Neil Farrell (U.S.) 43.6s Roald Larsen (NORWAY) Jaako Friman (FINLAND)
1932	John A. Shea (U.S.) 43.4*	Bernt Evensen (NORWAY) d.n.a.	Alexander Hurd (CANADA) d.n.a.
1936	Ivar Ballangrud (NORWAY) 43.4s*	Georg Krog (NORWAY) 43.5s	Leo Freisinger (U.S.) 44.0s
1948	Finn Helgesen (NORWAY) 43.1s*	Kenneth Bartholomew (U.S.) 43.2s Thomas Byberg (NORWAY) Robert Fitzgerald (U.S.)	
1952	Kenneth Henry (U.S.) 43.2s	Donald McDermott (U.S.) 43.9s	Arne Johansen (NORWAY) 44.0s Gordon Audley (CANADA)
1956	Yevgeniy Grischin (U.S.S.R.) 40.2s*	Rafael Gratsch (U.S.S.R.) 40.8s	Alv Gjestvang (NORWAY) 41.0s
1960	Yevgeniy Grischin (U.S.S.R.) 40.2s*	William Disney (U.S.) 40.3s	Rafael Gratsch (U.S.S.R.) 40.4s
1964	Richard McDermott (U.S.) 40.1s*	Yevgeniy Grischin (U.S.S.R.) 40.6s Alv Gjestvang (NORWAY)	
1968	Erhard Keller (W. GERMANY) 40.3s	Hasse Borjes (U.S.) 40.5s Magne Thomassen (NORWAY)	
1972	Erhard Keller (W. GERMANY) 39.44s*	Hasse Borjes (SWEDEN) 39.69s	Valeriy Mouratov (U.S.S.R.) 39.80s

1,500 METRES

GOLD	SILVER	BRONZE
1908–1920 Event not held		
1924 Clas Thunberg (FINLAND) 2m 20.8s	Roald Larsen (NORWAY) 2m 22.0s	Sigurd Moen (NORWAY) 2m 25.6s
1928 Clas Thunberg (FINLAND) 2m 21.1s	Bernt Evensen (NORWAY) 2m 21.9s	Ivar Ballangrud (NORWAY) 2m 22.6s
1932 John A. Shea (U.S.) 2m 57.5s	Alexander Hurd (CANADA) d.n.a.	William F. Logan (CANADA) d.n.a.
1936 Charles Mathiesen (NORWAY) 2m 19.2s	Ivar Ballangrud (NORWAY) 2m 20.2s	Birger Wasenius (FINLAND) 2m 20.9s
1948 Sverre Farstad (NORWAY) 2m 17.6s*	Ake Seyffarth (SWEDEN) 2m 18.1s	Odd Lundberg (NORWAY) 2m 18.9s
1952 Hjalmar Andersen (NORWAY) 2m 20.4s	Willem van der Boort (HOLLAND) 2m 20.4s	Roald Aas (NORWAY) 2m 21.6s
1956 Yevgeniy Grischin (U.S.S.R.) 2m 08.6s Yuriy Michailov (U.S.S.R.)		Toivo Salonen (FINLAND) 2m 09.4s
1960 Roald Aas (NORWAY) 2m 10.4s Yevgeniy Grischin (U.S.S.R.)		Boris Stenin (U.S.S.R.) 2m 11.5s
1964 Ants Antson (U.S.S.R.) 2m 10.3s	C. Verkerk (NETHS.) 2m 10.6s	V. Haugen (NORWAY) 2m 11.25s
1968 Cornelis Verkerk (NETHS.) 2m 03.4s*	Ard Schenk (NETHS.) 2m 05.0s Ivar Eriksen (NORWAY)	
1972 Ard Schenk (NETHS.) 2m 02.96s*	Roar Gronvold (NORWAY) 2m 04.26s	Goran Clässon (SWEDEN) 2m 05.89s

5,000 METRES

1924 Clas Thunberg (FINLAND) 8m 39.0s	Julius Skutnabb (FINLAND) 8m 48.4s	Roald Larsen (NORWAY) 8m 50.2s
1928 Ivar Ballangrud (NORWAY) 8m 50.5s	Julius Skutnabb (FINLAND) 8m 59.1s	Bernt Evensen (NORWAY) 9m 10.1s
1932 Irving Jaffee (U.S.) 9m 40.8s	Edward S. Murphy (U.S.)	William F. Logan (CANADA)
1936 Ivar Ballangrud (NORWAY) 8m 19.6s*	Birger Wasenius (FINLAND) 8m 23.3s	Antero Ojala (FINLAND) 8m 30.1s
1948 Reidar Liaklev (NORWAY) 8m 29.4s	Odd Lundberg (NORWAY) 8m 32.7s	Göthe Hedlund (SWEDEN) 8m 34.8s
1952 Hjalmar Andersen (NORWAY) 8m 10.6s	Kees Broekman (NETHS.) 8m 21.6s	Sverre Haugli (NORWAY) 8m 22.4s
1956 Boris Schilkov (U.S.S.R.) 7m 48.7s*	Sigvard Ericsson (SWEDEN) 7m 56.7s	Oleg Gontscharenko (U.S.S.R.) 7m 57.5s
1960 Viktor Kositschkin (U.S.S.R.) 7m 51.3s	Knut Johannesen (NORWAY) 8m 00.8s	Jan Pesman (NETHS.) 8m 05.1s
1964 Knut Johannesen (NORWAY) 7m 38.4s*	P. Moe (NORWAY) 7m 38.6s	F. Maier (NORWAY) 7m 42.0s
1968 F. Anton Maier (NORWAY) 7m 22.4s*	Cornelis Verkerk (NETHS.) 7m 23.2s	Petrus Nottet (NETHS.) 7m 25.5s
1972 Ard Schenk (NETHS.) 7m 23.6s	Roar Gronvold (NORWAY) 7m 28.2s	Sten Stensen (NORWAY) 7m 33.4s

10,000 METRES

1924 Julius Sknutnabb (FINLAND) 18m 04.8s	Clas Thunberg (FINLAND) 18m 07.8s	Roald Larsen (NORWAY) 18m 12.2s
1928 Event not held		
1932 Irving Jaffee (U.S.) 19m 13.6s	Ivar Ballangrud (NORWAY) d.n.a.	Frank Stack (CANADA) d.n.a.
1936 Ivar Ballangrud (NORWAY) 17m 24.3s	Birger Wasenius (FINLAND) 17m 28.2s	Max Stiepl (AUSTRIA) 17m 30.0s

	GOLD	SILVER	BRONZE
1948	Ake Seyffarth (SWEDEN) 17m 26.3s	Lauri Parkkinen (FINLAND) 17m 36.0s	Pentti Lammio (FINLAND) 17m 42.7s
1952	Hjalmar Andersen (NORWAY) 16m 45.8s	Kees Broekman (NETHS.) 17m 10.6s	Carl-Erik Asplund (SWEDEN) 17m 16.6s
1956	Sigvard Ericsson (SWEDEN) 16m 35.9s	Knut Johannesen (NORWAY) 16m 36.9s	Oleg Gontscharenko (U.S.S.R.) 16m 42.3s
1960	Knut Johannesen (NORWAY) 15m 46.6s*	Viktor Kositschkin (U.S.S.R.) 15m 49.2s	Kjell Bäckman (SWEDEN) 16m 14.2s
1964	Johnny Nilsson (SWEDEN) 15m 50.1s	F. Maier (NORWAY) 16m 06.0s	Knut Johannesen (NORWAY) 16m 06.3s
1968	Johnny Hoeglin (SWEDEN) 15m 23.6s*	F. Anton Maier (NORWAY) 15m 23.9s	Oerjan Sandler (SWEDEN) 15m 31.8s
1972	Ard Schenk (NETHS.) 15m 01.35s*	Cornelis Verberk (NETHS.) 15m 04.70s	Sten Stensen (NORWAY) 15m 07.08s

Speed Skating—Women

1908–1956 Events not held, but in 1932 there were three demonstration events for women speed skaters.

500 METRES

1960	Helga Haase (GERMANY) 45.9s	Natalie Dontschenko (U.S.S.R.) 46.0s	Jeanne Ashworth (U.S.) 46.1s
1964	Lydia Skoblikova (U.S.S.R.) 45.0s*	Irina Yegorova (U.S.S.R.) 45.4s	Tatyana Sidorova (U.S.S.R.)
1968	Ludmila Titova (U.S.S.R.) 46.1s	Mary Meyers* (U.S.) 46.3s Dianne Holum* (U.S.) Jennifer Fish* (U.S.)	
1972	Anne Henning (U.S.) 43.33s*	Vera Krasnova (U.S.S.R.) 44.01s	Ludmila Titova (U.S.S.R.) 44.45s

---

* Awarded a silver medal

1,000 METRES

1960	Klara Guseva (U.S.S.R.) 1m 34.1s	Helga Haase (GERMANY) 1m 34.3s	Tamara Rylova (U.S.S.R.) 1m 34.8s
1964	Lydia Skoblikova (U.S.S.R.) 1m 33.2s*	Irina Yegorova (U.S.S.R.) 1m 34.3s	K. Mustonen (FINLAND) 1m 34.8s
1968	Carolina Geijssen (NETHS.) 1m 32.6s	Ludmila Titova (U.S.S.R.) 1m 32.9s	Dianne Holum (U.S.) 1m 33.4s
1972	Monika Pflug (WEST GERMANY) 1m 31.40s*	Atje Keulen-Deelstra (NETHS.) 1m 31.61s	Anne Henning (U.S.) 1m 31.62s

1,500 METRES

1960	Lydia Skoblikova (U.S.S.R.) 2m 25.2s*	Elvira Seroczynska (POLAND) 2m 25.7s	Helena Pilejeyk (POLAND) 2m 27.1s
1964	Lydia Skoblikova (U.S.S.R.) 2m 22.6s*	K. Mustonen (FINLAND) 2m 25.5s	B. Kolokoltseva (U.S.S.R.) 2m 27.1s
1968	Kaija Mustonen (FINLAND) 2m 22.4s*	Carolina Geijssen (NETHS.) 2m 22.7s	Christina Kaiser (NETHS.) 2m 24.5s
1972	Dianne Holum (U.S.) 2m 20.85s*	Stein Baas-Kaiser (NETHS.) 2m 21.05s	Atje Keulen-Deelstra (NETHS.) 2m 22.05s

3,000 METRES

	GOLD	SILVER	BRONZE
1960	Lydia Skoblikova (U.S.S.R.) 5m 4.3s	Valentina Stenina (U.S.S.R.) 5m 16.9s	Eevi Huttunen (FINLAND) 5m 21.0s
1964	Lydia Skoblikova (U.S.S.R.) 5m 14.9s	Valentina Stenina (U.S.S.R.) 5m 18.5s	Pie Hwa (N. KOREA) 5m 18.5s
1968	Johanna Schut (NETHS.) 4m 56.2s*	Kaija Mustonen (FINLAND) 5m 01.0s	Christina Kaiser (NETHS.) 5m 01.3s
1972	Stein Baas-Kaiser (NETHS.) 4m 52.14s*	Dianne Holum (U.S.) 4m 58.67s	Atje Keulen-Deelstra (NETHS.) 4m 59.91s

Bobsleigh

2-MAN BOB

1932	U.S. I 8m 14.74s J. H. Stevens C. P. Stevens	SWITZ. I 8m 16.38s R. Capadrutt O. Geier	U.S. II 8m 29.15s J. R. Heaton R. Minton
1936	U.S. I 5m 29.29s I. Brown A. Washbond	SWITZ. 5m 30.64s F. Feierabend J. Beerli	U.S. II 5m 33.96s G. Colgate R. Lawrence
1948	SWITZ. II 5m 29.2s F. Endrich F. Waller	SWITZ. I 5m 30.4s F. Feierabend P. Eberhard	U.S. II 5m 35.3s F. Fortune S. Carron
1952	GERMANY I 5m 24.54s A. Ostler L. Nieberl	U.S. I 5m 26.89s S. Benham P. Martin	SWITZ. I 5m 27.71s F. Feierabend S. Waser
1956	ITALY I 5m 30.14s L. Dalla Costa G. Conti	ITALY II 5m 31.45s E. Monti R. Alvera	SWITZ. I 5m 37.46s M. Angst H. Warburton
1960	Event not held		
1964	G.B. 4m 21.90s A. Nash R. Dixon	ITALY II 4m 22.02s S. Zardini R. Bonagura	ITALY I 4m 22.63s E. Monti S. Siorpaes
1968	ITALY I 4m 41.54s Eugenio Monti Luciano de Paolis	WEST GERMANY I 4m 41.54s Horst Floth Pepi Bader	ROUMANIA I 4m 44.46s Ion Panturu Nicolae Neagoe
1972	WEST GERMANY I Wolfgang Zimmerer Peter Utzschneider 4m 57.07s	WEST GERMANY II Horst Floth Pepi Bader 4m 58.84s	SWITZ. I Jean Wicki Edy Hubacher 4m 59.33s

4-MAN BOB

1924	SWITZ. I 5m 45.54s E. Scherrer A. Neveu A. Schläppi H. Schläppi	G.B. 5m 48.83s R. H. Broome T. A. Arnold H. A. W. Richardson R. E. Soher	BELGIUM 6m 02.29s C. Mulder R. Mortiaux P. v.d. Broeck V. A. Verschueren or H. P. Willems
1928	U.S. II 3m 20.5s W. Fiske N. Tocker C. Mason C. Gray R. Parke	U.S. I 3m 21.0s J. Heaton D. Granger L. Hine T. Doe J. O'Brien	GERMANY 3m 21.9s H. Kilian V. Krempl H. Hess S. Huber H. Nägle
1932	U.S. I 7m 53.68s W. Fiske E. Eagan C. Gray J. O'Brien	U.S. II 7m 55.70s H. Homburger P. Bryant F. P. Stevens E. Horton	GERMANY I 8m 00.04s H. Kilian M. Ludwig Dr. H. Mehlhorn S. Huber
1936	SWITZ. II 5m 19.85s P. Mussy A. Gartmann C. Bouvier J. Beerli	SWITZ. II 5m 22.73s R. Capadrutt H. Aichele F. Feierabend H. Bütikofer	G.B. 5m. 23.41s F. McEvoy J. Cardno G. Dugdale C. Green
1948	U.S. II 5m 20.1s F. Tyler P. Martin E. Rimkus W. D'Amico	BELGIUM 5m 21.3s M. Houben F. Mansveld G. Niels J. Mouvet	U.S. I 5m 21.5s J. Bickford T. Hicks D. Dupree W. Dupree

Anthony Nash and Robin Dixon (Great Britain), hurtling down the bob run when they won a gold medal in the 1964 Games.

	GOLD	SILVER	BRONZE
1952	GERMANY 5m 07.84s	U.S. I 5m 10.48s	SWITZ. I 5m 11.70s
	A. Ostler	S. Benham	F. Feierabend
	F. Kuhn	P. Martin	A. Madörin
	L. Nierberl	H. Crossett	A. Filippini
	F. Kemser	J. Atkinson	S. Waser
1956	SWITZ. I 5m 10.44s	ITALY II 5m 12.10s	U.S. 5m 12.39s
	F. Kapus	E. Monti	A. Tyler
	G. Diener	U. Girardi	W. Dodge
	F. Alt	R. Alverá	C. Butler
	H. Angst	R. Mocellini	J. Lamy
1960	Event not held		
1964	CANADA I 4m 14.46s	AUSTRIA I 4m 15.48s	ITALY II 4m 15.60s
	V. Emery	E. Thaler	E. Monti
	P. Kirby	A. Koxeder	S. Siorpaes
	D. Anakin	J. Nairz	B. Rigoni
	J. Emery	R. Durnthaler	G. Siorpaes
1968	ITALY I 2m 17.39s	AUSTRIA I 2m 17.48s	SWITZ. 2m 18.4s
	E. Monti	E. Thaler	J. Wicki
	L. De Paolis	R. Durnthaler	H. Candrian
	R. Zandonella	H. Gruber	W. Hofmann
	M. Armano	J. Eder	W. Graf
1972	SWITZ. I 4m 43.07s	ITALY I 4m 43.83s	WEST GERMANY I 4m 43.92s
	J. Wicki	N. de Zordo	W. Zimmerer
	E. Hubacher	G. Bonichon	P. Utzschneider
	H. Leutenegger	A. Frassinelli	S. Gaisreister
	W. Carmichel	C. dal Fabbo	W. Steinbauer

Tobogganing (Lugeing)

SINGLE SEATER—MEN

	GOLD	SILVER	BRONZE
1964	Thomas Koehler (GERMANY) 3m 26.77s	Klaus Bonsack (GERMANY) 3m 27.04s	Hans Plenk (GERMANY) 3m 30.15s
1968	Manfred Schmid (AUSTRIA) 2m 52.48s	Thomas Koehler (EAST GERMANY) 2m 52.66s	Klaus Bonsack (EAST GERMANY) 2m 53.33s
1972	Wolfgang Scheidel (EAST GERMANY) 3m 27.58s	Harald Ehrig (EAST GERMANY) 3m 28.39s	Wolfram Fiedler (EAST GERMANY) 3m 28.73s

TWO-SEATER —MEN

	GOLD	SILVER	BRONZE
1964	AUSTRIA 1m 41.62s Josef Feistmantl Manfred Stengl	AUSTRIA 1m 41.91s Reinhold Senn H. Thaler	ITALY 1m 42.87s W. Aussendorfer S. Mair
1968	EAST GERMANY 1 m 35.85s Klaus Bonsack Thomas Koehler	AUSTRIA 1m 36.34s Manfred Schmid Ewald Walch	GERMANY 1m 37.29s Wolfgang Winkler Fritz Nachmann
1972	ITALY and EAST GERMANY 1m 28.35s Paul Hildgartner Walter Plaikner	Horst Hornlein Reinhard Bredo	EAST GERMANY Klaus Bonsack Wolfram Fiedler

SINGLE-SEATER—WOMEN

	GOLD	SILVER	BRONZE
1964	Otrun Enderlein (GERMANY) 3m 24.67s	Ilse Geisler (GERMANY) 3m 27.42s	Helene Thurner (AUSTRIA) 3m 29.06s
1968	Erica Lechner (ITALY) 2m 28.66s	Christa Schmuck (WEST GERMANY) 2m 29.37s	Angelika Duenhaupt (WEST GERMANY) 2m 29.56s
1972	Anna-Maria Muller (EAST GERMANY) 2m 59.18s	Ute Ruhrold (EAST GERMANY) 2m 59.49s	Margit Schumann (EAST GERMANY) 2m 59.54s

Ice Hockey

1920	1 CANADA Robert J. Benson Wally Byron Frank Fredrickson Chris Fridfinnson Mike Goodman Haldor Halderson Konrad Johannesson A. "Huck" Woodman	2 U.S. Raymond L. Bonney Anthony J. Conroy Herbert L. Drury J. Edward Fitzgerald George P. Geran Frank X. Goheen Joseph McCormick Lawrence J. McCormick Frank A. Synott Leon P. Tuck Cyril Weidenborner	3 CZECHO. Dr. Adolf Dusek Dr. Karel Hartmann Vilém Loos Jan Pallausch Jan Peka Dr. Karel Pesek Josef Sroubek Otakar Vindys
1924	1 CANADA Jack A. Cameron Ernest J. Collett Albert J. McCaffery Harold E. McMunn Duncan B. Munro W. Beattie Ramsay Cyril S. Slater Reginald J. Smith Harry E. Watson	2 U.S. Clarence J. Abel Herbert L. Drury Alphonse A. Lacroix John A. Langley John J. Lyons Justin J. McCarthy Willard W. Rice Irving W. Small Frank A. Synott	3 G.B. W. H. Anderson Lorne H. Carr-Harris Colin G. Carruthers Eric D. Carruthers Guy E. Clarkson Ross Cuthbert George Holmes Hamilton D. Jukes Edward B. Pitblado Blane N. Sexton

GOLD	SILVER	BRONZE
1928 1 CANADA	2 SWEDEN	3 SWITZ.
Charles Delahay	Carl Abrahamsson	Giannin Andreossi
Frank Fisher	Emil Bergman	Mezzi Andreossi
Dr. Louis Hudson	Birger Holmqvist	Robert Breiter
Norbert Mueller	Gustaf Johansson	Louis Dufour
Herbert Plaxton	Henry Johansson	Charles Fasel
Hugh Plaxton	Nils Johansson	Albert Geromini
Roger Plaxton	Ernst Karlberg	Fritz Kraatz
John G. Porter	Erik Larsson	Arnold Martignoni
Frank Sullivan	Bertil Linde	Heini Meng
Dr. Joseph Sullivan	Sigurd Oberg	Anton Morosani
Ross Taylor	Vilhelm Petersen	Dr. Luzius Rüedi
David Trottier	Kurt Sucksdorff	Richard Torriani
1932 1 CANADA	2 U.S.	3 GERMANY
William H. Cockburn	Osborn Anderson	Rudi Ball
Clifford T. Crowley	John B. Bent	Alfred Heinrich
Albert G. Duncanson	John Chase	Erich Herker
George F. Garbutt	John E. Cookman	Gustav Jaenecke
Roy Hinkel	Douglas N. Everett	Werner Korff
C. Victor Lindquist	Franklin Farrell	Walter Leinwever
Norman J. Malloy	Joseph F. Fitzgerald	Erich Römer
Walter Monson	Edward M. Frazier	F. Marquardt Slevogt
Kenneth S. Moore	John B. Garrison	Martin Schröttle
N. Romeo Rivers	Gerard Hallock III	Georg Strobl
Harold A. Simpson	Robert Cambridge Livingston	
Hugh R. Sutherland	Francis A. Nelson	
W. Stanley Wagner	Winthrop H. Palmer	
J. Aliston Wise	Gordon Smith	
1936 1 G.B.	2 CANADA	3 U.S.
Alexander Archer	Maxwell Deacon	John B. Garrison
James Borland	Hugh Farquharson	August F. Kammer
Edgar Brenchley	Kenneth Farmer	Philip W. LaBatte
James Chappell	James Haggarty	John C. Lax
John Coward	Walter Kitchen	Thomas H. Moone
Gordon Dailley	Raymond Milton	Eldridge B. Ross
John Davey	Francis W. Moore	Paul E. Rowe
Carl Erhardt	Herman Murray	Francis J. Shaugnessy
James Foster	Arthur Nash	Gordon Smith
John Kilpatrick	David Neville	Francis J. Spain
Archibald Stinchcombe	Ralph St. Germain	Frank R. Stubbs
Robert Wyman	Alexander Sinclair	
	William Thomson	
1948 1 CANADA	2 CZECHO.	3 SWITZ.
Murray-Alb Dowey	Vladimir Bouzek	Hans Bänninger
Bernard Dunster	Augustin Bubnik	Alfred Bieler
Orval Gravelle	Jaroslav Drobny	Heinrich Boller
Patrick Guzzo	Premysl Hajny	Ferdinand Cattini
Walter Halder	Zdenek Jarkovsky	Hans Cattini
Thomas Hibbert	Stanislav Konopásek	Hans Dürst
Ross King	Bohumil Modry	Walter Dürst
Henri-André Laperrire	Miloslav Pokorny	Emil Handschin
John Lecompte	Vaclav Rozinak	Heini Lohrer
George A. Mara	Dr. Mirosláv Sláma	Werner Lohrer
Albert Renaud	Karel Stibor	Reto Perl
Reginald Schroeter	Vilém Stovik	Gebhard Poltera
	Ladislav Troják	Ulrich Poltera
	Josef Trousilek	Beat Ruedi
	Oldrich Zábrodsky	Otto Schubinger
	Vladimir Zábrodsky	Richard Torriani
		Hans Trepp

GOLD	SILVER	BRONZE
1952 1 CANADA	2 U.S.	3 SWEDEN
George G. Able	Ruben E. Bjorkman	Gote Almqvist
John F. Davies	Leonard S. Ceglarski	Hans Andersson
William Dawe	Joseph J. Czarnota	S. "Tvilling" Andersson
Robert B. Dickson	Richard J. Desmond	Ake Andersson
Donald V. Gauf	Andre P. Gambucci	Lars Bjorn
William J. Gibson	Clifford N. Harrison	Gote Blomqvist
Ralph L. Hansch	Gerald W. Kilmartin	Thord Flodqvist
Robert R. Meyers	John F. Mulhern	Erik Johansson
David E. Miller	Joyn M. Noah	Gosta Johansson
Eric E. Paterson	Arnold C. Oss, Jr.	Rune Johansson
Thomas A. Pollock	Robert E. Rompre	Sven Johansson
Allan R. Purvis	James W. Sedin	Ake Lassas
Gordon Robertson	Allen A. Van	Holger Nurmela
Louis J. Secco	Donald F. Whiston	Hans Oberg
Francis C. Sullivan	Kenneth J. Yackel	Lars Pettersson
Robert Watt		Lars Svensson
		Sven Thunman
1956 1 U.S.S.R.	2 U.S.	3 CANADA
Yevgeniy Babitsch	Wendell Anderson	Denis Brodeur
Usevolod Bobrov	Wellington Burnett	Charles Brooker
Nikolay Chlystov	Eugene Campbell	William Colvin
Aleksey Guryschev	Gordon Christian	Alfred J. Horne
Juriy Krylov	William Cleary	Arthur Hurst
Alfred Kutschewskiy	Richard Dougherty	Byrle Klinck
Valentin Kusin	Willard Ikola	Paul Knox
Grigoriy Mkrttschan	John Matchefts	Kenneth Laufman
Viktor Nikiforov	John Mayasich	Howard Lee
Juriy Pantjuchov	Daniel McKinnon	James Logan
Nikolay Putschkov	Richard Meredith	Floyd Martin
Viktor Schuwalov	Weldon Olson	Jack McKenzie
Genrich Sidorenkov	John E. Petroske	Donald Rope
Nikolay Sologubov	Kenneth Purpur	Georges Scholes
Ivan Tregubov	Ronald Rigazio	Gerald Theberge
Dmitriy Ukolov	Richard Rodenhiser	Robert White
Aleksandr Uwarov	Edward Sampson	Keith Woodall
1960 1 U.S.	2 CANADA	3 U.S.S.R.
Roger A. Christian	Bob Attersley	Veniamin Aleksandrov
William Christian	Moe Benoit	Aleksandr Aljmetov
Robert B. Cleary	Jim Connelly	Juriy Baulin
William J. Cleary	Jack Douglas	Michail Bytschkov
Eugene Grazia	Fred Etcher	Vladimir Grebennikov
Paul Johnson	Bob Forhan	Yevgeniy Groschev
John Kirrane	Don Head	Viktor Jakuschev
John Mayasich	Harold Hurley	Yevgeniy Jerkin
Jack McCartan	Kenneth Laufman	Nikolay Karpov
Robert McVey	Floyd Martin	Alfred Kutschewskiy
Richard Meredith	Bob McKnight	Konstantin Loktev
Weldon Olson	Clifford Pennington	Stanislav Petuchov
Edwyn Owen	Donald Rope	V. Prjaschtschnikov
Rodney Paavola	Bob Rousseau	Nikolay Putschkov
Lawrence Palmer	George Samolenko	Genrich Sidorenkov
Richard Rodenhiser	Harry Sinden	Nikolay Sologubov
Thomas Williams	Darryl Sly	Juriy Tsitsinov

GOLD	SILVER	BRONZE
1964 1 U.S.S.R.	2 SWEDEN	3 CZECHO.
V. Konovalenko	K. Svensson	V. Dzurila
B. Zaitsev	L. Haeggroth	V. Nadrchal
V. Kuzkin	G. Blome	F. Gregor
E. Ivanov	R. Stoltz	R. Potsch
V. Davidov	N. Johansson	F. Tikal
A. Ragulin	B. Nordlander	S. Sventek
O. Zaitsev	N. Nilsson	L. Smid
A. Almetov	U. Sterner	J. Walter
V. Yakushev	T. Johansson	J. Golonka
V. Starshinov	R. Pettersson	J. Holik
K. Loktev	E. Maeaettae	V. Bubnik
B. Maiorov	L. Johansson	J. Klapac
A. Firsov	L. Lundvall	J. Dolana
S. Pyetukhov	C. Oeberg	S. Pryl
V. Aleksandrov	A. Andersson	M. Vlach
E. Maiorov	U. Oehrlund	J. Jirik
L. Volkov	H. Mild	J. Cerny
1968 1 U.S.S.R.	2 CZECHO.	3 CANADA
Viktor Zinger	Vladimir Nadrchal	Wayne Stephenson
Viktor Konovalenko	Vlado Dzurila	Kenneth Broderick
Vitaliy Davidov	Machac	Marshall Johnston
Viktor Blinov	Jan Suchy	Brian Glennie
Romishevskiy	Josef Horesovsky	Barry Mckenzie
Olyeg Zaitsev	Frantisek Pospisil	Paul Conlin
Aleksandr Ragulin	Karel Masopust	Edward Hargreaves
Viktor Kuzkin	Frantisek Sevcik	Terrence O'Malley
Boris Mayorov	Jan Havel	Raymond Cadieux
Anatoliy Firsov	Jan Hrbaty	Stephen Monteith
Evgeniy Zymin	Vaclav Nedomansky	William Macmillan
Viktor Polupanov	Josef Golonka	Francis Huck
Anatoliy Ionov	Petr Hejma	Gary Dineen
Vyacheslav Starchinov	Jiri Kochta	Danny O'Shea
Evgeniy Michakov	Jaroslav Jirik	Morris Mott
Vladimir Vikulov	Jiri Holik	Herbert Pinder
Yuriy Moiseyev	Josef Cerny	Roger Bourbonnais
Venyamin Aleksandrov	Jan Klapac	Gerry Pinder
1972 1 U.S.S.R.	2 U.S.	3 CZECHO.
Vladislav Tretiak	Michael Curran	Vado Dzurila
A. Pachkov	Peter Sears	Jiri Holocek
Viktor Kuzkin	James McElmury	Rudolf Tajcnar
Vitaliy Davidov	Thomas Mellor	Jaroslav Holik
Yevgeniy Michakov	Frank Sanders	Vaclav Nedomansky
Aleksandr Maltsev	Charles Brown	Vladimir Bednar
Aleksandr Iakuchev	Richard McGlynn	Frantisek Pospisil
V. Lutchenko	Walter Old	Jiri Holik
Aleksandr Ragulin	Kenneth Ahearn	Karal Vohralik
Igor Romichevskiy	Stuart Irving	Josef Horesovsky
G. Tsyganov	Mark Howe	Oldrich Machac
V. Kharlamov	Henry Bucha	Josef Cerny
Yuriy Blinov	Keith Christiansen	Bouslav Stastny
V. Petrov	Robbie Storek	Richard Farda
Anatoliy Firsov	Ronald Marsland	Ivzn Hlinka
Boris Mikhailov	Craig Farmer	Jiri Kochta
Vladimir Vikulov	Timothy Sheehy	Vlad Martinec

RESULTS—OLYMPIC GAMES 1972

EVENT	GOLD	SILVER	BRONZE
		ARCHERY (2 Events)	
International Round (Men)	....	....	....
International Round (Women)	....	....	....
		BASKETBALL	
Teams	....	....	....
		BOXING (11 Bodyweights)	
Light Flyweight Under 48 kg (7 st 7¼ lb)	....	....	....
Flyweight Max. 51 kg (8 st 0¼ lb)	....	....	....
Bantamweight Max. 54 kg (8 st 7 lb)	....	....	....
Featherweight Max. 57 kg (8 st 13¼ lb)	....	....	....
Lightweight Max. 60 kg (9 st 6¼ lb)	....	....	....
Light Welterweight			

Welterweight
Max. 67 kg (10 st 7½ lb) ------------------------- | -------------------------

Light Middleweight
Max. 71 kg (11 st 2½ lb) ------------------------- | -------------------------

Middleweight
Max. 75 kg (11 st 11½ lb) ------------------------- | -------------------------

Light Heavyweight
Max 81 kg (12 st 10½ lb) ------------------------- | -------------------------

Heavyweight
More than 81 kg (12 st 10½ lb) ------------------------- | -------------------------

CANOEING—MEN (8 Events)

Kayak 1 1,000 m. ------------------------- | -------------------------

Kayak 2 1,000 m. ------------------------- | -------------------------

Kayak 4 1,000 m. ------------------------- | -------------------------

Canadian 1 1,000 m. ------------------------- | -------------------------

Canadian 2 1,000 m. ------------------------- | -------------------------

K1 4 × 1,000 m. Relay ------------------------- | -------------------------

K1 Slalom ------------------------- | -------------------------

K2 Slalom ------------------------- | -------------------------

EVENT	GOLD	SILVER	BRONZE
		CANOEING—WOMEN (3 Events)	
Kayak 1 500 m.	....	....	....
Kayak 2 500 m.	....	....	....
Kayak 1 Slalom	....	....	....
		CYCLING (7 Events)	
1,000 m. Time Trial	....	....	....
1,000 m. Sprint	....	....	....
2,000 m. Tandem Sprint	....	....	....
4,000 m. Individual Pursuit	....	....	....
4,000 m. Team Pursuit	....	....	....
Road Team Time-Trial	....	....	....
Road Race Individual			

EQUESTRIAN EVENTS (6 Events)

Three Day Individual ························

Three Day Teams ························

Dressage Individual ························

Dressage Teams ························

Prix des Nations Individual ························

Prix des Nations Teams ························

FENCING—MEN (6 Events)

Foil Individual ························

Foil Teams ························

Épée Individual ························

Épée Teams ························

Sabre Individual ························

Sabre Teams ························

EVENT	GOLD	SILVER	BRONZE
FENCING—WOMEN (2 Events)			
Foil Individual	....	....	....
Foil Teams	....	....	....
FIELD HOCKEY			
Team	....	....	....
GYMNASTICS—MEN (8 Events)			
Floor Exercises	....	....	....
Pommelled Horse	....	....	....
Long Horse	....	....	....
Horizontal Bars	....	....	....
Parallel Bars	....	....	....
Rings	....	....	....
Combined Exercises	....	....	....
Team Event			

GYMNASTICS—WOMEN (6 Events)

Floor Exercises _____   _____   _____

Beam _____   _____   _____

Horse Vault _____   _____   _____

Assymetrical Bars _____   _____   _____

Combined Exercises _____   _____   _____

Team Event _____   _____   _____

HANDBALL

Team _____   _____   _____

JUDO (6 Events)

Lightweight _____   _____   _____

Welterweight _____   _____   _____

Middleweight _____   _____   _____

Middle Heavyweight _____   _____   _____

Heavyweight _____   _____   _____

Open _____   _____   _____

EVENT	GOLD	SILVER	BRONZE
		MODERN PENTATHLON (2 Events)	
Individual	....	....	....
Team	....	....	....
		ROWING (7 Events)	
Single Sculls	....	....	....
Double Sculls	....	....	....
Coxless Pairs	....	....	....
Coxed Pairs	....	....	....
Coxless Fours	....	....	....
Coxed Fours	....	....	....
Eights			....

EVENT	GOLD	SILVER	BRONZE
		SHOOTING (8 Events)	
50 m. Small Bore Rifle (3 positions)			
50 m. Small Bore Rifle (Prone position)			
Free Rifle			
Free Pistol			
Rapid Fire Pistol			
Olympic Trench (Clay Pigeon)			
Skeet			
Running Boar (50 m. Moving Target)			
		SOCCER (ASSOCIATION FOOTBALL)	
Teams			

SWIMMING, DIVING and WATER POLO—MEN (18 Events)

EVENT	GOLD	SILVER	BRONZE
Freestyle			
100 metres	————	————	————
200 metres	————	————	————
400 metres	————	————	————
1,500 metres	————	————	————
4 × 100 m. Relay	————	————	————
4 × 200 m. Relay	————	————	————
Breaststroke			
100 metres	————	————	————
200 metres	————	————	————
Butterfly			
100 metres	————	————	————
200 metres	————	————	————
Backstroke			
100 metres	————	————	————
200 metres	————	————	————

EVENT	GOLD	SILVER	BRONZE
Individual Medley			
200 metres	....	....	....
400 metres	....	....	....
Medley Relay			
4 × 100 metres	....		....
Springboard Dive	....	....	....
High Board Dive	....	....	....
Water Polo	....	....	....

SWIMMING AND DIVING—WOMEN (16 Events)

EVENT	GOLD	SILVER	BRONZE
Freestyle			
100 metres	....	....	....
200 metres	....	....	....
400 metres	....	....	....
800 metres	....	....	....
4 × 100 m. Relay	....	....	....

EVENT	GOLD	SILVER	BRONZE
Breaststroke			
100 metres	-------	-------	-------
200 metres	-------	-------	-------
Butterfly			
100 metres	-------	-------	-------
200 metres	-------	-------	-------
Backstroke			
100 metres	-------	-------	-------
200 metres	-------	-------	-------
Individual Medley			
100 metres	-------	-------	-------
200 metres	-------	-------	-------
Medley Relay			
4 × 100 metres	-------	-------	-------
Springboard Dive	-------	-------	-------
High Board Dive	-------	-------	-------

TRACK AND FIELD ATHLETICS—MEN (24 Events)

EVENT	GOLD	SILVER	BRONZE
100 metres			
200 metres			
400 metres			
800 metres			
1,500 metres			
5,000 metres			
10,000 metres			
Marathon			
110 m. hurdles			
400 m. hurdles			
3,000 m. Steeplechase			
4 × 100 m. Relay			
4 × 400 m. Relay			

EVENT	GOLD	SILVER	BRONZE
High Jump			
Pole Vault			
Long Jump			
Triple Jump			
Shot Putt			
Discus Throw			
Hammer Throw			
Javelin Throw			
Decathlon			
20 Km. Walk			
50 Km. Walk			

TRACK AND FIELD ATHLETICS—WOMEN (14 Events)

EVENT	GOLD	SILVER	BRONZE
100 metres			
200 metres			
400 metres			
800 metres			
1,500 metres			
100 m. hurdles			
4 × 100 m. Relay			
4 × 400 m. Relay			
High Jump			
Long Jump			
Shot Putt			
Discus Throw			
Javelin Throw			
Pentathlon			

EVENT	GOLD	SILVER	BRONZE
		VOLLEYBALL	
Team Men	....	....	....
Team Women	....	....	....

WEIGHTLIFTING (9 Events)

EVENT	GOLD	SILVER	BRONZE
Flyweight Max. 52 kg (8 st 2¼ lb)	....	....	....
Bantamweight Max. 56 kg (8 st 11¼ lb)	....	....	....
Featherweight Max 60 kg (9 st 6¼ lb)	....	....	....
Lightweight Max. 67½ kg (10 st 8½ lb)	....	....	....
Middleweight Max. 75 kg (11 st 11¼ lb)	....	....	....
Light Heavyweight Max. 82½ kg (12 st 13¾ lb)	....	....	....
Middle Heavyweight Max. 90 kg (14 st 2¼ lb)	....	....	....
Heavyweight Max. 110 kg (17 st 4¼ lb)	....	....	....
Super-Heavyweight Above 110 kg (17 st 4¼ lb)	....	....	....

WRESTLING—GRECO-ROMAN STYLE (10 Bodyweights)

Light Flyweight
Under 48 kg (7 st 7¼ lb) ....

Flyweight
Max 52 kg (8 st 11¼ lb) ....

Bantamweight
Max 57 kg (8 st 13¼ lb) ....

Featherweight
Max. 62 kg (9 st 10¼ lb) ....

Lightweight
Max. 68 kg (10 st 9¼ lb) ....

Welterweight
Max. 74 kg (11 st 9 lb) ....

Middleweight
Max. 82 kg (12 st 12¼ lb) ....

Light Heavyweight
Max. 90 kg (14 st 2¼ lb) ....

Heavyweight
Max. 100 kg (15 st 10¼ lb) ....

Extra Heavyweight
More than 100 kg (15 st 10¼ lb) ....

WRESTLING—FREESTYLE (10 Events)

EVENT	GOLD	SILVER	BRONZE
Light Flyweight Under 48 kg (7 st 7¼ lb)	....	....	....
Flyweight Max. 52 kg (8 st 11¼ lb)	....	....	....
Bantamweight Max. 57 kg (8 st 13¼ lb)	....	....	....
Featherweight Max. 62 kg (9 st 10¼ lb)	....	....	....
Lightweight Max. 68 kg (10 st 9¼ lb)	....	....	....
Welterweight Max. 74 kg (11 st 9 lb)	....	....	....
Middleweight Max. 82 kg (12 st 12¼ lb)	....	....	....
Light Heavyweight Max. 90 kg (14 st 2¼ lb)	....	....	....
Heavyweight Max. 100 kg (15 st 10¼ lb)	....	....	....
Extra-Heavyweight More than 100 kg (15 st 10¼ lb)			

YACHTING (6 Classes)

Finn Class
1 crew 14 ft 9 ins

Flying Dutchman
2 crew 19 ft 10 ins

Tempest Class
2 crew 21 ft 11¾ ins

Star Class
2 crew 22 ft 8 ins

Soling Class
3 crew 26 ft 9 ins

Dragon
3 crew 29 ft 2 ins

IMPRIMÉ EN FRANCE PAR BRODARD ET TAUPIN
6, place d'Alleray - Paris.
1306-5 - Usine de La Flèche, le 20-04-1972.
Dépôt légal 2ᵉ trimestre 1972.